Endorsements

"Though not as well known today as some Puritans, William Gouge was a giant of Reformed practical divinity. Dr. Rivera's excellent, broad-ranging study sheds much light on both Puritan theology and the Christian life in general, and on assurance of faith in particular. This work succeeds in unveiling how the Puritans combined academic theology with practical piety, so as to glorify God and do their souls good."
—**Joel R. Beeke**, President, Puritan Reformed Theological Seminary, Grand Rapids, Michigan

"Though they lived before the rise of modern experimental psychology, Puritan pastors often ministered as scientists of the soul—and William Gouge was one of their best. He served a Church of England congregation in London for 45 years, learning to help anxious sinners gain assurance of forgiveness and the presence of God in their lives during an especially uncertain and tumultuous time in England, particularly for its most restless evangelicals. Rivera's deft treatment of the ways in which he did this helps readers understand and even feel the beating heart of English Puritanism."
—**Douglas A. Sweeney**, Distinguished Professor of Church History and the History of Christian Thought, Trinity Evangelical Divinity School

"Digging deep into the work of a lesser known puritan, Eric Rivera has unearthed a treasure chest of timeless spiritual wisdom. This book shows how one godly pastor sought to shepherd his people by grounding them in faith, comforting them in sorrow, strengthening them against temptation and helping them to pray. It is a rich resource for all who seek to do the same today."
—**Colin S. Smith**, Senior Pastor, The Orchard Evangelical Free Church (Illinois)

"Though almost entirely forgotten today, the Puritan pastor and theologian William Gouge was one of the most influential church leaders in England during the first-half of the seventeenth century. Eric Rivera's masterful study of Gouge's practical divinity examines the theological convictions and practical commitments of a skilled pastor as he addressed his parishioners' most pressing concerns regarding Christian sanctification and the assurance of faith. In our present age where Christian leaders are routinely enticed by celebrity and size, Gouge's rich pastoral wisdom is both timeless and timely."

—**Scott M. Manetsch**, Professor of Church History, Trinity Evangelical Divinity School

CHRIST IS YOURS

The Assurance of Salvation in the Puritan Theology of William Gouge

CHRIST IS YOURS

The Assurance of Salvation in the Puritan Theology of William Gouge

ERIC RIVERA

STUDIES IN HISTORICAL AND SYSTEMATIC THEOLOGY

LEXHAM PRESS

Christ Is Yours: The Assurance of Salvation in the Puritan Theology of William Gouge

Copyright 2019 Eric Rivera

Lexham Press, 1313 Commercial St., Bellingham, WA 98225
LexhamPress.com

Print ISBN 9781683592471
Digital ISBN 9781683592488

Lexham Editorial Team: Todd Hains, Michael Haykin, Eric Bosell
Cover design: Bryan Hintz
Typesetting: Kathy Curtis

To Erikah, the "delight of my eyes," and
to our three precious children,
Keziah, Lukas, and Levi

Contents

Acknowledgments xi

1. Introduction: "From Blackfriars to Heaven" 1

2. The Foundation for Gouge's Practical Divinity 37

3. The Christian's Battle against the World, Flesh, and the Devil 72

4. Humiliation, Suffering, Death, and the Practice of Piety 109

5. Prayer and the Christian Home 144

6. Conclusion 179

Bibliography 192

Scripture Index 203

Subject Index 205

Acknowledgments

It has been a long and rewarding, though sometimes painful, journey. Many different people have poured into my life and contributed to seeing this book come to fruition. They have prayed for me, shared timely words of encouragement, and cheered me on even in the most trying times. I want to thank my doctoral advisor and academic mentor, Dr. Scott Manetsch. His consistent encouragements helped me stay the course, his editorial pen made me a better writer, and his teaching sparked my earliest thoughts about Puritan practical divinity. I would also like to thank Drs. Doug Sweeney and Richard Averbeck for reading, critiquing, and encouraging me in this work. Their insights were invaluable.

I am grateful for the Meeter Center of Calvin Studies at Calvin College that awarded me a research grant in the summer of 2016, which proved to be precisely what I needed to finish my last chapters. Karin Maag and Paul Fields were especially helpful during my time there. In addition, thank you Todd Hains and Lexham Press for taking on this project and assisting me in preparing it for publication. To my friend Joshua Phillips: thanks for making this book more accessible by taking on the tedious yet important task of compiling both the subject and Scripture indices.

To my "Blackfriars," the church family at The Brook, it has been my privilege to be called your pastor since we planted the church in 2013. I love to serve Jesus alongside of you. You have taught me much about the family of God, advancing this glorious gospel, and what it means to live life together. The contents of this book have entered your ears and hearts in a variety of ways. I am so encouraged to see you grow in the faith. Thank you for cheering me on as I left you for a month to write on two different occasions. I praise God for you!

To my parents, Roberto and Mary Rivera, and my siblings, Tito and Ivellise, I am so thankful for you. My parents have given me a legacy of faith in Jesus, the greatest thing I could ever ask for. I stand on your shoulders. Being a Puerto Rican family from Chicago that loves and serves the Lord is something that I hold dear to my heart. Thank you for spurring on my Christian walk and for your encouraging words along the way as I studied and wrote. I love you guys.

Erikah, you are not only my wife but also my best friend and my greatest cheerleader. You have known just the right words to say when I wanted to give up, just the right look to give when I needed a boost, and just the right prayer to pray when I was discouraged. You, along with our precious children, Keziah, Lukas, and Levi, have sacrificed a lot to make this PhD happen. I could not have done this without you. I love you, babe.

Lastly, all praise and glory be to you, my triune God. Father, you have chosen me according to your mercy. Jesus, your life, death, and resurrection have given me a new life. Spirit, you have regenerated my soul and are ever present with me. As is the heartbeat of this work, God, let me also be one who presents the majesty of who you are to comfort your afflicted, discouraged, and downtrodden children. Soli Deo Gloria.

Introduction: "From Blackfriars to Heaven"

DEFINING PURITANISM

In the middle of the sixteenth century, Protestant leaders sought to bring reformation to the English church. Harsh opposition met these efforts of reform during the reign of Henry VIII (1491-1547) before a new and hopeful day arrived for Protestants under the leadership of the child king, Edward VI (1547-1553). During his reign the Catholic mass was abolished and "replaced by a vernacular communion service," priests were allowed to marry, religious images were removed from churches, purgatory was rejected, and auricular confession to priests was no longer mandated.[1] However, much of the progress in ecclesiastical reform that was gained under Edward VI's Protestant leadership was brought to a sudden and bloody halt under the swift and heavy hand of Mary I (1553-1558) and her "Catholic (Counter-) Reformation."[2] After Mary's death, Elizabeth I (1558-1603) became queen of England following her half-sister's reign of terror. Elizabeth I needed to reestablish the nation's ecclesiastical and political stability and did so through what historians call the Elizabethan Settlement. Under the queen's leadership, the Church of England became theologically Protestant while retaining some similarities with Catholic practice, such as priestly vestments, genuflecting, statues, the burning of incense, the office of bishop, and the use of a liturgical guide for worship such as Thomas Cranmer's *Book of Common Prayer*. The queen's settlement did not please everybody and it is during her reign that the word "Puritan" finds its genesis.

---

1. Peter Marshall, "Britain's Reformations," in *The Oxford Illustrated History of the Reformation*, ed. Peter Marshall (Oxford: Oxford University Press, 2015), 201-3.
2. Marshall, "Britain's Reformations," 206.

Initially, the term "Puritan" was a label of insult and derision.[3] The
Puritans were those "nonconformist clergy within the newly reformed
Elizabethan church, zealous Protestants who refused to wear prescribed liturgical vestments, particularly the white surplice, and who
gained a reputation as 'opposers of the hierarchy and church-service.'"[4]
They believed that the Elizabethan Settlement prematurely halted
the progress of reformation in England, and further purification was
needed ecclesiologically, theologically, and morally. The majority of
these "Puritans" remained inside the state church and sought to reform
it from within, while others considered the church unredeemable,
separating from it entirely.[5]

The multifaceted context of the rise of Puritanism accentuates
the challenges of defining the movement when considering how the
movement developed in the seventeenth century.[6] Some historians have

---

3. Patrick Collinson states that "the invention of Puritanism in the sense that
it so largely took over as the brand name for a certain kind of Protestant religios-
ity, social conduct and politics was indeed a defining moment in English culture."
Patrick Collinson, "Antipuritanism," in *Cambridge Companion to Puritanism*, ed. John
Coffey and Paul Lim (Cambridge: Cambridge University Press, 2008), 23. Cf. Patrick
Collinson, *The Elizabethan Puritan Movement* (Oxford: Clarendon, 1967), 26–28.

4. John Coffey and Paul Lim, eds., *Cambridge Companion to Puritanism*
(Cambridge: Cambridge University Press, 2008), 1.

5. Theodore Dwight Bozeman, *The Precisianist Strain: Disciplinary Religion and
Antinomian Backlash in Puritanism to 1638* (Chapel Hill: University of North Carolina
Press, 2004), 3.

6. By multifaceted context, I have in mind the historical, cultural, theological,
methodological, geographical, and even political dimensions to the movement.
Historically, Puritanism begins as a term of disdain in Elizabethan England, but in
the seventeenth century became a term of honor. Culturally, Puritanism drew attention to the moral temperature of society. Theologically, some Puritans were Baptists
while others were paedobaptists. Most were Reformed in their theology, but the
Arminian leanings of John Goodwin demonstrates how not all endorsed all aspects
of Reformed theology. See Joel R. Beeke's discussion on John Owen's response to John
Goodwin's view of the saints' perseverance in *The Quest for Full Assurance: The Legacy
of Calvin and His Successors* (Carlisle, PA: Banner of Truth, 2000), 167–73. See also
Philip Benedict, who believes Goodwin was a "moderate Calvinist" who "searched
the middle ground between Arminianism and Antinomianism" while being recep-
tive to Amyraut. Philip Benedict, *Christ's Churches Purely Reformed: A Social History
of Calvinism* (New Haven: Yale University Press, 2002), 323. Methodologically, some
Puritans remained in the state church as non-conformists while others separated
from it. Geographically, while Puritanism originated in England, it spread into
Scotland, Wales, mainland Europe, and North America. Politically, the 1649 behead-
ing of Charles I was promoted by some Puritans while denounced by others.

found the term so problematic that they have proposed avoiding the word "Puritanism" altogether. However, other scholars have chosen to retain the name. Bozeman prefers the term because "it depicts accurately a substantive and often obsessive trait of the quest for further reformation: a hunger for purity" in English Protestantism.[7] In this same vein of thought, Coffey and Lim offer a definition that represents the diversity and challenges of research into Puritanism. Broadly speaking, they define it as an "intense variety of early modern Reformed Protestantism" within the Church of England. Still, their definition also narrows to encompass the ways in which Puritanism did not remain in neither England nor the Church of England but branched "off into divergent and dissenting streams" in other nations and lands.[8]

Coffey and Lim's definition takes into account the unique contexts of Puritanism's beginning, while recognizing the deviating directions of Puritanism seen in the seventeenth century. This understanding of Puritanism is assumed throughout this work.

PRESENTATION OF THESIS AND METHOD OF RESEARCH

As attempts to reform the Church of England in the late sixteenth century were met with resistance by the established Church, those Puritans seeking reform had to redirect their purifying goals from the institutional church to the individuals within. Their aim was to instruct the believer in the manner of how to lead a godly life. This Puritan approach to pastoral care came to be known as practical divinity. One of the primary concerns of this instruction was to provide Christians with grounds for personal assurance of their salvation, thus discerning whether they were truly elect and consoling the anxious soul.[9] Many of these practical matters are evident in the ministry and published works of William Gouge.

For Gouge and other Puritans, practical divinity encouraged rigorous reflection, introspection, and a disciplined life in order to help believers discern even the tiniest degree of faith that testifies that they

---

7. Bozeman, *Precisianist Strain*, 3.
8. Coffey and Lim, eds., *Cambridge Companion to Puritanism*, 1–2.
9. Benedict, *Christ's Churches Purely Reformed*, 320–21.

are elect, thereby bringing consolation to the anxious soul.[10] They were concerned that if one overemphasized justification and assurance at the neglect of a sanctified life, then moral standards would be lost. On the opposite side, they were equally concerned that if assurance was found in sanctification, the grace of God displayed at the cross of Christ might be neglected.[11] Thus, they sought to navigate a middle ground that emphasized Christ's finished work on the cross for the believer and a Christian life that bears fruit.[12]

Since the middle of the twentieth century, scholars such as Basil Hall and R. T. Kendall challenged the successfulness of the Puritans' practical agenda.[13] They maintain that the Puritan teaching on faith (which includes saving faith and temporary faith) fails to aid Christians in attaining a sense of assurance of salvation. Furthermore, they argue that this Puritan teaching failed because it grounded the locus of assurance on works of sanctification (signs of election) in the Christian's life rather than upon the finished work of Christ. Their arguments sparked a rigorous debate on the Puritan theology of assurance of salvation as it relates to their practical instruction that spans to the present day.

In light of the ongoing discussion and controversies related to Puritan practical divinity, I will focus this work on the practical divinity of William Gouge, who was prominent in his own day for this pastoral strategy. I will specifically argue that in his practical divinity, William Gouge does not represent a shift in emphasis in the Reformed tradition from assurance of salvation based on the promises of God to assurance being achieved through the introspective efforts of the Christian. Instead, we will see that William Gouge was a pastorally attentive minister who understood the spiritual needs of the church in England in general and those of his parishioners in particular—especially as it

---

10. Ibid., 321.

11. Bozeman, *Precisianist Strain*, 147–50; Benedict, *Christ's Churches Purely Reformed*, 322–23.

12. Charles E. Hambrick-Stowe, "Practical Divinity and Spirituality," in *The Cambridge Companion to Puritanism*, ed. John Coffey and Paul Lim (Cambridge: Cambridge University Press, 2008), 195.

13. Basil Hall, "Calvin against the Calvinists," in *John Calvin*, ed. Gervase E. Duffield (Grand Rapids: Eerdmans, 1966); R. T. Kendall, *Calvin and English Calvinism to 1649* (Oxford: Oxford University Press, 1979).

related to the practical outworking of their faith. We will also see that Gouge's practical divinity was born out of his understanding of the Bible, theology of atonement, and belief in God's providence and moved him to guide specifically Christians who struggled in their faith and doubted the reality of their salvation because of personal sin, physical ailments, and cultural circumstances. In summary, Gouge's practical divinity taught an assurance of salvation that placed the primary ground of assurance in the promises of God and the secondary grounds for assurance on the testimony of the Holy Spirit in the Christian's life.

Along the way, this work will also provide answers to a variety of important subsidiary questions: What do Gouge's writings tell us about his pastoral concerns and the spiritual needs of his audience? What were the goals of his teaching in practical divinity? What were the theological underpinnings to Gouge's practical divinity? How is Gouge's interpretive approach to the Bible reflected in his teaching? Concerning his writings, what do the years of publication tell us about the occasional nature of his instruction and to which matters of practical divinity did Gouge give prominence on these occasions? What types of opposition or resistance did Gouge face because of his teachings and approach to pastoral care? To what extent is his practical divinity a reflection or reworking of Catholic devotional practices?

This project will make a twofold contribution. First, it will advance the study of a respected and noteworthy seventeenth-century figure whose career, influence, and works on practical divinity are largely unknown.[14] Second, this study will contribute to the ongoing scholarly

---

14. This study will utilize Gouge's extant published works because they are representative of his most received and circulated teachings. Although this cannot be confirmed, it seems likely that any journals and personal notes of Gouge that existed were destroyed, along with certain parish records, in the Great London Fire of 1666. Brian Burch, in his study on the parish of St. Anne's writes, "The church of St. Anne, Blackfriars, was destroyed in the Great Fire and not rebuilt, the parish being united to St. Andrew by the Wardrobe. It may be supposed that the early records of the parish were also largely destroyed, and all that survives today is a complete set of registers," containing baptismal, marriage, and burial records. Burch, "Parish of St. Anne's Blackfriars," 1–2. Gouge's works have been accessed through Early English Books Online (EEBO) and microfiche as well as the combined rare book collections at Calvin College, the Newberry Library (Chicago), and the University of Chicago.

discussions on the nature of Puritan practical divinity. Gouge's instruction on the relationship between faith, assurance, and self-inspection in his practical divinity will be examined to determine whether he represents a shift in Reformed Christianity from christocentrism to introspection as grounds for assurance.

PRACTICAL DIVINITY AND ASSURANCE OF SALVATION

The Puritans recognized that people are sinners deserving of God's wrath and that salvation was found in the complete saving work of Jesus Christ on the cross. Therefore, how one might know that one is elect, and thus, in right standing with God was of utmost importance. Francis Bremer writes concerning how one might gain assurance:

> Some clergy suggested that men and women look to their lives, not in the hope that they could ever merit heaven, but on the assumption that grace changed the saints and that the fruits of that change would be godly behaviour. Others feared that such advice would lead people to come to rely on their works for assurance, subtly leading them to accept the discredited covenant of works. These Puritans relied instead on the sensation of God's caress that they had received at the first intimation that they had been elect and that they periodically were refreshed anew. Many drew on both of these methods of gaining assurance.[15]

Assurance of salvation reflected in a life of godliness gave way to practical divinity. For this reason, Michael P. Winship maintains that Puritan practical divinity was not simply a product of an ecclesiological shift from attempting to purify the church from without to doing so from within. Nor is it simply a by-product of ecclesiastical politics seeking to make a move from the Church of England's influence to that of the Presbyterians in the 1590s. While both of these approaches contributed to the rise and prominence of Puritan practical divinity, the underlying component is found in the desire of ministers to shepherd

---

15. Francis J. Bremer, "The Puritan Experiment in New England, 1630–1660," in *The Cambridge Companion to Puritanism*, ed. John Coffey and Paul Lim (Cambridge: Cambridge University Press, 2008), 134.

their people that they might be neither "carnal-gospelers" nor weary and distressed souls with no direction or hope for assurance.[16]

While Hambrick-Stowe, Bremer, and Winship effectively demonstrate the pragmatic questions that gave way to the emergence of Puritan practical divinity, this practical relationship raises important questions about the theological relationship that exists between practical divinity and assurance of salvation. What are the grounds by which a believer can be assured of his or her salvation? Is assurance of salvation of the essence of faith or is it something attained by only a few? Were the Puritans, represented by the Westminster Confession, following the theological trajectory of their Reformation predecessors like John Calvin or were they presenting something new in the Protestant tradition? These questions have spawned decades of vibrant dialogue among contemporary scholars.

In the 1960s, scholars such as Basil Hall and R. T. Kendall argued that the Puritans departed from the theological teachings of John Calvin and replaced them with a pseudo-Arminian teaching on assurance of salvation. They contend that the Puritans, exemplified in their works of practical divinity and in the Westminster Confession, changed the locus of assurance from the finished work of Christ on the cross and grounded it on the Christian's ability to discern signs of election in their lives (evidence of the Spirit's sanctifying work). According to Kendall, this teaching evidenced in the Confession, separated assurance from the essence of saving faith. Kendall contends that the plainest example of this shift is found in the Westminster Confession 18.3, which reads, "This *infallible assurance does not so belong to the essence of faith*, but that a true believer may wait long, and conflict with many difficulties, before he be partaker of it."[17]

Kendall challenges the assumption "that William Perkins and his followers were followers of the Genevan reformer John Calvin and that the theology embraced in the Westminster Confession of Faith was

---

16. Winship, "Weak Christians," 479–81.

17. "The Westminster Confession of Faith, 1647," in *Documents of the English Reformation*, ed. Gerald Bray (Minneapolis: Fortress, 1994), 500. Emphasis added.

true Calvinism, or, at least, the logical extension of his thought."[18] He contends that while Calvin taught a general atonement that places the primary ground of assurance in the finished work of Jesus, the Puritans taught a limited atonement that tells believers to search their lives for evidence of the Spirit's working (and of their election) that demonstrates that they are truly saved. Ultimately, the Puritans taught a kind of assurance that is grounded in a Christian's efforts. He concludes,

> The Westminster divines do not explicitly state that repentance is the condition of the new covenant. But they should have; for this is virtually what they finally say. While the Westminster divines never intended to make works the ground of salvation, they could hardly have come closer. Since saving faith is defined as "yeelding obedience" to God's commands, the "principall Acts" of faith being of the *will*, this seems to make the claims of "free grace" suspect.[19]

Basil Hall and Randall Zachman have similar interpretations as Kendall. They argue that Calvin's Genevan successor Theodore Beza and the English theologian William Perkins are largely responsible for this shift from the ground of assurance being in Christ to what Beza and the Puritans called the practical syllogism.[20] The practical syllogism is "a conclusion drawn from an action." In the case of faith, the actions or responses to faith, such as repentance, demonstrate the genuineness of one's belief. For William Perkins, the practical syllogism as it relates to assurance would be as follows:

18. R. T. Kendall, *Calvin and English Calvinism to 1649* (Oxford: Oxford University Press, 1979), 1.

19. Ibid., 205

20. Hall, "Calvin against the Calvinists," in *John Calvin*, ed. Duffield; Randall Zachman, *The Assurance of Faith* (Minneapolis: Fortress, 1993), 6–7, 246. Basil Hall writes concerning the shift he sees from Calvin's biblical exegesis to Beza's speculative theology, "Calvin's successors nevertheless distorted the balance of doctrines which he had tried to maintain. His successor at Geneva, Beza, together with the Heidelberg theologian Zanchius, the English Puritan Perkins, and their associates and followers, bear much of the blame for this. Even if we allow that theological change had to come in order to meet changing situations, yet it is not necessary to assume that only those changes that these men made were necessarily the right ones" (p. 25).

Major premise: Only those who repent and believe in Christ alone for salvation are children of God.

Minor Premise: By the gracious work of the Spirit, I repent and believe in Christ alone for salvation.

Conclusion: Therefore I am a child of God.[21]

Scholars such as Paul Helm, Richard Muller and Joel Beeke have persuasively challenged Kendall, Hall, and Zachman's proposal.[22] As it pertains to the historiographical trends that pit Calvin against Calvinists, Muller's primary contention is that they propose an unwarranted dichotomy. In the first place, it is incorrect to speak of "Calvin" as the sole representative of Reformed theology. In the second place, to speak of the successors of the Reformed tradition as "Calvinists" is to fail to recognize the varying differences within the Reformed tradition. In Muller's assessment, when discontinuities are being leveled, they usually are the fruit of having pulled the original meaning and/or approach of a particular writer out of its historical context to be dogmatized. While clear dissimilarities in the Reformed tradition exist when it comes to doctrinal method and nuance, theological continuity still remains in important topics such as views of predestination, the two natures of Christ, his atoning work on the cross, *sola Scriptura*, and the theology of covenant.[23]

With reference to the practical syllogism, Beeke contends, contra Zachman, that in the late sixteenth century, the practical syllogism was never meant to be the primary ground of salvation, but rather was a mode of reasoning whereby sanctification gives evidence of assuring faith.[24] Beeke argues that Calvin, Beza, and the Westminster Assembly teach three grounds for assurance: the promises of God in the gospel,

---

21. Joel R. Beeke and Mark Jones, *A Puritan Theology: Doctrine for Life* (Grand Rapids: Reformation Heritage, 2012), 593.

22. Paul Helm, *Calvin and the Calvinists* (Edinburgh: Banner of Truth, 1982). Joel R. Beeke, *The Quest for Full Assurance: The Legacy of Calvin and His Successors* (Carlisle, PA: Banner of Truth, 2000); Richard A. Muller, *After Calvin: Studies in the Development of a Theological Tradition* (Oxford: Oxford University Press, 2003).

23. Muller, *After Calvin*, 4, 16.

24. Zachman believes Calvin and Luther's understanding of saving faith "left the door open for the possibility that the foundation of faith might be reversed, as indeed happened immediately after the death of Calvin in the theology of Beza, with

the signs of grace in sanctification, and the inward testimony of the Holy Spirit, with the primary ground being the promises of God in the gospel. The Westminster Confession 18.2 reads,

> This certainty is not a bare conjectural and probable persua-sion grounded upon a fallible hope; but an infallible assurance of faith founded upon the divine truth of the *promises of salvation*, the *inward evidence* of those graces unto which these promises are made, the *testimony of the Spirit* of adoption witnessing with our spirits that we are the children of God, which Spirit is the earnest of our inheritance, whereby we are sealed to the day of redemption.[25]

Of this primary ground, Beeke says that "Beza differed little from Calvin. 'Faith in Jesus Christ is a sure witness of our election,' Beza wrote."[26] For Perkins, says Beeke, the practical syllogism never pointed away from Christ, the Spirit, or saving faith. Rather, Spirit-worked faith was chained to Christ.[27]

Donald Sinnema's reading of Beza's theology of assurance slightly differs from Beeke's, but nonetheless produces the same conclusion. Sinnema agrees with Beeke in that Beza's grounds for assurance have been sorely misinterpreted. "While Beza does recognize a role for good works in assurance, his position has sometimes been understood to mean that good works are a basis of assurance; that is incorrect."[28] However, where Beeke stresses Beza's pointing to Christ for assurance, Sinnema highlights that one ground of assurance even above Christ is the divine decree of election. For Beza, "Eternal election is the sole foundation (*fondement*) of all assurance," says Sinnema.[29]

---

the emergence of the practical syllogism (*syllogismus practicus*) as the foundation of faith and assurance." Zachman, *Assurance of Faith*, 6–7.

25. "Westminster Confession," 500. Emphasis added.

26. Beeke, *Quest for Full Assurance*, 76.

27. Ibid., 87, 93.

28. Donald Sinnema, "Beza's View of Predestination in Historical Perspective," in *Théodore de Bèze (1519–1605): actes du colloque de Genève (septembre 2005)*, ed. Irena Backus (Geneva: Librairie Droz, 2007), 235.

29. Ibid., 236.

Because the promises of God (or even the immutable plan of election to salvation) are the primary and highest ground of assurance, the signs of grace in sanctification and the inward testimony of the Spirit were lower grounds of assurance that might be more readily accessible for the afflicted conscience. For this reason, Beza and Perkins instructed believers to seek the lowest ground of assurance in order to climb to the higher and primary ground of God's promises. This graduated approach neither makes sanctification the primary ground for assurance nor makes each ground opposed to the other. In the same way, neither one of these grounds were meant to stand alone, rather the Holy Spirit is intimately involved in each aspect. It is the Spirit who enables the believer to trust the promises of God and it is the Spirit who illuminates the heart that the believer might examine it.[30]

The Puritans also distinguished between the direct act of faith and the reflex act of faith, each related to the practical syllogism. The direct act of faith is that evidence of grace whereby the believer is convinced that God's promises are specifically applied to him or her. The reflex act of faith is that evidence of grace whereby the Holy Spirit sheds light upon his own work in the believer enabling the believer to conclude that he or she is a child of God because his or her faith has a saving character to it.[31] Beeke quotes the Puritan minister Anthony Burgess (d.1664) who wrote, "So that when we believe in God, that is a direct act of the soul; when we repent of sin, because God is dishonoured, that

---

30. Beeke, *The Quest for Full Assurance*, 146–47. Quoting Beza, Sinnema provides what he sees as the clearest description of this graduated process of moving up from the lowest ground of assurance to the highest, "We ascend from good works to the gift of sanctification, and from sanctification to faith.... In like manner, we infer from these sure effects (by the surest connection of effects and causes) not just any calling at all but a calling that is efficacious; and from this calling, we infer election, and from election finally, we infer predestination in Christ.... Therefore, this doctrine of predestination is the only basis of our faith and hope, and we must apply it only in this way: that as the Apostle said already in Romans 8:30, by those same stages by which God descends to adopt us, we in turn may ascend to him." Sinnema, "Beza's View of Predestination," 237. For a similar perspective on Beza, see also Scott M. Manetsch, *Calvin's Company of Pastors: Pastoral Care and the Emerging Reformed Church, 1536–1609* (Oxford: Oxford University Press, 2013), 252–53.

31. Beeke, *Quest for Full Assurance*, 132, 232.

is a direct act; but when we know that we do believe, and that we do repent, this is a reflex act."[32]

While the practical syllogism is not a method of reasoning employed by John Calvin, the relationship between justification and sanctification is not absent from his thought. Calvin understands justification and sanctification to be reflections of God's "double grace" or *duplex gratia*. God's justifying work in the believer where he unites the believer with Christ by faith through imputation is the first grace. God's sanctifying work is the second grace, where "in Christ, through the Spirit, believers begin the slow process of moral transformation."[33] J. Todd Billings emphasizes how in Calvin's theology, these two graces of justification and sanctification are "distinct, yet inseparable." Alluding to the Chalcedonian formula, Billings summarizes Calvin, just as the divinity and humanity of Jesus can be distinguished but not separated, so also justification can be distinguished but not separated from sanctification.[34] In Puritan thought, the practical syllogism relates faith and works, justification and sanctification, in the same way as Calvin's explanation of the *duplex gratia*.

Several important questions remain. Is assurance of salvation of the essence of faith or is it something attained only by some? Were the Westminster Puritans following in the trajectory of their Reformation predecessors like John Calvin? In order to answer these questions, it is important to understand Calvin's view on the matter. In Book Three of his *Institutes of the Christian Religion* (1559), Calvin espouses a position that has appeared contradictory to some scholars. Calvin defines faith as "a firm and certain knowledge of God's benevolence toward us, founded upon the truth of the freely given promise in Christ, both revealed to our minds and sealed upon our hearts through the Holy Spirit," which seems to say that assurance, or certainty, is of the essence of faith.[35] Helm states the dilemma these words seem to pose: "If faith involves

32. Ibid., 132.

33. J. Todd Billings, *Calvin, Participation, and the Gift: The Activity of Believers in Union with Christ* (New York: Oxford University Press, 2007), 107.

34. Ibid., 107.

35. John Calvin, *Institutes of the Christian Religion*, 2 vols., ed. John T. McNeill, trans. Ford Lewis Battles (Philadelphia: Westminster, 1960), 551.

assurance, then all who believe must have this confidence about themselves in relation to God. If they fail to have confidence then they cannot truly be believers."[36] What accentuates the matter is Calvin's statement later in his *Institutes* where he acknowledges the deep-seated nature of unbelief inside the heart of the believer and that certainty of one's salvation can indeed be tinged with doubt. Helm does not see these statements as contradictory but of what faith ought to be and what it actually is in daily life. "So while faith *ought* to be assured faith, there is no such thing as perfect or total assurance, a completely doubt-free confidence that God's mercy applies to *me*."[37] Again, Helm writes,

> Calvin held that it was possible for a person to be assured of his own salvation, and normal to expect this. It was monstrous to teach that such assurance was impossible. But he recognized that saving faith is often accompanied by periods of doubt which eclipse assurance, and that even assured faith is never totally free from doubt.[38]

Zachman comes to a similar conclusion concerning Calvin's position on assurance. He writes, "Consonant with the simultaneity of faith and fear, Calvin does not want us to think that faith gives an assurance of conscience that is untouched by anxiety or doubt. The anxiety and doubt of conscience in the faithful do not mutually exclude, but rather reinforce, assurance and certainty in God's mercy."[39] According to Zachman, Calvin therefore taught that doubt concerning one's salvation comes when the knowledge of who people are as sinners seeks to overthrow the promises of God in the gospel. Doubt and anxiety,

---

36. Helm, *Calvin and the Calvinists*, 24.

37. Ibid., 25. Beeke quotes Calvin: "Surely, while we teach that faith *ought* to be certain and assured, we cannot imagine any certainty that is not tinged with doubt, or any assurance that is not assailed." Beeke then adds, "though Calvin was anxious to keep faith and assurance in close proximity by definition, he also recognized that in actual experience the Christian gradually grows into a more full faith in God's promises.... In short, Calvin distinguished between the 'ought to' of faith in its essence, and the 'is' of faith as wrestled out in daily life." Beeke, *Quest for Full Assurance*, 45.

38. Helm, *Calvin and the Calvinists*, 31.

39. Zachman, *Assurance of Faith*, 183.

therefore, drives the believer to turn to God in his Word, where his or her faith can be strengthened.[40]

Beeke provides a similar angle with an important distinction in Calvin's thought. While full assurance is not attained by all believers, Beeke demonstrates from Calvin's commentaries and *Institutes* that Calvin taught that a drop or germ of faith can be found in even the most immature of believers, and that assurance is found in that drop.[41] The believer may not be aware of this tiniest degree of faith, even though it is indeed present. "*Assurance may be possessed without always being known*," says Beeke.[42] Thus, it is appropriate to say that full or infallible assurance is not of the essence of faith, but that the tiniest drop of faith and assurance is. Beeke writes, "For Calvin, assurance is both essential for faith and contained in all its exercises, regardless of the believer's consciousness of his assurance."[43] It is in this way that the Westminster Confession is in line with Calvin.

By separating faith and full or certain assurance, the Puritans with Calvin, recognize that someone may be a child of God even if he or she lacks confident assurance of his or her salvation. This understanding of faith and assurance, however, does not transfer the primary ground of assurance from the work of Christ to the works of men and women. Beeke and Helm stress the importance of understanding the full statement found in 18.3 of the Westminster Confession, for in it one finds that the primary ground for assurance is still the enabling work of the Spirit of God and not found in meritorious works. It reads,

> This *infallible assurance* does not so belong to the essence of faith, but that a true believer may wait long, and conflict with many difficulties, before he be partaker of it: yet, being *enabled by the Spirit* to know the things which are freely given him of God, he may, without extraordinary revelation in the right use of ordinary means, attain thereunto. And therefore it is the duty of every one to give all diligence to make his calling and election

---

40. Ibid., 183–85.
41. Beeke, *Quest for Full Assurance*, 44–52.
42. Ibid., 53.
43. Ibid.

sure, that thereby his heart may be enlarged in peace and joy in the Holy Ghost, in love and thankfulness to God, and in strength and cheerfulness in the duties of obedience, the proper fruits of this assurance; so far is it from inclining men to looseness.[44]

Thus, both Calvin and the Calvinist Puritans of Westminster taught that full assurance "doth not so belong" to the essence of faith but that every believer possesses a drop of assuring faith although he or she may not be aware of it. "How Faith can grow in any to a full Assurance, if there be no Assurance in the Nature of it, I cannot comprehend," said the Scottish Puritan, Thomas Boston (1676–1732).[45] Even though full assurance of salvation may, if ever, come after a long and difficult season, it is still attained as one is enabled by the Holy Spirit. Therefore, the promises of God are the primary grounds for assurance and God's working through his Spirit is the means by which one grows in assurance. In this way, the Westminster divines did not differ from Calvin on assurance nor did they follow a trajectory different from him.

These various studies and approaches to Puritan practical divinity and the assurance of salvation in the latter part of the sixteenth and into the seventeenth century have given way to studies of the Puritan legacy as it relates to assurance of salvation in the centuries that follow.

GODLINESS AND THE CONSOLATION OF AFFLICTED CONSCIENCES

Through their proclaimed sermons and written works of practical divinity, William Gouge and other Puritans encouraged rigorous reflection, introspection, and a disciplined life. They wanted to provide tools for believers to find consolation for their spiritual anxieties. They did so by instructing them to search their hearts to discern even the smallest degree of faith that testifies to their justification.[46] While no single or exhaustive printed work demonstrating the marks of Puritan practical divinity was ever developed, efforts to this end were in place. Historian Anthony Milton reports that John Dury (1596–1680), the

---

44. "Westminster Confession," 500. Emphasis added.
45. Quoted in Beeke, *Quest for Full Assurance*, 147–48.
46. Benedict, *Christ's Churches Purely Reformed*, 321.

Scottish Protestant who sought to unite European Protestant churches, attempted to compile such a complete body of practical divinity in the 1630s. He desired to make available a work that would equip continental Protestant pastors for the purpose of reforming personal and public piety. Milton notes that Dury contacted Gouge and other London Puritans for assistance in this task. These Puritans expressed a willingness to do so, while suggesting that James Ussher (1581–1656), Archbishop of Armagh, lead the project. Although this work never came to fruition, it does provide important insight into contemporary perceptions of Gouge's considerable contribution to the genre of practical divinity.[47]

Scholars trace the roots of Puritan practical divinity to Richard Greenham (c. 1540–1594), while attributing its methodical and systematic development to men like William Perkins (1558–1602) and Richard Rogers (1551–1618).[48] Greenham published little in his life, devoting most of his time to caring for his flock in Dry Dayton. Much of what is known about his teaching comes from the notes of his students that were edited and revised after his death. As a youth, Greenham enrolled at Pembroke Hall, Cambridge in 1559 and became a Fellow there in 1567. Pembroke had suffered immensely under Mary Tudor's short reign with many martyrs and exiles belonging to its ranks. Historians Parker and Carlson state that by the time Greenham matriculated at Pembroke the leading voice at the school was its Master, later Archbishop of York then

---

47. Anthony Milton, "Puritanism and the Continental Reformed Churches," in *The Cambridge Companion to Puritanism*, ed. John Coffey and Paul Lim (Cambridge: Cambridge University Press, 2008), 117.

48. See Kenneth L. Parker, "Richard Greenham's 'Spiritual Physicke': The Comfort of Afflicted Consciences in Elizabethan Pastoral Care," in *Penitence in the Age of Reformations*, ed. Katharine Jackson Lualdi and Ann T. Thayer (Burlington, VT: Ashgate, 2000), 73. Parker and Carlson state, "Greenham's ability to use the metaphysical and theological assumptions of the godly, mixed with a talent for assessing persons in distress, made his work with afflicted consciences paradigmatic as Reformed casuistry in the late Elizabethan period developed. While a prolific publisher like Perkins is normally credited with the origins of this casuistic tradition, it should not escape notice that the most renowned practitioners of this skill in the next generation, Arthur Hildersham, Richard Rogers, Henry Smith and others, received their first formation in this 'facultie' at Dry Dayton," where Greenham ministered. Kenneth L. Parker and Eric J. Carlson, *"Practical Divinity": The Works and Life of Revd Richard Greenham* (Aldershot, England: Ashgate, 1998), 95.

Canterbury, Edmund Grindal (c. 1519-1583). "The spirit brooding over the waters of Master Grindal's ecclesiology was Martin Bucer and, if Greenham's later words and actions are any evidence, the young scholar not only drank deeply from but also washed often and thoroughly in those waters."[49] Martin Bucer (1491-1551), the German reformer exiled to England in 1549, held the pastoral ministry in high esteem. He was an influencing voice in the life of Thomas Cranmer (1489-1556) and wanted to see Bible-centered ministry take place among ministers.[50] While at Cambridge, Bucer's ideal for ministry inspired young ministers like Greenham. Thus, in 1570, Greenham accepted the role of rector of Dry Dayton where he served for the next twenty years considering that calling one of great responsibility.

During his career at Dry Dayton, Greenham's household seminary became famous for training university students on the responsibilities of caring for the spiritual lives of people. "It was the first of its kind and a truly significant innovation in clerical education, filling a crucial gap: the absence of any *practical* training for ministry."[51] Most importantly, Greenham gained popularity for his ability to care for afflicted consciences, which is at the foundation of Puritan practical divinity. "Greenham assessed the situation of each afflicted conscience. These took the form of physical illness, doubts about the state of one's soul, fears of things to come, and tragedies like the death of a child or a natural disaster. Considering each case in context, Greenham comforted, guided and admonished as each circumstance required."[52]

Like Greenham, William Perkins was central in the development and popularization of caring for the wounded conscience. Blacketer calls Perkins "a pioneer in the field of Protestant practical theology" and states that his writings on "practical piety" were influential in and outside of England.[53] His most important work of practical

---

49. Parker and Carlson. "*Practical Divinity*," 9.

50. Diarmaid MacCulloch, *The Later Reformation in England, 1547-1603* (New York: St. Martin's, 1990), 16-17, 69; Parker and Carlson, "*Practical Divinity*," 10-11.

51. Parker and Carlson, "*Practical Divinity*," 21.

52. Ibid., 87.

53. Raymond A. Blacketer, "William Perkins (1558-1602)," in *The Pietist Theologians*, ed. Carter Lindberg (Malden, MA: Blackwell, 2005), 38. O'Banion argues

divinity related to assurance of salvation was *A Treatise Tending unto a Declaration, Whether a Man be in the Estate of Damnation or the Estate of Grace* (1588). In the preface to this work, Perkins states the problem for which he wrote this treatise, "Good reader, it is a thing to be considered that a man may seeme both unto himself & to the church of God to be a true professor of the gospel & yet indeed be none."[54] Perkins made an appeal for appropriate reflection upon one's sin in order that the redeemed might experience assurance of salvation, and the unconverted become aware of spiritual hypocrisy and the need for redemption.[55]

Having sat beneath the teaching of Greenham while at Cambridge and having visited him when he was a minister, Richard Rogers followed Greenham's footsteps as one who tended to afflicted consciences.[56] In his *Seven Treatises* (first published in 1592), Rogers called for a "life of personal spiritual and moral discipline through rigorous daily devotional practices" involving self-inspection.[57] Rogers' instruction on the

---

that Perkins followed the influence of Jerome Zanchi (1516–1590), who spent time in England as Perkins and Greenham developed their practical divinity. He concludes, "If Heinrich Heppe, the great nineteenth-century historian of doctrine, could describe William Perkins as the father of pietism, then Zanchi, 39 years Perkins's senior and a major influence on his thinking, must be regarded as its grandfather." Patrick O'Banion, "Jerome Zanchi, the Application of Theology, and the Rise of the English Practical Divinity Tradition," *Renaissance and Reformation/ Renaissance et Reforme* 29, nos. 2–3 (2005): 110–11.

54. William Perkins, "A Treatise Tending vnto a Declaration, Whether a Man be in the Estate of Damnation, or in the Estate of Grace," in *Workes of that Famovs and Worthy Minister of Christ in the Vniuersitie of Cambridge, Mr. William Perkins.* vol. 1 (London: Iohn Legatt, 1626), 355.

55. Charles E. Hambrick-Stowe, "Practical Divinity and Spirituality," in *The Cambridge Companion to Puritanism*, ed. John Coffey and Paul Lim (Cambridge: Cambridge University Press, 2008), 194–95; Michael P. Winship, "Weak Christians, Backsliders, and Carnal Gospelers: Assurance of Salvation and the Pastoral Origins of Puritan Practical Divinity in the 1580s," *Church History* 70, no. 3 (September 2001): 472–77.

56. In his journal, Rogers tells of a visit he had to Dry Dayton, where Greenham was located. See Marshall M. Knappen, ed., *Two Elizabethan Puritan Diaries by Richard Rogers and Samuel Ward* (Chicago: American Society of Church History, 1933), 59.

57. Hambrick-Stowe, "Practical Divinity," 194. Winship ("Weak Christians," 462–81) discusses Richard Greenham as one who promoted puritan practical divinity before Perkins and Rogers' ordered work.

introspective searching of one's heart came from personal experience. He wrote in his journal on October 30, 1587,

> It is an other thing that I desire, to know mine owne hart better, where I know that much is to be gotten in understaunding of it, and to be acquainted with the diverse corners of it and what sin I am most in daunger of and what dilig[ence] and meanes I use against any sin and how I goe under any afflict[tion]. To conclude, I hope it shal somewhat further my desire and purpose to please god which I taught yesterday, Exod[us] 18:21, that it is the worck and occupation of a christian to learne to understand the lawes of god and to walk in his ways, and thus that should be the chiefest thinge which should be looked after and from thing to thinge practized.[58]

Rogers' concern for his personal godliness is also reflected in his concern for fellow believers. In this manner, Rogers was also a pioneer in Puritan practical divinity.

Greenham, Perkins, and Rogers blazed a trail for other Puritan pastors in this matter of caring for the afflicted soul. These pastors, like Gouge, who followed their example, provided the Christian with reflective tools and practical guides so that they might lead a godly life such as is pleasing to God. The title of Lewis Bayly's (c. 1575–1631) popular 1617 book sums up practical divinity well, *The Practice of Piety: Directing a Christian How to Walke That He May Please God*.[59]

THE LIFE OF WILLIAM GOUGE

William Gouge was born on November 1, 1575, in Stratford-Bow in the southeast county of Middlesex to a family with Puritan convictions.[60]

---

58. Knappen, *Two Elizabethan Puritan Diaries*, 62.

59. Lewis Bayly, *The Practise of Pietie, Directing a Christian how to walke, that he may please God*, 9th ed. (London: I. Hodgetts, 1617). This copy of Bayly's work is available in the rare book collection at the Newberry Library in Chicago, IL.

60. Two biographies of Gouge written shortly after his death provide the bulk of the details known about his life. Those biographies are from his son Thomas Gouge, "A Narrative of the Life and Death of Doctor Gouge," in *A Commentary on the Whole Epistle to the Hebrews, Being the Substance of Thirty Years' Wednesday's Lectures at Blackfriars, London*, by William Gouge, vol. 1 (Edinburgh: James Nichol, 1866), and

His mother was the sister of two Puritan preachers, Samuel and Ezekiel Culverwell and her sisters both married Puritan preachers, William Whitaker and Laurence Chaderton, "so as by the mother's side he came of a stock of preachers."[61] Gouge married his wife Elizabeth on February 11, 1604. They were married for twenty-two years and had thirteen children (eight of whom reached adulthood, six sons and two daughters) before Elizabeth's death on October 26, 1625. The couple moved to Blackfriars, London in 1608 where he became the minister at St. Anne's parish and the rector in 1621 after the death of Stephen Egerton.[62] William continued his educational endeavors at Cambridge during his years in Blackfriars. From Cambridge he earned his Bachelor of Divinity degree in 1611 and his Doctor of Divinity degree in 1628.

Gouge frequently received offers to more prominent places of ministry with more generous salaries and greater notoriety than Blackfriars.[63] However, his son Thomas recounts his father's sentiments when he says, "the height of his ambition was to go from Blackfriars to heaven."[64] He remained at Blackfriars for forty-five years, preaching twice on the Lord's Day and once on Wednesday. Gouge preached a preparation sermon once a month on the Saturday before his parish partook of the Lord's Supper. Thomas estimates that during his father's tenure at Blackfriars thousands were converted, having "the first seed of grace

---

his pastoral successor, William Jenkyn, *A Shock of Corn Coming in its Season. A Sermon Preached at the Funeral of that Ancient and Eminent Servant of Christ William Gouge, Doctor of Divinity and Late Pastor of Black-Friers, London, December the 16th, 1653. With the Ample and Deserved Testimony that then was Given of His Life* (London: Samuel Gellibrand, 1654). Kenneth Allen East adds, "The sermon preached at the funeral of William's wife, Elizabeth, provides biographical information previously overlooked by Gouge's biographers. In addition, biographical specifics can be culled from Gouge's own writings to fill out the picture provided by the other materials." See Kenneth Allen East, "William Gouge: Preacher and Scholar" (PhD diss., University of Chicago, 1991), 170. For a discussion on the apparent discrepancy between the November 1, 1575 birthday given by his son Thomas Gouge and the December 25, 1578 birthday in The *Dictionary of National Biography*, see East, "William Gouge," 5n1.

61. Thomas Gouge, "Narrative," v.

62. Brian Burch, "The Parish of St. Anne's Blackfriars, London, to 1665," *The Guildhall Miscellany* 3 (October 1969): 26.

63. One known offer, according to Jenkyn, was for Gouge to take the post of Provost at Kings College, Cambridge. Jenkyn, *Shock of Corn*, 36–37. Thomas Gouge, "Narrative," ix.

64. Thomas Gouge, "Narrative," ix.

sown into their souls by his ministry," and spiritually equipped for the Christian life by his father's efforts.[65] In 1643, Gouge's reputation, learning and pastoral influence led him to be selected by Parliament to join the Westminster Assembly of Divines.[66]

Like many other Puritans, Gouge remained within the Church of England as a non-conformist. From all accounts, he did not use *The Book of Common Prayer* as a liturgical guide, nor did he support the ecclesiastical structure of the Church of England, which are reflections of his Presbyterian convictions. In 1618 as well as in 1633, Gouge refused to have the "Book of Sports and Recreations" read at his church on the Lord's Day, seeing the very command to do so as deplorable.[67] However, Gouge was flexible in the manner in which people received the Lord's Supper, understanding the importance of the Supper to be bound up not with the external modes of reception but with the sacrament itself.

Although the Church of England required genuflecting, Gouge neither required the same, nor prohibited it. He was content administering the sacrament to those who chose to genuflect, sit or stand. In this manner, Gouge was more prepared to conform to the state Church than was his predecessor at Blackfriars.[68] Because of this flexibility, Gouge was able to appease ecclesiastical authorities while at the same time administer the elements to other non-conformist Puritans.[69] Jenkyn says Gouge was to older Puritans "a sweet refreshing shade and shelter,

---

65. Ibid. Gouge's concern for the unbeliever is also evident in his signature recommending the evangelization of the Indians in New England. See the Society for the Propagation of the Gospel in New England, *Strength out of weaknesse, or, A glorious manifestation of the further progresse of the gospel among the Indians in New-England* (London: M. Simmons, 1652).

66. While serving in the assembly, his attendance was said to be "assiduous, not being observed during the whole time of that session to be one day absent, unless it were in case of more than ordinary weakness." Thomas Gouge, "Narrative," xi.

67. Leslie Stephen and Sidney Lee, eds., *Dictionary of National Biography* (New York: Macmillan, 1890), 22:272; Thomas Gouge, "Narrative," xii.

68. "Unlike Egerton Gouge felt no scruples about conformity." East, "William Gouge," 178.

69. Summarizing historian Paul Seaver, East states that Gouge was called to stand before ecclesiastical authorities on at least two occasions and was questioned concerning his administration of the Lord's Supper. His explanation satisfied the authorities, enabling him to continue on with his method. East, "William Gouge," 194-95.

and even as streams in a dry scorching wildernesse" because he admin-istered the Lord's Supper to them when their non-conformist stances prevented them from receiving it elsewhere.[70] Gouge's discretion allowed him to minister at Blackfriars unhindered until his death, despite his non-conformist position.

In 1621 Gouge spent nine weeks in prison at the hands of King James I (1566–1625), not for his Puritan convictions, but for publishing Sir Henry Finch's work on the restoration of the Jews that the King deemed threatening.[71] Gouge ran afoul with the crown again in 1632 because of activities that began six years earlier. In 1626, Gouge, Puritan ministers Richard Sibbes (1577–1635), John Davenport (1597–1670), and Charles Offspring (d.1659) along with eight other feoffees (four lawyers and four lay members) formed a society that raised money to purchase lay impropriations. Their aim was to see the gospel advance into other parts of the country through the pulpits of Puritan ministers they themselves could appoint.[72] In 1632, then Bishop William Laud and the King's attorney William Noy prosecuted the feoffees recognizing the agenda of the society to be an attempt to reform the English Church from within according to Puritan ideals. As a result, the society was brought to trial. "Those who had engaged in the impropriations scheme ... having been thus summoned before the Star-Chamber, were dealt with, not as honourable and good men, but as 'criminals and traitors.' The verdict was—CONFISCATION of the funds and BANISHMENT of the men."[73] Although banishment was not enforced, the men suffered

---

70. Jenkyn, A Shock of Corn, 35. This description given by Jenkyn appears to be a reference to Isaiah 32:2, "Each will be like a hiding place from the wind, a shel-ter from the storm, like streams of water in a dry place, like the shade of a great rock in a weary land." Unless otherwise stated, all biblical quotations are taken from The Holy Bible: English Standard Version (Wheaton, IL: Standard Bible Society, 2001). Although Gouge ran into problems with the King, he nonetheless vehemently opposed the execution of Charles I. See his signature in Cornelius Burges, The dissenting ministers vindication of themselves, from the horrid and detestable murther of King Charles the First, of glorious memory. With their names subscribed, about the 20th of January, 1648. Signed: C. Burges ... Will. Gouge ... Edmund Stanton ... [and others] (London, 1648; repr., 1704).

71. Finch, Calling of the Ievves.

72. Thomas Gouge, "Narrative," xi.

73. The Star Chamber was a court of law made up of judges in the Palace of Westminster. Alexander B. Grosart, "Memoir of Richard Sibbes, D.D.," in

humiliation and the King confiscated the money and properties they obtained, except for that which they gave out of their own pockets.[74]

In addition to challenging circumstances like these, Gouge was stricken with various illnesses throughout his adult life, such as what appear to be kidney stones and severe asthma. "I have heard him groan a thousand times," said Jenkyn, "yet never did I hear him grumble once."[75] He was a man of both longsuffering and conviction. Gouge's personal trials and illnesses qualified him to address the important topic of the Christian and suffering, as he did at various points in his career.[76] Gouge died on December 12, 1653 and only nine years after his death, was included in Samuel Clarke's (1599-1683) composition titled, *A Collection of the Lives of Ten Eminent Divines, Famous in Their Generation for Learning, Prudence, Piety, and Painfulness in the Work of the Ministry* (1662).[77]

Alex F. Mitchell, the nineteenth-century editor of the minutes of the Westminster Assembly, numbered Gouge among the greatest churchmen and preachers of his era. He writes, "the age is acknowledged to have been an age of greater preachers; and in the first rank of these there fall to be numbered Dr. Gouge, 'the father of the London Puritan ministers,' on whose preaching [James] Ussher and other scholars then congregated in the metropolis did not disdain at times to attend."[78] Mitchell's comments are a fitting tribute for Gouge, an

---

The Complete Works of Richard Sibbes, D.D. (Edinburgh: James Nichol, 1862), lxxiv-lxxv.

74. See William Haller, *The Rise of Puritanism* (New York: Columbia University Press, 1938), 80–82. See also Ronald H. Fritze's helpful article on the matter, "Feoffees for Impropriations (1626-1633)," in *Historical Dictionary of Stuart England, 1603-1689*, ed. Ronald H. Fritze and William B. Robinson (Westport, CT: Greenwood, 1996), 244–46.

75. Jenkyn describes his kidney stones as the "bitterness of his pains by the stone and sharpnesse of urine" and in Gouge's own words, his asthma as "*lethalis arundo*," the deadly arrow in his side. *Shock of Corn*, 32.

76. See chapter 6.

77. Samuel Clarke, *A Collection of the Lives of Ten Eminent Divines, Famous in Their Generation for Learning, Prudence, Piety, and Painfulness in the Work of the Ministry* (London: Samuel Gellibrand, 1662). This account is a reworking of the Thomas Gouge biography found in the preface to William Gouge's commentary on Hebrews.

78. Alex F. Mitchell and John Struthers, eds., *Minutes of the Sessions of the Westminster Assembly of Divines While Engaged in Preparing Their Directory for Church Government, Confession of Faith, and Catechism (November 1644 to March 1649) from Transcripts of the Originals Procured by A Committee of the General Assembly of the Church of Scotland* (Edinburgh: William Blackwood and Sons, 1874), xxxiv-xxxv.

influential yet widely unknown Puritan churchman of the first half of
the seventeenth century.

REVIEW OF THE SECONDARY LITERATURE ON GOUGE

Despite his influence in the seventeenth century, Gouge is largely
unknown in the present day. While references to Gouge can be found
in scattered biographical segments, such as in the *Dictionary of National
Biography*, and in works on the Puritans, these accounts heavily rely
upon the biographies written by Gouge's son, Thomas, and the sermon
preached at Gouge's funeral.[79] Other references to Gouge's works can be
found in scholarly works on Puritan providentialism, family structures
and practices in seventeenth-century England, funeral messages in
Jacobean and Stuart England, catechisms, and Puritan teachings on
prayer. I will discuss these works at the appropriate chapters in this
book. Nevertheless, few writers deal with the extent of Gouge's writings
and the works that he produced.

Gouge published nineteen different works between 1616 and his
posthumous *magnum opus*, a three-volume commentary on Hebrews,
in 1655.[80] His teachings cover an array of topics and genres, several of
which underwent multiple editions. He produced full-length books on
topics such as domestic duties, the armor of God (his book, *The Whole
Armour of God* was published six times between 1616 and 1647), blas-
phemy against the Holy Spirit, the Lord's Prayer, keeping the Sabbath

---

James Ussher (1581-1656) was the Irish Archbishop of Armagh and Primate of All
Ireland from 1625 to 1656.

79. Stephen and Lee, *Dictionary of National Biography*. Benjamin Brook, *The
Lives of the Puritans: Containing a biographical account of those divines who distin-
guished themselves in the cause of religious liberty, from the reformation under Queen
Elizabeth, to the Act of Uniformity, in 1662* (1983; repr., Pittsburgh: Soli Deo Gloria,
1994), 3:165-70; James Reid, *Memoirs of the Westminster Divines* (Edinburgh: Banner of
Truth, 1811), 1:343-63; William S. Barker, *Puritan Profiles* (Ross-Shire: Mentor, 1999),
35-43; John L. Carson and David W. Hall, eds., *To Glorify and Enjoy God* (Edinburgh:
Banner of Truth, 1994), 52-54; Joel R. Beeke and Randall J. Pederson, *Meet the Puritans*
(Grand Rapids: Reformation Heritage, 2006), 284-89. Other common references to
Gouge are found in studies of English household roles that utilize his *Of Domestical
Duties*, discussions on Divine providence, and seventeenth-century millennialism.

80. William Gouge, *A learned and very vsefvl commentary on the whole Epistle to
the Hebrewes* (London: A. M., T. W. and S. G., 1655).

holy, and thanksgiving in suffering.[81] Gouge also published a number of his sermons that addressed topics like God's providence, seeking God's favor in times of national difficulty, and recovering from spiritual apostasy.[82] He originally delivered these published sermons to diverse audiences such as his parishioners in Blackfriars, other congregations, to Parliament, and to an artillery company. He preached on weekdays, the Sabbath, and days of public fasts. Between 1615 and 1637, Gouge published eight editions of his catechism, which also included mealtime, morning, and evening family prayers.[83] At least five of his works were translated into foreign languages, four into Dutch and one into French.[84]

---

81. William Gouge, *Of Domesticall Dvties: eight treatises* (London: Iohn Haviland, 1622); *Panoplia tou theou. The whole-armor of God* (London: Iohn Beale, 1616); *Treattise of the Sinne Against the Holy Ghost* (London: I. Beale, 1639); *A Guide to Goe to God or, an Explanation of the Perfect Patterne of Prayer, the Lords Prayer* (London: G. M. and R. B., 1626); *Sabbath Sanctification* (London: George Miller, 1641); *The Saints Sacrifice: Or, A Commentarie On the CXVI. Psalme* (London: George Miller, 1632). Other books and exegetical works of Gouge include *Gods three arrovves : plagve, famine, svvord, in three treatises* (London: George Miller, 1631); *An Exposition on the VVhole Fifth Chapter of S. Iohns Gospell: also notes on other choice places of Scripture* (London: H. Lownes and R. Young; and J. Beale, 1630); "First Kings through Esther" in *Annotations Upon all the Books of the Old and Nevv Testament* (London: Evan Tyler, 1657).

82. William Gouge, *Extent of God's Providence* (London: George Miller, 1631); *The Progresse of Divine Providence* (London: George Miller, 1645); *The Right VVay: or A direction for obtaining good successe in a weighty enterprise* (London: A. Miller, 1648); *The Saints Svpport* (London: George Miller, 1642); *A Recovery from Apostacy* (London: George Miller, 1639); Other sermons of Gouge include *Mercies Memorial* (London: George Miller, 1645); *Dignitie of Chivalry, set forth in a sermon, preached before the artillery company of London, June xiii, 1626*, 2nd ed. (London: Edward Brewster, 1631); *A Funeral Sermon preached by Dr. Gouge of Black-Friers London, in Cheswicke Church, August 24, 1646, at the funeralls of Mrs. Margaret Ducke* (London: A. Miller, 1646).

83. William Gouge. *A briefe method of catechizing wherein are briefely handled the fundamentall principles of Christian religion, needfull to be knowne by all Christians before they be admitted to the Lords Table. Whereunto are added sundry prayers, with thanksgivings before and after meale*, 8th ed. (London: John Beale, 1637). In 1642, he produced a similar work titled *Briefe Ansvvers to the Chiefe Articles of Religion* (London: George Miller, 1642).

84. Cornelius W. Schoneveld's, *Intertraffic of the Mind in Studies in Seventeenth-Century Anglo-Dutch Translation with a Checklist of Books Translated from English into Dutch, 1600–1700* (Leiden: Brill, 1983), proved most helpful in tracking down Dutch translations. However, Schoneveld mistakenly confuses Gouge's *Sinne Against the Holy Ghost* for *Recovery from Apostacy*. Gouge's works translated into Dutch: *Sinne Against the Holy Ghost* translated *Een Verhandeling van de sonde tegen den H. Geest* (Amsterdam: Ernestest Bach, 1659); *God's Three Arrows* translated *De Drie Pylen Gods. Namelijk, Peste, Honger, Sweert. In drie verhandelingen, I. De plaaster voor de Peste, II.*

In addition to his own literary works, Gouge contributed a number of dedications to other authors' books and republished two books by a notable churchman, Sir Henry Finch (c. 1558–1625).[85] The only letters that remain of his correspondence are a letter he coauthored with three other ministers seeking financial support for an aging friend in 1647 and a letter written to the future Archbishop, William Laud (1573–1645) in 1631.[86]

The crown jewel of his works is his Hebrews commentary. He commented on all but the second half of the final chapter of this New Testament book, only his death preventing its completion. His son Thomas finished the final half chapter in preparation for the posthumous publication. This work was the result of thirty years of Wednesday public expositions that made Gouge a prominent pastoral figure in London. William Jenkyn (1613–1685), Gouge's pastoral successor, attested to the popularity of Gouge's midweek messages when he wrote, "when the godly Christians of those times came to London, they thought not their businesse done un-less they had been at Black-friers Lectures."[87] Gouge's finished commentary was admired for its theological profundity and expositional precision. Over two hundred years later, Charles H. Spurgeon commended the worth of this exposition when he writes, "We greatly prize Gouge. Many will think his system of

---

De Doot des Dieren-Tijts, III. Des Kerks overwinninge over het Sweert. In 't Engels beschreven, en in 't Nederduytsch vertaalt door Petrus Heringa (Amsterdam: Johannes van Someren, 1666); Progresse of Divine Providence translated De Uytstrekkinge van Godts Voorsienigheyt (Amsterdam, Johannes van Someren, 1666); and Dignitie of Chivalry translated De Waerdigheyt vsn de Krijgshandel (Amsterdam: Johannes van Someren, 1666). Gouge's works translated into French: Whole Armour of God translated L'Armure Complette de Dieu (Geneva: Jacques Chouet, 1643).

85. See Gouge's dedications in Robert Bolton's Certaine devout prayers of Mr. Bolton upon solemne occasions (London: George Miller, 1638); Nicholas Byfield's A commentary: or, Sermons vpon the second chapter of the first Epistle of Saint Peter: (London: H. Lownes, 1623), Clement Cotton's A complete concordance to the Bible of the last translation (London, 1635); Ezekiel Culverwell's A Treatise of Faith (London: J. Dawson, 1623); Thomas Sheafe's Vindiciæ senectutis, or, A plea for old-age (London: George Miller, 1639); Those works of Finch are An exposition of the Song of Solomon (London: Iohn Beale, 1615) and The calling of the Ievves (London: William Bladen, 1621).

86. William Gouge, Thomas Foxley, Richard Hiller, and Henry Hickford, To men, fathers and brethren," 26 June 1647 (London, 1647); Gouge to Laud, 19 October 1631, National Archives SP 16/202/3. Laud became the Archbishop of Canterbury in 1633.

87. Jenkyn, Shock of Corn, 28.

observations cumbrous, and so, perhaps it is; but upon any topic which he touches he gives outlines which may supply sermons for months."[88]

Originally printed in 1655, his Hebrews commentary was republished in 1866 and again in 1980 and 2006.[89] In this commentary Gouge engages the Greek text in a sophisticated fashion demonstrating his linguistic and literary capabilities (perhaps this is why Spurgeon thinks some will view it as "cumbrous"). Furthermore, his commentary is filled with thousands of Scripture references to both the Old and New Testaments, displaying his wide grasp of the biblical text. While his Hebrews commentary is at times grammatically meticulous, it does not overlook applying the biblical text to present life situations. This kind of biblical exposition and practical application to life is consistent throughout Gouge's published works.

Only one in-depth study of his life exists, the valuable doctoral dissertation by Kenneth A. East entitled, "William Gouge: Preacher and Scholar." East contends that Gouge was a "major figure" in his era who was "know[n] to and highly respected by his contemporaries" making the study of Gouge's career crucial for interpreting seventeenth-century Puritanism.[90]

East begins his work recreating the intellectual culture in which Gouge was educated in order to determine what elements of his education remained important to him as an adult. By a careful study of the 2,500 marginal citations to over 300 different authors in Gouge's collected works, East concludes that Gouge's exposure to Latin and Greek writers proved valuable to him in his pastoral ministry.[91] Some of the authors that Gouge cites, like Cicero and Ovid, were introduced to him in his early educational years. East also determines that it was

---

88. Charles H. Spurgeon, *Commenting on Commentaries: Lectures addressed to the students of the Pastor's College, Metropolitan Tabernacle, with a list of the best biblical commentaries and expositions, also a lecture on eccentric preachers, with a complete list of all of Spurgeon's sermons with the Scripture texts used* (New York: Sheldon, 1876), 254.

89. William Gouge, *A Commentary on the Whole Epistle to the Hebrews Being the Substance of Thirty Years' Wednesday's Lectures at Blackfriars, London* (Edinburgh: James Nichol, 1866); William Gouge, *Commentary on Hebrews* (Grand Rapids: Kregel, 1980); Gouge, *A Commentary on the Epistle to the Hebrews: Exegetical and Expository*, 2 Vols. (Birmingham: Solid Ground Christian Books, 2006).

90. East, "William Gouge," 1–2.

91. Ibid., 25, 395–96.

during Gouge's Divinity training that he likely drank from the wells of the Church Fathers, which figure prominently in his works. The author Gouge cites most frequently is Augustine followed by Jerome, Chrysostom, and the medieval mystic, Bernard of Clairvaux, says East.[92]

Gouge received a quality education up to age twenty, but it was not extraordinary since many others had similar opportunities.[93] However, what separated Gouge from his classmates, according to East, was his assiduousness. He bypassed opportunities for leisure with fellow classmates in order to study even more. East argues that Gouge went beyond the normal curriculum in order to broaden his learning. One example of Gouge's diligence occurred when a rabbi visited London in order to teach Hebrew. Gouge was the only student to seize this opportunity; his classmates later expressed regret for not doing the same. Furthermore, Gouge's studies excelled beyond not only the requirements of his educational programs but also beyond the recommendations that came from one of the earliest Puritans, Thomas Cartwright (1535-1603).[94] East concludes,

> Gouge's citations point to an intellectual universe which had broadened significantly from that of Cartwright. Not only does he make extensive use of contemporary scholarship, even that written by Catholics, he also has reappropriated areas of the literature—such as Latin commentaries and Scholastic works— that Cartwright recommended avoiding.[95]

For East, these examples demonstrate how Gouge expanded his learning by going beyond the expected learning program.

Another goal of East's work is to provide a picture of Gouge's parish and writing responsibilities. As a minister, Gouge preached on Sundays, administered the sacraments, catechized children, provided spiritual guidance, preached funeral sermons, gave oversight for building projects and delivered messages for unique occasions. As a writer, Gouge published practical writings that influenced Christians beyond

---

92. Ibid., 86, 108–9.
93. Ibid., 39.
94. Ibid., 80.
95. Ibid., 117–18.

Blackfriars. East demonstrates that Gouge's skill as a minister and as a writer placed demands on Gouge that at times agitated the men and women of his parish.[96] Although Gouge apologized to his people for his occasional absence, he continued writing and speaking at other churches because he understood these as opportunities to instruct the godly beyond his parish on how to live in a manner that pleases God. As a minister and as a writer, East determines that Gouge used his learning to "practical and casuistical ends," turning to ancient writers such as Augustine, Chrysostom, Jerome, and Bernard of Clairvaux for practical examples through which he instructed believers. "Gouge devoted most of his life and work to showing people how they could lead upright and moral lives. He was a Puritan casuist."[97]

Although East succeeds in writing an informative and detailed biography of William Gouge that lays the groundwork for future studies such as the present one, his study falls short in two areas. First, East does little to engage contemporary scholarship in a significant way. Perhaps the most noteworthy example of dialogue he has is with William Haller. Haller was critical of the Puritan tendency to write large tomes, which he says "began to find the road toward manifest futility."[98] According to Haller, what advanced Puritanism was not these technical and polemical works, but its prophetic and poetic works. Haller views Gouge's writings to be "arid" and reflective of a technician. East agrees that Gouge was no prophet or poet, but contends that technicians like Gouge did indeed advance Puritan ideas. East says that as a technician Gouge sought to nurture spiritual growth through expounding the theological ideas at the foundation of godly living. "Gouge may not fit neatly into Haller's four types of Puritan—prophets, poets, technicians, and polemicists," says East, "But he was definitely in the Puritan mainstream. He may have polished and reworked his sermons more than most of his contemporaries, but his preaching and writings were extremely popular with both his immediate contemporaries and the

---

96. Ibid., 171. In this list, East includes the *Whole Armour of God, Of Domestical Duties, A Guide to Goe to God, Gods Three Arrowes, Saints Sacrifice,* and *Commentary on Hebrews.*

97. East, "William Gouge," 301, 311–12.

98. Quoted in East, "William Gouge," 296.

printed works maintained their influence after his death."[99] Beyond this discussion, little significant interaction takes place with contemporary writers except for explanatory and descriptive purposes.

Second, East's work also lacks a penetrating thesis statement or research question. While East successfully demonstrates that Gouge was an erudite pastor who through his learning not only sought "to support technical or theological points" but more importantly provided "practical examples and advice or evidence of spiritual witness in his sources," this aim was too general.[100]

Despite these shortcomings, East's dissertation contains a treasure trove of original research demonstrating the significance and importance of Gouge to his contemporaries in the seventeenth century. Furthermore, it lays essential groundwork for further studies into the life and work of William Gouge.

PRACTICAL DIVINITY AND MEDIEVAL SPIRITUALITY

While ministers such as Greenham, Perkins, and Rogers developed an innovative theology and approach to pastoral care, this kind of work is not without historical precedence. Hambrick-Stowe argues that practical divinity does not find its genesis with the Puritans, but resembles medieval Catholic spirituality.

> Despite the Puritans' strong opposition to the Roman Catholic church, they never isolated themselves from long-established devotional traditions. The rise of Puritanism and the settlement of New England ought to be understood as a significant episode in the ongoing history of Christian spirituality. In private devotional practice especially—in the disciplines of meditation and prayer—continuity with earlier traditions may be traced as clearly as may the more easily recognizable discontinuity.[101]

---

99. East, "William Gouge," 296–97.

100. Ibid., 311.

101. Charles Hambrick-Stowe, *The Practice of Piety: Puritan Devotional Disciplines in Seventeenth-Century New England* (Chapel Hill: University of North Carolina Press, 1982), 25.

Hambrick-Stowe proposes that rather than inventing a new genre for spirituality, Puritan writers adapted "classical practices" by "pirating and protestantizing Catholic materials."[102]

Practical divinity resembles Catholic spirituality in that it included the spiritual exercises of daily readings, meditation, and prayers in general and journal keeping, spiritual autobiography, and meditative poetry in particular. Like their medieval Catholic predecessors, Puritan works of spirituality contained visual devotional aids with meditative verse, "thus continuing the iconographic traditions in an age of increasing literacy."[103] Conversely, Puritan spirituality differed from Catholic spirituality in that it made no distinction between the spirituality of the clergy and that of the laity. The Puritans "offered a spirituality for life in the world, without any sense that a purer form of devotion might be found in a religious cloister." Therefore, implanted into Puritan practical divinity is a recognition of the Reformed doctrine of the priesthood of believers.[104] There was also a difference between the practice of meditation in Catholic spirituality and that of practical divinity. The Puritans uniquely emphasized allowing the biblical text to stand in judgment of the believer, where the text not only exposes sin but also provides consolation. "The biblical promises made possible the resolution of misery for one's sinfulness into joy for one's salvation."[105]

In *Penitence in the Age of Reformations* Katharine Lualdi, Anne Thayer, and the contributors to the volume propose that sixteenth- and seventeenth-century Protestants, including the Puritans, actually retained elements of the Catholic penitential system such as self-examination, confession, and discipline in their own practice, even though they rejected penance as a sacrament.[106] Thomas Tentler

---

102. Hambrick-Stowe, "Practical Divinity," 196.
103. Ibid., 203. Hambrick-Stowe, *Practice of Piety*, 29.
104. Hambrick-Stowe, "Practical Divinity," 197.
105. Ibid., 203–4.
106. "The chapters in this volume ... reveal that Protestants did not simply abandon the sacrament of penance, but searched for alternatives that would address similar religious and social needs in keeping with their distinctive convictions concerning sin and salvation." Katharine Jackson Lualdi and Anne T. Thayer, "Introduction," in *Penitence in the Age of Reformations*, ed. Katharine Jackson Lualdi and Anne T. Thayer (Burlington, VT: Ashgate, 2000), 2. Cf. Parker, "Richard Greenham's 'Spiritual Physicke,'" 71–83.

writes, "We can see that the penitential systems of the Reformation represent, simultaneously and paradoxically, a continuation of medieval mentalities and practices and a revolutionary break with them."[107] Theodore Dwight Bozeman also recognizes this continuity and discontinuity between Puritan practical divinity and the medieval Catholic penitential system.

In his study, Bozeman relates practical divinity to the doctrine of assurance of salvation and rightly determines that there were two principal ends of practical divinity. First, the purpose of practical divinity was "to reassure saints in doubt about the reality of their conversion and of their standing before God" and second "to enhance moral purity."[108] Bozeman suggests that as practical divinity progressed into the seventeenth century, a gradual shift took place and practical divinity began to drift theologically into what better resembled the Catholic penitential system than Protestant devotion. The survey of personal sins fed "the late-medieval phenomenon of the sin-anguished conscience," says Bozeman. Where personal reflection was meant to bring comfort, in reality it did the opposite.[109] "In the Stuart years the examen of self had evolved into an aggressive, punctilious, and repeated survey of sins tied completely to the question of assurance." In Puritan writers like John Downame, Bozeman sees "the complete [Catholic] confession in Protestant dress!"[110] Downame appeals to the Ten Commandments as the standard by which one examines self. In addition, he calls his readers to catalogue each sin and determine its severity and degree. The cataloguing process led to a fear of the last days and God's final judgment. In Bozeman's mind, practical divinity had become a "devotional re-Catholicization" because it reflected not only the methods but

---

107. Thomas Tentler, "Postscript," in *Penitence in the Age of Reformations*, ed. Katharine Jackson Lualdi and Ann T. Thayer (Burlington, VT: Ashgate, 2000), 240.

108. Theodore Dwight Bozeman, *The Precisianist Strain: Disciplinary Religion and Antinomian Backlash in Puritanism to 1638* (Chapel Hill: University of North Carolina Press, 2004), 106.

109. Ibid., 148. See also Louis Bouyer, *Orthodox Spirituality and Protestant and Anglican Spirituality*, History of Christian Spirituality 3 (Minneapolis: Seabury, 1969), 154–64.

110. Bozeman, *Precisianist Strain*, 149–50.

also the theology of medieval Catholicism.[111] Along with Downame, he makes his point citing numerous Puritan writers, including Gouge. If Bozeman's reading of Gouge and Puritan practical divinity is correct, which this thesis argues against, then it raises important questions about how a Christian can be assured of his or her salvation and the grounds by which this assurance is maintained.

THE BEBBINGTON THESIS: THE LEGACY OF THE PURITANS ON ASSURANCE

In his seminal work, *Evangelicalism in Modern Britain: A History from the 1730s to the 1980s* (1989), David W. Bebbington proposed that Evangelicalism was a movement that began in the 1730s.[112] According to Bebbington, four characteristics distinguish Evangelicalism of the 1730s onward from past generations of Protestants. He writes,

> There are four qualities that have been the special marks of Evangelical religion: *conversionism*, the belief that lives need to be changed; *activism*, the expression of the gospel in effort; *biblicism*, a particular regard for the Bible; and what may be called *crucicentrism*, a stress on the sacrifice of Christ on the cross. Together they form a quadrilateral of priorities that is the basis of Evangelicalism.[113]

Most pertinent for the present study is Bebbington's proposal of *conversionism* as it relates to the doctrine of assurance of salvation, and *activism* as it relates to self-examination and the pursuit of holiness.

Bebbington states that for Evangelicals assurance of salvation accompanies conversion and that this understanding of assurance was central in the Evangelical Revivals of the eighteenth century. Bebbington does not claim that assurance of salvation appeared for the first time in the eighteenth century, but argues that while "assurance had been an important theme of pre-Evangelical Protestant spirituality … the experience had never been regarded as the standard possession

---

111. Ibid., 150.
112. David W. Bebbington, *Evangelicalism in Modern Britain: A History from the 1730s to the 1980s* (London: Unwin Hyman, 1989).
113. Ibid., 2–3.

of all believers. The novelty of Evangelical religion ... lay precisely in claiming that assurance normally accompanies conversion."[114] With relation to the Puritans, Bebbington states, "Whereas the Puritans had held that assurance is rare, late and the fruit of struggle in the experience of believers, the Evangelicals believed it to be general, normally given at conversion and the result of simple acceptance of the gift of God."[115] Bebbington cites numerous eighteenth-century Evangelicals who understood their doctrine of assurance to be a departure from that of their Puritan and Calvinistic predecessors. According to this understanding, Puritan practical teaching encouraged believers to doubt their justification in order to examine further whether they were truly saved. Bebbington quotes the Methodist, Thomas Payne, who said, "Hence I was persuaded that ... I must doubt my justification, which those wretched casuists lay down as one mark of sincerity. For want of knowing better, I listened to these, till I lost the witness of the Spirit." Bebbington concludes, "The age of such Puritan casuists was passing."[116]

Bebbington's thesis has been challenged in a number of ways, including on the matter of assurance. A number of scholars believe that Bebbington overlooked important continuities between the Protestant Reformers and the Evangelicals of the eighteenth century. Using Bebbington's quadrilateral, these scholars conclude that Evangelicalism is a movement that precedes the eighteenth century with continuities that can be found as early as with a figure like Martin Luther in the early sixteenth century.[117]

A. T. B. McGowan disputes Bebbington's claim that a theological shift in the doctrine of assurance took place in the 1730s. McGowan contends, "There was no change in the doctrine of assurance in Reformed theology. Rather, there were always these two elements to the doctrine, assurance by a direct act of faith and assurance as a reflex act of faith. Different scholars at different times may have put more emphasis

---

114. Ibid., 7.
115. Ibid., 43.
116. Ibid., 46.
117. See Michael A. G. Haykin and Kenneth J. Stewart, eds., *The Advent of Evangelicalism: Exploring Historical Continuities* (Nashville: B & H Academic, 2008).

on the one than on the other but there was no change."[118] McGowan argues that assurance of salvation was of the essence of saving faith for the seventeenth-century divines as it was for the eighteenth-century evangelicals.

Bebbington also believes that the *activism* found in the eighteenth century is the primary quality that is lacking in the Puritans of the seventeenth century. He highlights revival meetings, joining societies, the discipline of self-examination, prayer meetings, and a missionary impulse to be qualities that are distinctly found in eighteenth-century Evangelicalism. While evangelicals from the 1730s onward had a greater zeal for certain aspects of activism, such as world missions, it is not correct to conclude that activism is missing in seventeenth century among believers such as the Puritans. Beeke provides examples of how Puritans and those in the Dutch Further Reformation possessed activist qualities.[119] One will find this activist quality in Puritan practical divinity, which emphasized self-examination and the pursuit of holiness.

When one considers the wording of the Westminster Confession and the teachings of the Puritans in this perspective, one finds that it is incorrect to state that Beza, Perkins, and the Puritans departed from the teachings of Calvin. Instead, it is better to understand the differences to be ones of advancing Calvin's thought, not departing from it. There are quantitative differences between Calvin and the Reformers that followed him, and not qualitative ones.[120]

The relationship between practical divinity and assurance of salvation among the Puritans is an important matter to consider as

---

118. A. T. B. McGowan, "Evangelicalism in Scotland from Knox to Cunningham," in *The Advent of Evangelicalism*, ed. Haykin and Stewart, 82. In the same volume, Joel R. Beeke states that "the doctrine of assurance in Puritan and Dutch Further Reformation theology, which influenced Edwards, the Great Awakening and later eighteenth-century evangelicalism, is more nuanced than Bebbington allows." Beeke, "Evangelicalism and the Dutch Further Reformation," *The Advent of Evangelicalism*, ed. Haykin and Stewart, 165.

119. Beeke, "Evangelicalism and the Dutch Further Reformation," 154–67.

120. Beeke makes this distinction, borrowing his language from John S. Bray's *Theodore Beza's Doctrine of Predestination* (Nieuwkoop: DeGraaf, 1975), when he writes, "I am convinced that Calvinism's wrestlings with assurance were *quantitatively* beyond, but not *qualitatively* contradictory to, that of Calvin." Beeke, *Quest for Full Assurance*, 3–4.

demonstrated in this chapter. The present study will advance this discussion through the lens of William Gouge. Because Gouge was a prominent, learned, and pastorally keen minister in the seventeenth century, he is, therefore, an invaluable and rich resource that needs to be mined for insight into this discussion on Puritan practical divinity and assurance of salvation.

2

The Foundation for Gouge's Practical Divinity

GOUGE'S PASTORAL CALL AND PRACTICAL DIVINITY

While traveling to Richard Greenham's house seminary in Dry Dayton, one of practical divinity's trailblazers, Richard Rogers, writes in his diary, "I gave my selfe oft to medit[ation]" and that "much confer[ence] was betwixt me and mr. Cu[lverwell]."[1] He refers to fellow Puritan and neighbor Ezekiel Culverwell (1554–1631), son of Nicholas Culverwell and brother to Samuel, both of whom were Puritan preachers. Rogers and Culverwell were close friends who shared likeminded pastoral concerns and a passion for learning. On August 30, 1587, Rogers writes, "I was occupied in privat study for my Sabbaths exercize ... and the Monday after mr. C[ulverwell] and I studied privatly togither."[2] On November 17 of the same year, Rogers calls his time with Culverwell "sweet."[3] Culverwell knew firsthand and admired the ways in which life and doctrine intersected in Rogers' life.

What makes their friendship important in our discussion is that Ezekiel Culverwell was William Gouge's uncle, twenty-two years his senior. Gouge spent three years under his uncle's teaching while he went to school at Felsted in Essex during the same period that Rogers refers to his friendship with Culverwell in his diary.[4] Gouge expressed how his time learning from Culverwell successfully made him "much built up in

---

1. Marshall M. Knappen, ed., *Two Elizabethan Puritan Diaries by Richard Rogers and Samuel Ward* (Chicago: American Society of Church History), 59.
2. Ibid., 58.
3. Ibid., 63.
4. Gouge would later write the preface of Ezekiel Culverwell's *A Treatise of Faith* (London: J. Dawson, 1623).

his holy faith."[5] With an uncle like Culverwell who was close friends with Richard Rogers and was familiar with Greenham's teaching, it is no surprise that Gouge's ministry at Blackfriars mirrored the practical and theological concerns of the aforementioned Puritans.

Gouge had a great esteem for the pastoral ministry because to be a pastor was to be called by God to be a preacher of the Word of God, and through the Word given opportunity to care for the souls of the people in his church. When reflecting upon his own calling, he writes, "Among the many great blessings which the Lord hath beene pleased to bestow on me, his poore seruant, vnworthy of the least, I account this to be an high Fauour, that he hath put me in his Seruice, and appointed me to be one of the Ministers of his Word."[6] For Gouge, because the Bible is the Word of God, it is therefore authoritative in its instruction for life and doctrine. Thus, he is hard-pressed to find any other calling to be of greater importance than the pastoral one, and is humbled that God had appointed him to it. He writes,

> Basely is this calling accounted of by the greater, and vulgar sort of people: but my conscience beareth me witnesse that I receiue such contentment therein, and hold my selfe so honoured thereby, as I preferre it to all other callings, and am prouoked thereby to giue some euidence of my thankefull acceptance thereof: which better I know not how to doe, then by imploying and improuing to my poore power, the Talent which my Master hath committed to my charge. I am not ignorant how insufficient I am thereunto.[7]

From this statement, it is evident that Gouge believed in a particular pastoral calling whereby God assigns the pastoral task to particular

---

5. Thomas Gouge, "A Narrative of the Life and Death of Doctor Gouge" in William Gouge, *A Commentary on the Whole Epistle to the Hebrews Being the Substance of Thirty Years' Wednesday's Lectures at Blackfriars, London*, vol. I (Edinburgh: James Nichol, 1866), v.

6. The pagination for William Gouge's preface to *The Whole Armour of God. Or, A Christians spirituall furniture, to keep him safe frō all the assaults of Satan*, 5th ed. (London: I. Beale, 1639) is incorrect. Therefore, the first page of his preface will be A1 hereafter.

7. Ibid., A1.

individuals. Gouge believed he was a recipient of this call and chose to accept it along with the responsibilities that accompany the call. Feeling unworthy to receive this divine assignment, Gouge set his mind to labor in such a way that improved his pastoral abilities and thereby strived to be a good steward of the gifts that God has given him. So sure of his calling and commitment to fulfill it, he adds, "I am the seruant of Christ, and of his Church; so long as my life, health, strength, liberty, or any ability is by the good prouidence of God preserued vnto me, my desire is to spend it in the seruice of Christ, and of his Church."[8]

Over his fifty-five years of ministry at St. Anne's parish in Blackfriars, London, Gouge undertook this pastoral task through preaching as well as publishing. As it pertains to preaching as part of his ministerial call, Gouge writes,

> I account Preaching the most principall part of my function: for this is Christs charge, Goe preach the Gospell; and this is that Ordinance wherein and whereby God doth ordinarily, and most especially manifest his owne power, and bestow his blessing. This is it therefore which hitherto I haue most attended vpon, and intend so to continue as long as God shall affoord mee ability and liberty.[9]

What Gouge states here is true in his extant works: that preaching was his principal task and that the gospel should be the central message of that preaching. As for preaching being his primary task, most of Gouge's printed works are expanded from his sermons, which sounded forth from that Blackfriars pulpit multiple times a week. As for the gospel, his works demonstrate how the gospel message is indeed the most prominent theme of his pastoral ministry. The reason for this, says Gouge, is that through the preached gospel message God manifests his power in unique ways.

If preaching the gospel message is of such importance and power, then why would Gouge choose to allocate many of his pastoral hours to publishing books? He says that he has done so in order "to seek the

---

8. Ibid., A4.
9. Ibid., A2–A3.

edification of Gods Church" beyond those in St. Anne's parish. Gouge wrote, "hoping that many whom I neuer knew, nor saw, may reape some benefit by my paines." Furthermore, publishing allows the content of his pastoral ministry to have a longer lasting influence because, "that which is Printed lieth by a man, and may againe and againe be read, and throughly pondered, till a man come to conceiue the very depth of that he readeth."[10]

But Gouge's concerns were not mere instruction to increase learning as an end in itself, but were practical in nature. Through printing and publishing, he said to his parishioners, "I intend your good, whose proper and peculiar Minister I am, and for whose soules I watch, as hee that must giue an account." Similarly in 1622, when addressing his Blackfriars parishioners, Gouge calls himself, "The Watch man of your soules," expressing the rather burdensome task of caring for their spiritual well-being.[11] Gouge believed that God had entrusted not only the minds of his people to him, but also their very souls. Knowing he will one day give an account for his shepherding work before God, Gouge preached and published seeking to instruct the church on both right doctrine and right living. He desired that those who heard his sermons and read his works would conform their lives to the teaching of the Bible and become more devoted followers of Jesus. Here is the heart of Gouge's practical divinity: The ministry of the Word of God was inseparably linked with shepherding the people of God.

His extant writings provide the historian access to the nature of his pastoral teaching along with his biblical-theological framework that informed his practical divinity. The remainder of this chapter will examine Gouge's approach to interpreting and expounding the Bible as well as his understanding of the gospel and divine providence. These three motifs—the Bible, the gospel, and God's providence—factor heavily in his pastoral teaching and practical divinity. As Gouge instructs and consoles the burdened and distressed Christian, he provides guidance from the Bible pointing Christians to the Word of God where the character of God and the gospel are revealed. Thus, it is apparent in Gouge's practical

---

10. Ibid., A3–A4.

11. William Gouge, *Of Domesticall Dvties: eight treatises* (London: Iohn Haviland, 1622), vii.

divinity that the Bible is the primary source of his instruction. Second, he consoles Christians with the gospel message reminding them that it is what saves sinners and brings consolation in dark times. Third, he teaches the theology of divine providence, namely, God's sovereign hand overarching the dealings of humanity on earth, interconnected with the practical implications of that doctrine. In this way, the Bible, the gospel, and divine providence prove to be the foundation of his practical divinity.

GOUGE, THE BIBLE, AND HIS EXEGETICAL METHOD

As stated above, the preaching of the Word was central to Gouge's understanding of his pastoral call. Nearly all of his extant writings were biblical expositions, excluding his catechetical writings. Still, his catechisms, through their question and answer format, shed light on why he was convinced of the centrality of the Bible in his ministry. Consider the following:

> Q. What meanes hath God sanctified to breed and increase these graces [of repentance] in us?
> A. 1. The ministry of the Word. 2. The administration of his sacraments.
> Q. How is the ministry of the Word made profitable?
> A. By giving diligent heed thereto, and by mixing faith with hearing.
> Q. When is faith mixed with hearing?
> A. When the Word as a truth is believed, and withal applied as a truth which concerneth ourselves in particular.[12]

Gouge is committed to the Scriptures because the ministry of the Word is a means of grace through which God brings about genuine repentance in the Christian. When the Christian gives diligent attention and faithful obedience to the Scriptures, he demonstrates fruit of genuine faith. It is a small wonder why Gouge castigates the pope for

---

12. William Gouge, *A briefe method of catechizing wherein are briefely handled the fundamentall principles of Christian religion, needfull to be knowne by all Christians before they are admitted to the Lords Table. Whereunto are added sundry prayers, with thanksgivings before and after meale*, 8th ed. (London: John Beale, 1637), 7.

withholding the Bible from the laity by keeping it in the less-familiar Latin tongue and failing to encourage people to read it for themselves. Concerning the Bishop of Rome, he writes "He denieth to the people liberty to search the rolls wherein this testament is registered; for he suffers not people to read the Scriptures. Oh presumptuous guide! Oh blind people!"[13] Christ's death ratified a new covenant, which should "incite us to search the Scripture, wherein Christ's last will and new testament is registered. Therein observe the promises made to us."[14]

In order for the Bible to minister effectively to people, faithful exegesis must be accompanied by thoughtful exposition.[15] Gouge called the organizing of the text into understandable and memorable points "dividing the Word aright." When this organizing is done well, "thus will the understanding of hearers be much informed with a distinct knowledge of the mysteries of godlinesse, & thus shall they much better discerne the great depth of those mysteries, and the rich treasure that is contained in them."[16] Gouge does not dogmatically propose one method of dividing and explaining over against another. Instead, he reminds his readers that preachers are gifted in different ways and will therefore utilize diverse methods of organizing and delivering the

---

13. William Gouge, *Wherein every word and particle in the originall is explained, and the emphasis thereof fully shewed. The sense and meaning of every verse clearly unfolded. Each chapter and verse logically, and exactly analysed. Genuine doctrines naturally raised, and applied from the severall words, and particles in the whole Epistle. The manifold types of Christ clearly, and largely unveiled. Divers cases of conscience satisfactorily resolved. Severall controversies pithily discussed. Various common-places thoroughly handled. Sundry errors and heresies substantially confuted. Very many dark and obscure places of Scripture, which occasionally occur, perspicuously opened. Being the substance of thirty years Wednesdayes lectures at Black-fryers* (London: A. M., T. W. and S. G., 1655), 642.

14. Gouge, *Commentary on Hebrews*, 642.

15. Gouge emphasizes the necessity of preaching what is in the text, rather than imposing a foreign idea onto the text. In his treatise, *Dignitie of Chivalry*, Gouge defends how the thrust of his message is drawn out of the text (2 Chron 8:9) and not forced upon the text. He says, "the *Dignity of Chivalry* ... is the Pearle that is enclosed in the casket of my Text." He continues, "Bee pleased therefore to take notice of the generall Scope whereat the holy Ghost aimeth in this Chapter [i.e., 2 Chron 8]: thereby you may discerne that the forenamed point, *The dignity of Chivalry*, is not violently wrested, but properly ariseth out of my Text." William Gouge, *Dignitie of Chivalry, set forth in a sermon, preached before the artillery company of London, June xiii, 1626*, 2nd ed. (London: George Miller for Edward Brewster, 1631), 1-2.

16. Gouge, *Whole Armour of God*, 433-34.

passage in their preaching.[17] Gouge himself favored Ramism as a method for expositing the biblical text and aiding application.[18] The French logician Pierre de la Ramée (1515–1572) taught a simplified method of logical analysis, which employed bifurcational divisions of the content being analyzed.

Consider Gouge's teaching on public prayer in *The Whole Armour of God* as an example of Ramism. He states that the place of public prayer must be such that allows all to come without hindrance. He continues, then, to speak of what that prayer gathering should consist. In Ramist fashion, he divides public prayer into two parts stating that it must be done with "unanimitie" and "uniformitie." Being "unanimous," that is, of one accord, is further divided into the two categories of being "audible" and "intelligible" in public prayer. "Intelligible" is then divided into "praying in a known tongue" and "of the aberrations contrary to praying with understanding."[19] This form of exposition is common in his treatises and is evidence of his attempt to interpret properly the Scriptures and apply them to the laity. Even when Gouge's exposition of a text or subject was weighty in matter, his utilization of Ramism allowed for thorough application, which helps to demonstrate his concern for practical Christian living.

After Gouge's death, his son Thomas reflected on his father's expositional approach from the pulpit when he wrote,

---

17. Ibid., 434.

18. Raymond A. Blacketer, "William Perkins (1558–1602)," in *The Pietist Theologians*, ed. Carter Lindberg (Malden, MA: Blackwell, 2005), 41, emphasizes the "self-consciously practical and goal-oriented" nature of the system. It is important to note that Ramist methodology did not influence the content of the matter. For instance, Blacketer points out that Jacob Arminius employed this methodology coming up with very different theological conclusions than did Perkins, Blacketer, 41. See also Sinclair B. Ferguson's foreword to William Perkins's *The Art of Prophesying* (Edinburgh: Banner of Truth, 2002), xii. Donald K. McKim, in his essay, "William Perkins' Use of Ramism as an Exegetical Tool" in *A Commentary on Hebrews 11 (1609 Edition): With Introductory Essays*, ed. J. H. Augustine (New York: Pilgrim, 1991), lists Laurence Chaderton, William Perkins, George Downame, Paul Baynes, Arthur Hildersham, and William Ames as other Puritans who "used the Ramist philosophy and logic not only for presenting their systematic theological writings but also as a method of approaching and exegeting Scripture" (p. 32).

19. Gouge, *Whole Armour of God*, 447–48.

His preaching it was all waies very distinct, first opening the true literall sense of the text, then giving the *Logical Analysis* thereof, and then gathering such proper observations as did thence arise, and profitably and pertinently applying the same; so as his Ministery proved very profitable to his hearers. Many have acknowledged, that in a *Logical Revolution* of his text, he went beyond all that ever they heard, as also in clearing of diffi-cult and doubtfull places, as they came in his way. As his method was clear, so his expressions pl[a]in, all waies delivering the solid points of Divinity in a familiar stile, to the capacity of the meanest.[20]

His son's report allows the reader to hear the simplicity and engag-ing nature of Gouge's sermon delivery so that deep truths are com-municated in such a way that the "meanest" (i.e., average person) has the capacity to understand. Gouge taught and modeled diligence and faithfulness to the biblical text by carefully defining words, parsing verbs, cross-referencing other biblical passages, consulting learned scholars, and communicating the message to the believing community. His approach to the Scriptures is of great importance because it not only provides insight into how he comes to textual conclusions and his preaching style, but also gives present-day historians insight into his "pre-critical" exegesis.

In an essay titled "The Significance of Precritical Exegesis," Richard A. Muller and John L. Thompson defend the value of pre-critical exe-gesis in contrast to the historical-critical method of the twentieth cen-tury.[21] They argue that a common trend among many modern exegetes and students of the history of interpretation is to "spend far more time vilifying these earlier interpreters than understanding them."[22] Muller and Thompson maintain that such "vilifying" is reflective of what

---

20. Thomas Gouge, "Narrative," x.

21. Richard A. Muller and John L. Thompson, "The Significance of Precritical Exegesis" in *Biblical Interpretation in the Era of the Reformation*, ed. Richard A. Muller and John L. Thompson (Grand Rapids: Eerdmans, 1996), 335–45.

22. Ibid., 336.

C. S. Lewis called "chronological snobbery."[23] Instead, David Steinmetz proposes that "knowledge of the exegetical tradition of the church is an indispensable aid for the interpretation of Scripture."[24] Muller and Thompson see four primary distinctives, or "assumptions" as they call them, in pre-critical exegesis. First, pre-critical exegetes understand that the story the text recounts resides in the actual text and "not under or behind it." This is to say that the meaning of the text is in its literal sense.[25] Second, the meaning of the text is administered within the

---

23. C. S. Lewis defines "chronological snobbery" as "the uncritical acceptance of the intellectual climate common to our own age and the assumption that whatever has gone out of date is on that account discredited." Rather than approaching history as such, Lewis says, "You must find why it went out of date. Was it ever refuted (and if so by whom, where, and how conclusively) or did it merely die away as fashions do? If the latter, this tells us nothing about its truth or falsehood." Clive S. Lewis, *Surprised by Joy* (Orlando: Harcourt, 1955), 207.

24. Quoted in Richard Muller's essay, "Biblical Interpretation in the Era of the Reformation: The View from the Middle Ages," in *Biblical Interpretation in the Era of the Reformation* (Grand Rapids: Eerdmans, 1996), 7. Through the influence of Steinmetz and others, there has been a renewed interest in the history of exegesis among contemporary scholars. See for example Thomas C. Oden, ed., *Ancient Christian Commentary on Scripture*, 25 vols. (Downers Grove: InterVarsity, 1998); Henri de Lubac, *Medieval Exegesis*, vol. 1, trans. Mark Sebanc (Grand Rapids: Eerdmans, 1998); Timothy George and Scott Manetsch, eds., *Reformation Commentary on Scripture*, 28 vols. (Downers Grove: InterVarsity, 2011); Craig S. Farmer, *The Gospel of John in the Sixteenth Century: The Johannine Exegesis of Wolfgang Musculus* (New York: Oxford University Press, 1997); David Steinmetz, *Calvin in Context* (New York: Oxford University Press, 1995) and David Steinmetz, *Luther in Context* (Grand Rapids: Baker Books, 2002).

25. Some scholars broadly categorize early Christian exegesis under the Antiochene School of Interpretation and the Alexandrian School of Interpretation. The Antiochene School of interpretive method had as its trademark, a "literal" hermeneutic exemplified by Diodore of Tarsus (died c. 392) and his pupils John Chrysostom (347–407) and Theodore of Mopsuestia (c. 350–428). Duane Garrett highlights four interpretive categories that are unique to the Anitchone hermeneutic: *tropikos*, *allegoria*, *sugkatabasis*, and *theoria*. However, Donald Fairbairn argues that the Antiochene-Alexandrian distinction is overly simplified, concluding that the differences were more theological than hermeneutical. That is to say, their theology led them to interpret the Scripture literally or allegorically and not that their literal or allegorical hermeneutic led them to their theology. See Diodore of Tarsus, *Commentary on Psalm 1–51: Writings from the Greco-Roman World*, trans. R. C. Hill. (Atlanta: SBL, 2005), 4; Duane A. Garrett, *An Analysis of the Hermeneutic of John Chrysostom's Commentary on Isaiah 1–8 with an English Translation*, Studies in the Bible and Early Christianity 12 (Lewiston: Edwin Mellen, 1992), 21–22; Robert A. Krupp, *Shepherding the Flock: The Pastoral Theology of John Chrysostom* (New York: Peter Lang, 1991), 71; Bradley L. Nassif, "The 'Spiritual Exegesis' of

larger scope of the book, which too is set within the larger context of
the goal of divine revelation.[26] "Christian exegetes traditionally have
assumed that a divine purpose and divine authorship unite the text
of the entire canon."[27] Third, the primary reference of the literal and
grammatical sense of the text is not the historical community that
gave rise to the text but the believing community that once received
and continues to receive the text.[28] On this point, Steinmetz clearly
states that "the text cannot mean anything a later audience wants it
to mean" but that a range of viable meanings must be considered and
approached as such.[29] Fourth, for the pre-critical exegete, exegesis was
meant to be done within the larger community of interpretive history including people from the present and the past.[30] "Admittedly, the

---

Scripture: The School of Antioch Revisited," *Anglican Theological Review* 75, no. 4
(1993): 437–70; Donald Fairbairn, "Patristic Exegesis and Theology: The Cart and
the Horse," *Westminster Theological Journal* 69 (2007): 1–19.

26. Sheppard argues that the usage of the English term "scope" among
English expositors is derivative from the ancient Greek church's usage of *skopos*.
He points out that both Athanasius and Irenaeus use this language by way of cor-
respondence "to the creedal core found clearly within the larger text of Scripture
and, from this vantage point, delimits the purpose of any part of Scripture on
the basis of the whole. In this way, the description of a text's scope vacillates
between a vision of the larger context and appeals to the core content of Christian
Scripture." Gerald T. Sheppard, "Between Reformation and Modern Commentary:
The Perception of the Scope of Biblical Books," in *A Commentary on Galatians: With
Introductory Essays*, by William Perkins, ed. Gerald T. Sheppard (New York: Pilgrim,
1989), lix–lx.

27. Muller and Thompson, "Significance of Precritical Exegesis," 340.

28. Ibid., 340–41. David C. Steinmetz believes that the primary issue historical-critical exegetes have with pre-critical exegesis is what they see as a common
tendency with pre-critical exegetes to have multiple levels of meaning within a
text, which brings about a sharp distinction between the interpretive tradition of
Origen and the historical-critical tradition of Benjamin Jowett. Steinmetz argues
that the departure from the interpretive tradition of Origen's hermeneutics brought
many gains in exegesis, but also losses. He defends the validity of the pre-critical
approach when confronted by difficult texts such as Psalms 127, stating that the
dashing of Babylonian children on stones must have more than one possible meaning than its "literal" sense. David C. Steinmetz, "The Superiority of Pre-Critical
Exegesis," *Theology Today*, (April 1980): 27–38. For a critical analysis of Steintmetz's
article, see Daniel Treier's, "The Superiority of Pre-Critical Exegesis? Sic Et Non,"
Trinity Journal (Spring 2003): 77–103.

29. Steinmetz, "Superiority of Pre-Critical Exegesis," 32.

30. Muller and Thompson state that this thesis is accurate even among
Reformation exegetes who boldly championed *sola Scriptura*. "Significance of

Reformers considered the biblical text to be clear and authoritative in itself, capable of being interpreted both grammatically and canonically by the comparison of difficult passages with clearer passage. But interpretation, for them, was not a conversation between a lonely exegete and a hermetically sealed text!"[31]

William Gouge approaches the text in a manner largely consistent with Muller and Thompson's observations. Gouge's Hebrews commentary, his *magnum opus* and the product of thirty years of Wednesday expositions, is his most helpful work when it comes to getting a fruitful understanding of his exegetical method. Originally printed posthumously in 1655, his Hebrews commentary was republished in 1866, 1980, and 2006. In this publication, Gouge works from the Greek text of Hebrews whereby Greek words, discussions on Greek prepositions, or Greek declensions appear on most pages. He often considers figures of speech such as metonymy, synecdoche, and metaphor demonstrating not only his linguistic, but also his literary capabilities. Furthermore, his commentary is filled with thousands of Scripture references to both the Old and New Testaments, which presents the wider scope of biblical revelation and demonstrates his grasp of the Scriptures as a unified whole. He also utilizes 595 footnotes spanning authors from Greek philosopher Aristotle (384–333 BC) to the English Puritan William Whitaker (1548–1595).[32]

Gouge's interpretation of Hebrews 4:12 provides a helpful sample of his exegetical method: "For the word of God is living and active, sharper than any two-edged sword, piercing to the division of soul and of spirit,

---

Precritical Exegesis," 341.

31. Ibid., 342.

32. It is difficult to know exactly why Gouge's works have largely been forgotten. It is possible that his writings that were most influential in his day were overshadowed by later Puritans in the generation following him. For instance, his great commentary on Hebrews may have been overshadowed by that of John Owen. His detailed exposition on the armor of God, which underwent several reprints in Gouge's day, is not as popular as William Gurnall's *magnum opus*, *The Christian in Complete Armour*. His influential works on practical divinity may have been overlooked due to the prolific works of someone like Richard Baxter in his *Christian Directory*. Not to mention that his lengthy work on *Domestical Duties* seems to have partially fallen out of date. Yet, as we have seen, Gouge was respected and admired in his own day as an eminent scholar. In recent days, Gouge has been quoted in new works and reprinted as in the case of his Hebrews commentary.

of joints and of marrow, and discerning the thoughts and intentions of the heart." The interpretive *sine qua non* of this passage lays with the phrase "the word of God" (ὁ λόγος τοῦ θεοῦ). Consistent with Muller and Thompson's first distinction, we see that Gouge aims to find the literal or grammatical sense of the text and does not attempt an allegorical, tropological, or anagogical approach to interpretation.[33] Gouge proposes and evaluates what he sees to be the three primary potential literal renderings of the subject of verse 12. First, the phrase "word of God" could refer to the Son of God. Jesus is referred to as the *essential* Word of God in several Johannine texts, acknowledges Gouge. However apart from the Apostle John, Gouge writes, "in no other place of the New Testament do I find [ὁ λόγος τοῦ θεοῦ] given to the Son of God."[34] Second, Gouge admits that the written word is the "usual" way the "word of God" is referred to in Scripture. However, Gouge provides a third option that understands the "word of God" as "God's word preached" or "the preached Scriptures." Gouge comes to this exegetical conclusion

---

33. The medieval church had great affection for the church fathers. The doctrinal formulations and exegetical decisions of the fathers became the predominant way of biblical understanding. Exegesis, therefore, was done by interpretive glosses, which were "Scripture annotations or commentaries from the fathers that were written in the margins or between the lines of the Bible." William Klein, Craig L. Blomberg, and Robert L. Hubbard, *Introduction to Biblical Interpretation* (Nashville: Thomas Nelson, 2004), 43. As these glosses became the norm for exegesis, so too did Origen's proposal of a threefold sense of Scripture beyond the literal sense. By the mid fourteenth-century, the fourfold senses—literal, allegorical, tropological, and anagogical—had been put into a saying as a memory aid: *The Letter teaches events, allegory what you should believe, morality teaches what you should do, anagogy what mark you should be aiming for.* Henri de Lubac notes that Nicholas of Lyra cites this creedal poem c. 1330. See Henri de Lubac, *Medieval Exegesis: The Four Senses of Scripture*, trans. Mark Sebanc (Grand Rapids: Eerdmans, 1998), 1:1, 142–59, 161–224. With the rise of scholasticism and humanism in the middle ages, an array of interpretive proposals arose distancing various interpreters from Origen's heritage. Thus, such alternatives ought to prevent the assumption that medieval exegesis was mere allegorism. Rather, a number of scholastic and humanist scholars stressed the literal meaning of the text. Muller and Thompson write, "Not only does medieval exegesis manifest a considerable variety of interpretive patterns, but it also displays what can only be called an increasing interest in both the text and its literal sense and thereby situates itself along a trajectory pointing toward the Reformation rather than away from it." Muller and Thompson, "Significance of Precritical Exegesis," 344.

34. Gouge, *Commentary on Hebrews*, 324.

through a series of interpretive decisions that reflect the other three "fundamental assumptions" of pre-critical exegesis proposed Muller and Thompson.

Like Muller and Thompson's second stated "assumption" suggests, Gouge interprets the phrase "word of God" in both its immediate literary context as well as in the larger "scope" of the book of Hebrews and all of biblical revelation. In Hebrews 3, the Israelite hope of entering into God's "rest" is a prominent theme (3:11, 18; 4:1, 3, 5, 8, 9, 10, 11) that, according to Gouge, should inform the reader's interpretation of the phrase "word of God" in Chapter 4. For Gouge, this context is significant because, "By this word," that is, the preached word, "have God's people in all ages been called to enter into that rest, whereof the apostle hath spoken so much before."[35] However, it is not only the immediate context that leads him to this interpretation, but also the *analogia fidei*, that is, the usage of Scripture to interpret Scripture.[36] He references no less than 120 biblical references in his exposition of verse 12 alone, making use of thirteen different Old Testament books and eighteen different New Testament books.[37] In doing so, Gouge demonstrates how Hebrews 4:12 relates to the goal of God's canonical revelation.[38] As one who had a role in the crafting of the Westminster Confession of Faith, Gouge's exposition of Hebrews 4:12 coincides with Chapter 1, Article 9 of the Confession which says, "The infallible rule of interpretation of Scripture is the Scripture itself: and therefore, when there is a question about the true and full sense of any Scripture (which is not manifold, but one), it must be searched and known by other places that speak more clearly."[39]

---

35. Ibid., 324.

36. William Perkins defines the analogy of faith as "a summary of the Scriptures, drawn from its well-known and clear parts." Perkins, *Art of Prophesying*, 26–27.

37. Old Testament books: Genesis, 1 Samuel, 2 Samuel, 1 Kings, 2 Kings, 2 Chronicles, Psalms, Isaiah, Jeremiah, Ezekiel, Hosea, Jonah, and Zechariah. New Testament books: Matthew, Luke, John, Acts, Romans, 1 Corinthians, 2 Corinthians, Galatians, Ephesians, Philippians, 1Thessalonians, 2 Timothy, Philemon, Hebrews, James, 1 Peter, 1 John, and Revelation.

38. Muller and Thompson, "Significance of Precritical Exegesis," 340.

39. "The Westminster Confession of Faith, 1647," in *Documents of the English Reformation*, ed. Gerald Bray (Minneapolis: Fortress, 1994), 488–89.

According to Muller and Thompson, the believing community that receives and continues to receive the text is the primary recipient of the literal grammatical sense. This third assumption of pre-critical exegesis is seen in the way Gouge's pastoral instincts keep his interpretation close to the life of the believing community of his day. When he explains that the "preached word" is what is meant by the phrase "word of God," he notes how John the Baptist, Christ, and the Apostles *preached* the word of God while the Scribes and Pharisees failed to do so, preaching instead the traditions of their elders. Gouge correlates this text with the life of the church in the decades that preceded him when he states that Luther and the Reformers preached God's word whereas the friars preached "popish legends."[40] The message came as a rebuke for his contemporaries who lay trust in their own word and neglect to preach the word of God. These pastoral observations reminded ministers to be "diligent and faithful in preaching" and for "people to attend upon the ministry of this word."[41]

Muller and Thompson's fourth distinctive states that pre-critical exegetes did not do their exegetical work in "isolation." Gouge's exposition of Hebrews 4:12 does show some sign of conversation with past and present interpreters. In presenting the position that the "word of God" might refer to the Son of God, Gouge displays knowledge of the interpretations of patristic exegete Ambrose of Milan (337–397), the medieval exegete Theophylactus of Achrida (1055–1107), and the Catholic reformation exegete Cardinal Cajetan (1469–1534). Furthermore, his own exegesis was done not only in conversation with the community of other interpreters, but also in the community of other translators speaking of a "former" English translation and the "last" English translation when expounding the word "quick" (i.e., "living").[42]

Gouge may have also utilized Calvin's commentary without necessarily referencing it. Some similarities exist, such as when Calvin poses the question, "Is this word to be understood of the Law or the Gospel?" In like manner, Gouge applies both Law and Gospel to the word

---

40. Gouge, *Commentary on Hebrews*, 324.
41. Ibid., 325.
42. Ibid., 324.

envisioning each to be one of the sword's two edges.[43] Furthermore, Gouge, like Calvin, places an emphasis on the preached word and its efficacy. Another significant similarity is their exposition of the words "piercing of soul and spirit." Calvin writes, "The word *soul* means often the same with *spirit;* but when they occur together, the first includes all the *affections*, and the second means what they call the *intellectual* faculty.[44] Gouge similarly writes, "The *soul*, as distinguished from the *spirit*, is put for the *will* and *affections*.... The spirit is put for the *understanding* or *mind*."[45] Gouge, like Calvin, likens the soul to the affections and the spirit to the intellect. Although it cannot be proven at this juncture, we may tentatively suggest that Gouge could have interacted with Calvin's comments on this verse.

In this survey of Gouge's exposition of Hebrews 4:12, we see that this seventeenth-century Puritan commentator employed an exegetical method consistent with the four fundamental distinctives of pre-critical exegetes as proposed by Muller and Thompson.

GOUGE'S THEOLOGICAL OUTLOOK ON THE GOSPEL

The cross of Jesus Christ finds its way into all of Gouge's works with varying degrees of emphasis. The reader of Gouge is hard pressed to find a one- or two-sentence definition of the Christian gospel in Gouge's writings. Even in his catechism, the reader will not find a discreet question, "What is the gospel?" Instead, what is found is a grouping of questions, the answers to which collectively expound Gouge's view of the gospel. These questions include: "What is the punishment due to sin?" "Was it necessary that our Saviour should bee both God and man?" "What did Christ to make that satisfaction?" "How appeareth it that he became a curse for us?" "How did he manifest his victory over death?" "How can those things which Christ did, and suffered in his owne person, be made availeable for us?"[46] His clearest and most substantive

---

43. Ibid., 326.

44. John Calvin, *Calvin's Commentaries, The Epistle of Paul the Apostle to the Hebrews and the First and Second Epistles of St. Peter*, trans. by W. B. Johnston and ed. by D. W. Torrance and T. F. Torrance (Grand Rapids: Eerdmans, 1970), 52.

45. Gouge, *Commentary on Hebrews*, 327. Emphasis added.

46. Gouge, *Briefe Method of Catechizing*, 5–7.

descriptions of the gospel are found in his Hebrews commentary, where we see the gospel explained theologically by way of biblical exegesis and in his *Whole Armour of God*, where gospel descriptions predominantly stem from practical and theological reflection. Both of these approaches provide the reader with a clear picture of Gouge's gospel understanding from which his practical divinity takes root.

Beginning with its etymology, Gouge reminds his readers that the English "gospel" comes from the Greek "εὐαγγέλιον" which is to speak of a "good message" or "good tidings." The English "*spell* in ancient time signified *speech*: Gospel then is *good speech*," writes Gouge. This simple etymological explanation of the gospel, for Gouge, begs the question of "what is the good speech, or good news?" At various places, Gouge provides perspicuous theological descriptions of the gospel, such as,

> The Gospell revealeth Christ Iesus, who being the true eternall Sonne of God, even very God, and so able to beare the infinite wrath of his Father, and procure his favour, tooke upon him, into the vnity of his person mans nature, wherein he suiected himself to the Law, and both fulfilled the righteousnesse, and also underwent the curse thereof.[47]

When discussing the phrase "gospel of peace" in Ephesians 6:15, he communicates man's need and the solution offered in Christ. The following quote, though lengthy, demonstrates his clear description of the gospel.

> In the beginning God made man after his owne Image, by virtue whereof, there was a sweet harmony and concord betwixt God and man; God having revealed unto man what was his good will, pleasing and acceptable unto him; man being both able, and also willing to doe that which was acceptable to God. But long this Peace did not last: it was soone broken, and that wholly, and onely through mans default. For man wittingly sinned against his Creator, and thereby justly provoked his wrath: thus came enmity betwixt God and man. Such a breach was made by mans rebellion, that all creatures in Heaven and earth were not able to make it up. Christ therefore, the eternall, true, naturall, proper,

---

47. Gouge, *Whole Armour of God*, 221.

onely begotten Sonne of GOD, tooke upon him to be a Mediator betwixt God and man. He satisfied his Fathers Justice, pacified his wrath, procured favour towards man, whereby God was moved to offer reconciliation unto man; with all he gave unto man his sanctifying Spirit, to breed faith in him, that thereby man might receive and embrace this reconciliation.[48]

The clarity and exactness with which he writes provide a window into Gouge's pastoral priorities. His gospel proclamation begins with the Garden of Eden and the fall of man and brings his readers to God's solution for man's sin—the cross of Jesus. While his description confronts his readers with the enmity that resulted from man's rebellion in the Garden, it also provides balm for those sinful wounds in declaring to them the saving hope found in Jesus, the Mediator between God and man. Gouge's words remind Christians what Christ has done on their behalf and tugs at the hearts of unbelievers who are in need of putting their faith in the Christian gospel.

In these examples one can see that Gouge's understanding of the gospel and his atonement theology are two sides of the same coin, which may also explain why Gouge does not provide a succinct definition of the gospel. The gospel has levels of depth where no brief definition is altogether adequate. Gouge's gospel descriptions are expounded in a biblical-theological way under the banner of what Christ's death has accomplished rather than under a category of systematic theology, such as theories of the atonement.[49] Still, Gouge's atonement theology equates what is now understood as the penal substitutionary atonement theory (although he does not use this exact kind of language) while giving proper weight and importance to the truthfulness of other dimensions of the atonement.[50] Gouge's theology of atonement has four

---

48. Ibid., 166.

49. In this chapter, the terms theory and model interchangeably are used to describe a particular theological approach to Jesus' atoning work on the cross (i.e., ransom theory is synonymous with ransom model).

50. From the earliest days of the Church the ransom theory of Jesus' atoning work on the cross has been an important, if not central, atonement model. Through the Middle Ages and Reformation era, other atonement theories were articulated ranging from Anselm's satisfaction theory, Abelard's moral influence theory, the substitutionary emphasis of the Reformers, and Grotius' moral government theory.

essential elements to it, namely, (1) Jesus offered himself as a sacrifice on the behalf of man, (2) to satisfy infinite justice and pacify the wrath of God which, (3) removed the curse of the Law and, (4) vanquish the devil and death resulting in the freeing of those who believe who were once held captive by sin, the Law, and Satan.[51]

Indeed, the gospel fuels Gouge's practical divinity. When he declares the gospel message (reflecting his atonement theology) he often does so in order to remind Christians that the gospel matters in their day-to-day lives. When confronted with the spiritual battle and hardships of life, it is the hope of the gospel that will comfort and sustain believers through hard times as well as instruct them on how to endure and hope in God. After his gospel proclamation quoted above, he follows with these practical applications that result from a sinner being reconciled with God, "As fruits of this peace there flow from it remission of sinnes, quietnesse and comfort of conscience, joy of heart, willingnesse and ability to doe that which is pleasing unto God, freedome from the dominion of sinne, from the power of the Divell, from the evill of all crosses,

---

In the nineteenth century, the penal substitutionary model became prominent among many who come from the Reformation tradition, almost at the expense of other theories. In recent years, reformed scholars have responded to this sort of pendulum swing and have shown the diversity of understanding of Reformers like Luther and Calvin arguing that no one theory should stand alone, while at the same time defending the centrality of penal substitution in Jesus' atoning work. See Alister McGrath, "Irenaeus on the 'Ransom' Theory of the Atonement," in The Christian Theology Reader 2nd ed., ed. Alister McGrath (Oxford: Blackwell, 2001), 328. Gustaf Aulén calls this the "classic" or "dramatic" view in his Christus Victor: An Historical Study of the Three Main Types of the Idea of Atonement, trans. A. G. Herbert (New York: Macmillan, 1969). See Graham A. Cole's discussion of penal substitution in God the Peacemaker: How Atonement Brings Shalom, New Studies in Biblical Theology (Downers Grove: InterVarsity, 2009), 233–41. See the essays "The Atonement in Martin Luther's Theology" by Timothy George and "The Atonement in John Calvin's Theology" by Henri Blocher in Charles E. Hill and Frank A. James III, eds. The Glory of the Atonement: Essays in Honor of Roger Nicole (Downers Grove: IVP, 2004).

51. I have chosen to combine the "satisfaction of justice" and "pacification of wrath" rather than separate the two because in Gouge's language, the two are closely intertwined. It would not properly represent Gouge to divide these similar yet unique dimensions of what took place at the cross. The same is true of Jesus "vanquishing the devil" and "vanquishing death" in Gouge's thought. Because the devil holds the power of death, and Jesus vanquished Satan and death by himself dying, the two ideas will then be discussed together.

from the sting of death, and of the grave, and from the feare and fire of hell."[52] Thus the Christian is capable of walking in a manner that brings God glory because he has been freed from sin and the curse of the law through the atoning death of Jesus Christ. The gospel is, therefore, the starting point of the Christian life and the foundation from which the Christian lives. When trials, and fear, and failure enter the Christian's life, they can first turn to the gospel where they find assurance of faith, comfort, and instruction on how to live.

In his Hebrews commentary in particular, Gouge's theology of the atonement comes in the form of biblical theology, stemming from his exegesis and exposition of the biblical text. Gouge devotes seventy-six double-columned small-font pages to explain Hebrews 2:6–18.[53] At various junctures reference will be made to John Owen's (1616–1683) comments on Hebrews 2:6–18 in his magisterial Hebrews commentary.[54] The intention is not to evaluate the strengths of one commentary against the other *per se*, but rather to compare the commentaries and note the theological and expositional differences and consistencies between the two. John Owen will be employed as a conversation partner for the following reasons. First, Owen's commentary on Hebrews is widely regarded as among the best Hebrews commentaries produced by an English-speaking Reformed Protestant in the seventeenth century.[55] Second, comparing Gouge's exposition with Owen's will provide insight into the quality of Gouge's commentary further validating the significance of Gouge's contribution as a pastoral and theological voice among

---

52. Gouge, *Whole Armour of God*, 167.

53. That is, in its 2006 publishing, William Gouge, *Commentary on Hebrews: Exegetical and Expository Vol. 1 and Vol. 2* (Birmingham: Solid Ground Christian Books, 2006). Gouge invests another twenty-eight pages covering the atonement while commenting on Hebrews 10:1–18. These two lengthy discussions are not the only discussions on the gospel and atoning work of Jesus in his commentary, but are the most detailed and substantive. While helpful, these other sections in his commentary do not add anything new to the atonement theology expounded in Hebrews 2:6–18.

54. Owen began publishing his commentary in 1668, fifteen years after Gouge's death.

55. Alexander Grosart, Richard Sibbes' biographer, says that Gouge's "great 'Exposition of Hebrews' is worthy of a place beside the kindredly-massive folios of John Owen." Alexander B. Grosart, "Memoir of Richard Sibbes, D.D.," in *The Complete Works of Richard Sibbes, D.D.* (Edinburgh: James Nichol, 1862), xx.

Puritans. Third, although Owen does not explicitly quote Gouge, he at least on one occasion engages Gouge as a conversation partner.[56] Fourth, in both Gouge and Owen, the reader will find a non-reductionistic theology of the atonement born out of their exposition of the biblical text.

A Sacrifice on Man's Behalf

The first component of Gouge's atonement theology states that Jesus died on man's behalf. He does not use the exact language of "substitute" or "vicar" to discuss why Jesus had to die but instead tends to use the word "surety" in that Jesus was the guarantee on behalf of those who believe. He also provides the concept of substitution where one stands in the place of another. Commenting on Hebrews 2:9 where it says that Jesus "taste[d] death for everyone," Gouge writes, "He was our *surety*, and took *our sins on him*, and undertook to make full satisfaction for them (italics added)."[57] For this reason Jesus had to become a man, in order to die on man's behalf. Plainly stated, Jesus' self-giving sacrifice is only of importance because he was fully man. For Gouge, the incarnation is the necessary starting point in considering Christ's atoning work. In Hebrews 2:6-8a the writer to the Hebrews quotes Psalm 8:4-6 and then expounds this quotation in 2:9 saying, "But we see him who for a little while was made lower than the angels, namely Jesus, crowned with glory and honor because of [διὰ] the suffering [τὸ πάθημα] of death, so that by the grace of God he might taste death for everyone."[58] Important for Gouge is the preposition διὰ, which in this passage is followed by the accusative τὸ πάθημα thereby "signifieth the

---

56. Owen explicitly mentions Gouge in his comments on Hebrews 9:13-14 speaking of the priestly and sacrificial work of Jesus on the cross. Owen writes, "A late learned commentator on this epistle [whose name Owen unfortunately does not provide] takes occasion in this place to reflect on Dr. Gouge, for affirming that Christ was a priest in both natures; which, as he says, cannot be true. I have not Dr Gouge's Exposition by me, and so know not in what sense it is affirmed by him; but that Christ is a priest in his entire person, and so in both natures, is true, and the constant opinion of all protestant divines." Here we see Owen siding with Gouge against another "learned commentator" affirming that Jesus was priest in both his human and divine natures. John Owen, *The Works of John Owen*, vol. 20, *Exposition of the Epistle to the Hebrews with Preliminary Exercitations*, 7 vols., ed. W. H. Goold (Edinburgh: T&T Clark, 1862), 3:295.

57. Gouge, *Commentary on Hebrews*, 133.

58. Unless otherwise stated, all biblical quotations are taken from the ESV.

final cause" and accordingly should be rendered, "But we see Jesus, who was made a little lower than the angels *for the suffering of death* ..." The writer to the Hebrews is communicating that the purpose for which Christ was made lower than the angels (taking on human flesh) was so that he could actually die. John Owen concludes as does Gouge that the preposition διὰ should be taken as the "*final end of the humiliation of Christ*" rather than the "*meritorious cause of his exultation.*"[59]

As God, Jesus could not die, but as a man he could and did die. Gouge writes, "I supposed that the main scope of the apostle is, to set out the end of Christ's being made lower than angels, namely, that he might be a sacrifice to expiate man's sin; and thereby to make reconciliation betwixt God and man."[60] Christ could not have tasted death for everyone had he not become a man. "Had not Christ assumed a human nature ... he could not have died," he continues, "For Christ died not as a private person to pay his debt, but as a surety for man, and a redeemer of man." This task of redemption surpasses the power of angels, but in order to accomplish it, Jesus had to be made lower than the angels. Gouge writes, "As by being man he was made fit to suffer, so that manhood being united to the Deity, was made able to endure whatsoever should be laid upon it." With great awe, Gouge continues, "Behold here the wonder of wonders. Christ undertakes a task above the power of all the angels [i.e., the redemption of humanity], and to effect it he is made lower than angels. If ever power were made perfect in weakness, it was in this."[61]

Christ's death as a man was on behalf of humanity based not upon the merits of men and women but upon the grace of God. "It was therefore of God's grace that Christ was given to man, and that he did what he did, and endured what he endured *for man*." God's grace is manifest through "the satisfaction that Christ hath made *for our sins.*"[62] Jesus' death "for man" was not simply to provide his followers with an example to follow of one who suffers unjustly. He was no mere moral exemplar, but an actual atoning sacrifice. The substitutional nature of

---

59. Owen, *Epistle to the Hebrews*, 3:355.
60. Gouge, as most commentators in the seventeenth century, is taking the author of Hebrews to be the apostle Paul. Gouge, *Commentary on Hebrews*, 130–31.
61. Ibid., 131.
62. Ibid., 132. Emphasis added.

Jesus' death is evident in Gouge's usage of prepositions such as "for" and prepositional phrases such as "on behalf of." Furthermore, the substitutional nature of Gouge's thought is connected with the satisfactory nature of that sacrifice.

SATISFYING INFINITE JUSTICE, PACIFYING INFINITE WRATH

In 1098, Anselm the Archbishop of Canterbury penned his famous work, *Cur Deus Homo*, where he endeavors to answer the question why God had to become a man. His treatise comes in a question and answer format where he articulates a theory of the atonement that has come to be known as the "satisfaction theory." Anselm himself does not claim any bit of novelty, "what should be enough has been said by the holy Fathers on the subject," he writes. The value of his work is found in his ability to compile the teachings of the Fathers and distill them into one treatise that is often praised for its brevity and the clarity of its reasoning. Intertwined with the question of why God had to become man is the question of why satisfaction needs to be provided. According to Anselm, what God is owed above all is honor from his creatures. Therefore, it is sin when humanity fails to give him this deserved honor. "If angelic beings, or men, always repaid to God what they owe (i.e., honor), they would never sin ... thus to sin, is nothing else but to not repay God one's debt."[63] Satisfaction is needed when one offends God's honor by failing to repay God the honor due to him. "Whoever renders not unto God this due honour, takes away from God that which is His, and does God dishonor.... Thus, therefore, each sinner ought to repay the honour of which he has robbed God: and this is the satisfaction which every sinner ought to make to God."[64] Anselm continues in arguing that neither mercy alone nor divine will can satisfy this failure to give God honor because sin cannot be left unatoned without punishing it. This is the great dilemma and plight of humanity, where God had to become a man and atone for the sin of humanity thereby satisfying divine honor.

Although Gouge presents a satisfaction model for the atonement that has some similarities to Anselm, he deviates from him in at least

---

63. Anselm, *Cur Deus Homo: To Which Is Added a Selection from His Letters* (Edinburgh: John Grant, 1909), 23.
64. Ibid., 24.

one important way. Where Anselm argues for a satisfaction of divine *honor*, Gouge, like other reformers, argues for a satisfaction of divine *justice*. In Hebrews 2:2, the writer to the Hebrews speaks of a "just retribution" or "just judgment," due to "every transgression or disobedience." Gouge states, that by metonymy of *effect*, every "transgression" refers to every "transgressor" as every act of "disobedience" refers to the one who is "disobedient."[65] Because God is just, punishment is due to disobedient transgressors, according to the phrase "just (i.e., righteous) judgment." Gouge's atonement theory is penal, and he reiterates this point at several junctures with statements such as, "For man therefore he was to satisfy infinite justice."[66] Owen writes from the same theological perspective as Gouge, fifteen years after him speaking of the necessity of death and the demands of divine justice, "Such is the desert of sin, and such is the immutability of the justice of God, that there was no way possible to bring sinners unto glory but by the sufferings and death of the Son of God, who undertook to be the captain of their salvation."[67]

Gouge and Owen see a glorious and perhaps even paradoxical display of God's grace in the way Jesus satisfies divine justice. As stated above, the justice of God was satisfied by his giving of his Son Jesus Christ as a substitute for humanity, which is a reflection of God's grace. Concerning this encounter of justice and grace Gouge writes,

> More grace is manifested in God's not sparing his Son, but giving him to death for us, than if by his supreme authority and absolute prerogative he had forgiven our sins, and saved our souls. We that partake of the benefit of Christ's death, nor do, nor can make any satisfaction at all. For God to impute another's satisfaction

---

65. As Gouge states, this is metonymy of *effect*, "Transgression, therefore, by a metonymy of the effect, is put for a transgressor." Gouge, *Hebrews*, 98. Metonymy of *effect* is the opposite of metonymy of *cause*. Bullinger states that one has a metonymy of *cause* "when the cause is put for the effect: i.e., when the doer is put for the thing done; or where the action is put for the effect produced by the action." Thus we see as Gouge points out that the thing done, "transgression," stands for the doer, "transgressor." E. W. Bullinger, *Figures of Speech Used in the Bible* (London: Eyre & Spottiswoode, 1898), 538.

66. Gouge, *Commentary on Hebrews*, 131, 132, 136.

67. Owen, *Epistle to the Hebrews*, 4:466.

to us, and to accept it for us, is mere grace; and that the rather, because he that is true God, even the proper Son of God, made that satisfaction. Thus we see how, in working out our redemption, divine grace and justice meet together, and sweetly kiss each other: justice, in reference to the Son of God, who hath satisfied God's justice to the full; grace, in reference to us, who neither have made, nor can make, any satisfaction at all.[68]

Further deepening the wonder of the intersection or "kiss" between grace and justice is the necessary dimension of God's burning anger toward sin. The satisfaction of infinite justice is inseparable from the pacification of divine wrath. Through the rebellion of His creatures, says Gouge, "the just Creator was provoked to wrath."[69] God's justice demands reparation for sin, and his wrath is the means by which that reparation is made. For Gouge, it is God's justice and not his honor that necessarily demands recompense for sin in the form of divine judgment which although may be "violent," is always just.[70]

> The *justice* of God hath been made known in all ages by judgments executed on wicked sinners; as the punishment of our first parents, the drowning of the old world, the destroying of Sodom and Gomorrah with fire and brimstone, the casting off the Jews, the casting of the wicked angels and reprobate men into hell fire; but to exact the uttermost of the Son of God, who became a surety for man, and so to exact it as in our nature, he must bear the infinite wrath of his Father, and satisfy his justice to the full, is an instance of more exact justice than ever was manifested.[71]

The author of Hebrews further demonstrates this point when he says that "he had to be made like his brothers in every respect, so that he might become a merciful and faithful high priest in the service of God, to make propitiation for the sins of the people" (2:17). No priest could

---

68. Gouge, *Commentary on Hebrews*, 132.
69. Ibid., 136.
70. See Gouge's comments on Hebrews 2:2 in *Commentary on Hebrews*.
71. Gouge, *Commentary on Hebrews*, 136.

satisfy infinite justice and pacify divine wrath except the God-Man, the Priest who made atonement "once for all."

In Owen's exposition this "kiss" between grace and justice is found in the transition from Hebrews 2:9 to 2:10. In 2:9, it was the grace of God that led Jesus to taste death for men. It is in 2:10 that the result of this gracious death is to "bring many sons to glory." The very fact that sons need to be brought to glory says that there is a need that Christ met in his tasting of death. The reality of sin has created this need, to which God "had, according to the exigence of his justice, denounced and declared death and judgment to be brought upon all that sinned, without exception."[72] Here we see the implications of sin with reference to the justice of God. Just as Gouge at this juncture of his exposition marveled at God's provision for the utter lostness of humanity, so too does Owen. He writes, "Yet such was his infinite love and grace, that he determined or purposed in himself to deliver some of them, to make them sons, and to bring them unto glory."[73]

In Gouge's thought, the atonement was a violent event. Not only was physical violence done to the body of Jesus, but the violence of death itself was necessary to appease the "violent" wrath of the Father. As the God-Man, Jesus would absolutely pacify divine wrath, which the destruction of the flood, the fire over Sodom and Gomorrah, or the sacrificial work of a high priest could never accomplish. For this reason the priest had to atone for the sins of the people every year and Jesus had to suffer but "once for all." "None could pacify God's wrath, none could satisfy his justice, none could procure his favour, none could purge away sin, none could bring sinners into God's presence, but Christ."[74] Commenting on Hebrews 2:10, Gouge remarks that all of Christ's sufferings from his entering into the world until his departure, "were all ordered by God, and all tended to the very same end that is here intended, namely, the bringing of sons to glory."[75] Furthermore,

---

72. Owen, *Epistle to the Hebrews*, 4:401. "Exigence" is defined as "an urgent need or demand," according to Catherine Soanes and Angus Stevenson. *Concise Oxford English Dictionary*, 11th ed. (Oxford: Oxford University Press, 2004).

73. Ibid., 1:401.

74. Gouge, *Commentary on Hebrews*, 188.

75. Ibid., 142.

elsewhere in his commentary Gouge stresses the voluntary nature of Christ's offering, being a freewill offering.[76] As God in human flesh, through his God-ordained sufferings, Jesus was able to be man's substitute thereby satisfying divine justice and pacifying divine wrath.

These theological truths have practical implications as they relate to the Christian's assurance of faith as well as the Christian's daily life. Gouge changes from indicative description of Jesus' atoning work to exhortative language for his readers. Just as the apostle Paul relishes in God's grace toward humanity, Gouge adds, "Let us be like minded. Let us acknowledge the grace of God to us, and ascribe all the good we have thereunto. Let us so deeply meditate thereon, as we may be ravished therewith. Let us so apply it to ourselves, as we may render all the praise of what we have, or are able to do, to this grace of God."[77] Gouge wants Christians to "deeply meditate" on God's grace demonstrated in Christ's atoning work and to be "ravished," that is, overwhelmed or overcome with gratitude by these truths. By reflecting on the way Jesus satisfied divine justice and pacified divine wrath, the Christian is stirred to "render all praise" to God with the giving of one's entire life to God.

THE CURSE OF THE LAW REMOVED

Gouge adds a third benefit of Jesus' atoning work on the cross, namely, he has removed the curse of the law that binds humanity and brings death. With Hebrews 2:9 in view, Gouge does not fully explain the removal of the curse of the law at that point, but includes the following kind of explanations in most places where expounding on the atonement in his Hebrews commentary: "removed the insupportable curse of the law," "hereby was the curse of the law removed," and "removed the curse of the law." Gouge takes his readers to Galatians 3:13 where death on a cross is said to be a cursed death.[78] He reflects upon man's deservedness of suffering and Jesus enduring suffering in place of sinful humanity and asks, "Who is able to 'comprehend the breadth, and length, and depth, and height of Christ's love to us, which passeth

---

76. Ibid., 685.

77. Ibid., 132.

78. Ibid., 131, 135, 168. Owen notes the shamefulness of this death, which is an effect of the curse of sin. *Epistle to the Hebrews*, 1:397.

knowledge?' What now should not we do and endure for Christ's sake, thereby to testify our love to him?"[79] While Gouge speaks mainly of the "curse" of the Law, Owen begins with a stronger emphasis on that which brings the curse, namely, sin. "Sin is the worst and most obstinate" enemy for those who believe on Christ, says Owen. Sin's design is to first, reign in the believer, and second, to condemn the believer. The means by which it has sought to rule over man is the Law. Christ has removed the Law and placed the Christian under grace, thus "the reign of sin comes to an end."[80]

When commenting on Hebrews 2:6–18, in each instance where Gouge makes mention of the removal of the curse of the Law, he follows with a word on the breaking of the bonds of death and the vanquishing of Satan. In like manner, Owen closely links the two when expounding Hebrews 2:10. He understands this verse as the "sum of the gospel and the doctrine of it" because it provides a proper description of the nature and work of the Messiah versus a Jewish misunderstanding of a temporal deliverer. He writes, "The salvation and deliverance that God had promised and intended to accomplish by the Messiah was spiritual and eternal, from sin, death, Satan, and hell, ending in everlasting glory; not temporal and carnal ... as they (i.e., the Jews) vainly imagined."[81] Both Gouge and Owen present a textured view of what Jesus accomplished on the cross. While the satisfaction of God's justice and the pacification of his wrath present the great need for atonement, victory over death and the devil were also accomplished.

Death and the Devil Vanquished

Although it is the curse of the Law that brings death, Hebrews 2:14–15 states that it is the devil who has the power of death which is his instrument by which he keeps mankind enslaved to fear. Even though the biblical text is straightforward in this manner, what is significant in Gouge's comments is the careful theological development of this point. Gouge does not attempt to reduce the atoning work of Christ to a single dimension, but presents it as a multi-dimensional and all-encompassing

---

79. Gouge, *Commentary on Hebrews*, 131.
80. Owen, *Epistle to the Hebrews*, 1:393.
81. Ibid., 1:356.

triumph whereby Jesus offered himself as a sacrifice on the behalf of man to satisfy infinite justice and pacify the wrath of God, which removed the curse of the Law and vanquished the devil and death. Jesus had to become flesh and blood in order that he might die. He had to die in order to destroy the devil who has the power of death, says Gouge. Thus, the general end for which Christ took on flesh and blood was so that he might die. The mighty or powerful effect of this general end is that he would thus conquer death and he who holds its power.[82]

Gouge asks what the writer to the Hebrews means by stating that Jesus "destroyed" the devil. Is not the enemy still roaming around like a roaring lion? Does he not remain desirous of stealing, killing, and destroying? Has he then truly been vanquished? In making sense of this phrase, Gouge begins in the Greek text and undertakes a lexical study of the word translated "destroy" (καταργήσῃ). The word καταργήσῃ, he argues, finds its lexical root in the noun ἔργον, a work. When the particle α is prefixed to the verbal form it results in the negative, "not working" (ἀργός). Furthermore, when the word κατα is compounded with ἀργός one has in its verbal form the word καταργέω, which means "to bring to naught things that are" (1 Cor 1:28; see also 1 Cor 6:13 "God shall destroy"). After his technical discussion on the lexical roots of καταργήσῃ, Gouge continues, "By the aforesaid derivation and various signification of the word, it appeareth that it doth not always signify to annihilate a thing ... for the devil that is here spoken of still retains his being and substance ... but it implieth that he is so vanquished, as he shall never prevail against the members of Christ." In sum, what the writer to the Hebrews means by saying that the devil is destroyed is that he will "never prevaileth against God's children; but that they in all assaults remain conquerors."[83]

Jesus would suffer death, being assaulted by the devil; but he conquered death thereby conquering the devil. In a very practical way, Gouge reiterates that this truth should result in great comfort against the terror of the devil, for Jesus "knowing what flesh and blood is, and what our enemies are, hath first himself vanquished them, and then

---

82. Gouge, *Commentary on Hebrews*, 166.
83. Ibid., 166.

provided sufficient armor for his children to stand safe against them, Eph. vi. 12, &c."[84] Thus the Christian does not need to be afraid of Satan because of what Jesus has accomplished on the cross on his behalf.

Furthermore, the foundational nature of the gospel in Gouge's practical divinity is visible in that the Christian is comforted at the realization that Jesus has removed the curse of the law and vanquished death and the devil. Gouge writes,

> This ministereth much comfort and hope in death. In this respect we may, after an holy manner, insult over death, and say, 'O death, where is thy sting?' 1 Cor. xv. 55. Though death may arrest us, yet we need not fear that judgment and execution shall be got against us ... Christ was saved from death, not as a private person, but as a public person, and as an head to save all his members from death.[85]

The afflicted Christian need not fear death, but can instead rest in what Jesus has accomplished on his behalf.

In order for people to understand the terrible nature of death and thus the glorious nature of Christ's victory over it, they must explore how it is that Satan holds the power of death, says Gouge. He lays out six ways in which the devil has the power of death. First, like a hangman, he is the executioner of God's just judgment. Second, like a hunter, he hunts for the life of reasonable men. Third, like a thief, he continually lays in wait for the precious life of man. Fourth, like a tempter, he allures men into sin, which results in death. Fifth, like an accuser he presses God's just law against men calling for judgment against them. Sixth, like a tormentor, he frightens men with the terror of death and damnation, which is the consequence of sin.[86]

With this understanding of the power and sting of death, Christ's victory over it is magnified and his glory amplified. Gouge emphatically remarks (with similar words as quoted above),

---

84. Ibid., 166.

85. Ibid., 363.

86. Gouge writes, "In general, nothing is more terrible than death. In this respect death is called the king of terrors, Job xviii. 14." *Commentary on Hebrews*, 167.

The glory of that victory appeareth herein, that he hath overcome so potent an enemy as had the power of death; the benefit thereof herein appears, that he hath overcome so malicious and mischievous an enemy as exercised his power by all manner of death. Hence ariseth the ground of this holy insultation, 'O death, where is thy sting?' 1 Cor. xv. 55. He who had the power of death being destroyed, death now can have no more power over them that are redeemed by Christ.... The means whereby Christ overcame him that had the power of death, is expressly said to be death.[87]

Gouge proceeds into triumphant prose dwelling on how death was conquered by death. No angelic army was assembled for this victory. Rather, Jesus conquered death and the devil through laying down his life and not by taking up arms. He went to the cross. Like a trophy upon which the spoils of an enemy are hung, the cross was displayed upon which Christ hung and death was spoiled. By conquering death, Jesus altered the original nature of death, says Gouge, and now made a passageway into heaven. Where the passage from this world naturally leads into hell and bondage, believers are snatched out of the clutches of Satan, which represents the spoiling of the devil's power.

Gouge further illustrates the triumphant nature of Christ over the devil with two illustrations. The first is that of a bee which has lost its stinger. He "might buz and make a noise, but could not sting." The second illustration comes when considering the great shame that is brought upon the devil. Gouge notes that the devil was not only vanquished in his own kingdom, but with his own weapon. It is with death that the devil holds people enslaved by fear, and it is by death that he is conquered. He illustrates, "The strongest and sharpest weapon that Satan had was death, and by it he did most hurt. Christ dealt in this case as Benaiah did with an Egyptian, he plucked the spear out of his hand, and slew him with his own spear, 2 Sam. xxiii. 21."[88]

Although the satisfaction of divine justice and the pacification of divine wrath feature prominently in Gouge's articulation of the atoning

---

87. Ibid., 168.
88. Ibid.

work of Christ, Jesus' victory over his foes does not go unnoticed. This *Christus victor* perspective is seen in Gouge's atonement summary.

> Christ, by his death, offered himself up a sacrifice whereby such a price was paid for our sins, as satisfied God's justice, pacified his wrath, removed the curse of the law, and so spoiled Satan of all his power, wrestled his weapons out of his hands, set free those whom he held captive, and brought himself into captivity.[89]

While it is true that Christ satisfied justice, pacified wrath, and removed the curse of the law, it is equally true that "Christ's death proved Satan's destruction." Although people might scoff at "our crucified God," says Gouge, believers in Jesus Christ find the cross to be grounds for rejoicing and much glory. For this reason he reminds his readers that Paul would boast in nothing but the cross of Christ.[90]

PRACTICAL DIVINITY: THE FREEDOM OF THOSE HELD CAPTIVE

Interspersed throughout Gouge's exposition on these atonement verses is the reminder that regular reflection on Jesus' atoning work should elicit various responses from the Christian. Because Christ voluntarily offered himself as our substitute, "this should move us to labour after holiness."[91] The magnitude of Christ's sacrifice should compel the believer to walk in holiness, to live a pure life. Gouge is espousing the purifying effect of meditation on sound theology. In addition, the example of Christ in his suffering leaves for the Christian a model to be imitated when in the midst of his own trials. In his suffering, Jesus proves to be the ultimate guide to follow.[92] For all, suffering ultimately leads to death. Jesus set the captives free in order to give them a hope that transcends this life. He conquered death. Therefore, the Christian can take comfort with hope in the face of death and declare, "Death, where is your victory?"

The gospel further drives Gouge's practical divinity in this way. As stated above, God's justice is met by God's grace. When the Christian

---

89. Ibid., 168.
90. Ibid., 168–69.
91. Ibid., 691.
92. Ibid., 143.

is "ravished" by this truth displayed at the cross he is driven to praise God and devote all of his life to follow him.[93] Again, Gouge makes it unmistakably clear that the theological truths of God's Word are matters to be meditated upon and applied to one's life resulting in praise and adoration of God.

Jesus offered himself as a substitutionary sacrifice for humanity, which satisfied God's infinite justice and pacified his burning wrath toward sin. Jesus, by his atoning death on the cross, removed the wretched curse of the Law that was necessarily upon humanity and vanquished the devil and death through death resulting in the freeing of those who believe who were once held captive by sin, the Law, and Satan. These theological riches that sanctify the believer are to be found in the meditation upon Scripture and prayer. A priority of Puritan practical divinity reflected in Gouge's atonement teaching is that Christians lead holy lives. Gouge calls his readers to return to the Scriptures and return to prayer that they might be sanctified by the same. "That we may receive grace from Christ, we must be well informed in the means which he hath sanctified to sanctify us," writes Gouge. He continues, "These are his holy ordinances: in special, his word, and prayer, 1 Tim. iv. 5."[94] The Scriptures not only elicit praise from the lips of God's people, but they also have a purifying effect upon them. Then, as one sees himself growing in holiness and finds "any sanctifying grace wrought in us, we ought, with thankfulness ... to acknowledge from whence it cometh; and withal, we ought to use what we receive to the glory of him that hath sanctified us."[95]

Even in his gospel and atonement theology, Gouge presents the finished work of Christ that brings about salvation through saving faith as a motivation for a more dedicated Christian life. His practical teaching in his pastoral theology does not present the Christian life as something to be faithfully lived in order to merit God's favor or to make man's effort the primary ground for assurance, but rather believers live for God as a grateful response to his favor directed toward them. Furthermore, good works are not the basis for salvation nor are they the way in which the

---

93. Ibid., 132.
94. Ibid., 146.
95. Ibid., 146.

atoning work of Jesus is applied to believers. Rather, Christians express their gratitude to God for his gracious and unmerited atoning work on their behalf by performing sanctifying works.[96]

Gouge's gospel understanding and atonement articulation come from an exegetical and theological framework. In a variety of places, Gouge and Owen share striking similarities in their expositional approach to a text or phrase as well as in their conclusions. Neither Puritan was dependent on the other, and yet, with like-minded biblical conviction, the two present a multi-faceted theology of the atonement. What is evident in Gouge in particular, is that sound theological belief must never be distant from the affective response in the heart and change in life. Gouge teaches that pure theology is purifying theology, which elicits praise from the lips of God's people. Such is the case with the gospel and the atoning work of Jesus Christ on the cross, where grace and justice kiss resulting in the salvation of those who believe.

GOUGE'S THEOLOGICAL OUTLOOK ON DIVINE PROVIDENCE

A second theological theme that features prominently in Gouge's writings is divine providence. Although this topic will be covered in greater depth in Chapter 4 (under providence and suffering), it is appropriate to give a brief introduction to the theme at this juncture. "How did God govern all things?" Gouge's catechism asks. The answer: "As by wise prouidence he preserveth all, so he disposeth them to his own glory and his childrens good."[97] Again, his catechism asks, "What beleeve you concerning Gods Decree in generall?" with the proper answer being, "That he ordained all things before all times, according to his will."[98] Even the falling of a sparrow is ordered by God and does not happen apart from his decree. In response to these words of Matthew 10:29, Gouge writes concerning the extent of divine providence, "Not the greatest as the whale in the water, the elephant or lion on the earth, the eagle in the aire, but a little bird, a *sparrow* ... to prove that the most casuall things are ordered by God's providence, he saith not of this little bird, it is *fed*,

---

96. This discussion on the relationship between faith and assurance will be unpacked with great detail in the following chapter on spiritual warfare.

97. Gouge, *Briefe Method of Catechizing*, 3.

98. Ibid., 2.

or *preserved*, but it *falleth not*, indefinitely."[99] This same God, says Gouge, who orders these matters is the God who has given the greatest gift, "namely Iesus Christ his onely begotten Sonne, in him to adopt us to be his children, and to provide for us as for his children."[100]

For Gouge, this belief in the providence of God is not a polemical tool to inject fear into people or to invoke a deterministic approach to life, but rather an exegetically informed theological belief that matters in the practical aspects of one's life. Gouge's understanding of divine providence says something about God, namely, that he is omniscient, omnipotent, and sovereign. It also reminds Christians, especially in times of suffering and chaos that God is in control and that all things can be viewed as part of the larger framework of God's sovereign and wise plan. Christians can therefore trust God as they live out their lives in pursuit of giving him glory through their faith and obedience. In Gouge's mind, to reject divine providence is to be left with a belief in chance, fortune, luck, and coincidence, which are untrustworthy and devoid of God in the equations of life.

By exploring Gouge's understanding of Scripture, gospel and atonement theology, and his theology of God's providence, we are reminded of the intertwined nature of belief and practice in Gouge's work. These twin emphases are consistent with the broader picture of Puritan practical divinity. Hambrick-Stowe writes,

> In full range of Puritan programmatic visions, the work of theology was inseparable from ecclesiastical reform, the moral reformation of society and the revival of piety at the personal and family levels. Indeed, Puritans as theologians did not consider personal spiritual experience and the reform of church and society to be theologically derivative or secondary—as if they were mere applications of theology—but considered them at the heart of the theological enterprise.[101]

---

99. William Gouge, *Extent of God's Providence, set out in a sermon, preached in Black-Fryers Church, V. Nov. 1623. On occasion of the downe-fall of papists in a chamber at the said Black-Fryers, 1623. Oct. 27* (London: Edward Brewster, 1631), 374.

100. Ibid., 375.

101. Hambrick-Stowe, "Practical Divinity and Spirituality," in *Cambridge Companion to Puritanism*, ed. Coffey and Lim, 192.

In like manner, theology and practice are inseparably intertwined in Gouge's works. The subsequent chapters of this project will further demonstrate this point.

3

The Christian's Battle against the World, Flesh, and the Devil

SPIRITUAL WARFARE AND THE CHRISTIAN LIFE

Sorrowed by the occasion, William Gouge addressed the solemn assembly gathered to reinstate into the church a shamed and downtrodden twenty-year old young man. The young man's life had taken many unsuspecting turns bringing about this circumstance. His name was Vincent Jukes, a Christian Englishman trained as a cook near Stepney Church. His culinary career began aboard a ship that safely completed a five-month round trip voyage to Greenland. The following year, in 1636, Jukes again served as a cook on a voyage to Genoa that would change his life forever. While at sea, Turkish pirates spotted the English vessel and aggressively commandeered it. A violent fight ensued, the aftermath of which left seven Englishmen dead and about twenty severely wounded. Jukes was among the thirty-three survivors who now found themselves as prisoners rerouted to Algiers where they would be sold into slavery in the marketplace.

Jukes was bought as a slave and sent to the court of the King of Algiers before being passed on to the King's brother who in turn sold Jukes to a Muslim man of African descent. This slave owner repeatedly beat and threatened Jukes in an attempt to make the young man renounce his Christian faith. The slave owner prevailed, compelling Jukes to deny Christ and acknowledge Mohammed as the great Prophet. Jukes was circumcised as a Muslim and conformed to Turkish ritual and attire before he was again sold to a Grecian who made him a soldier aboard a Turkish ship. On board that ship were twenty native Turks, two English Christians, and a Scandinavian who, like Jukes, was circumcised as a

Muslim. Jukes, along with the three other foreigners on the ship, conspired to free themselves from their enslavement at an opportune time. That moment came when they saw five unsuspecting Turks alone below the deck. The four men, armed only with their knives, rushed upon the sailors stabbing them and seizing their muskets. They proceeded to kill five more and injuring another five before taking the ten living soldiers hostage. In similar form to Jukes's own captivity, the four men sailed to St. Lucas, Spain, where they sold the ship and prisoners, dividing the money amongst themselves.

Rather than remain in Catholic Spain as the other three did, on April 30, 1638, Jukes sailed back to his native England and its Protestant faith. It was now over a year from the time in which he was first taken hostage. Once back in England, "hee was much troubled night and day, and ... could not well sleepe through horror of conscience for denying his Christian Faith."[1] Jukes confessed his apostasy to the ancient curate in his parish who brought the unusual circumstance to the vicar of Stepney Church. In like manner, the vicar relayed the situation to his superior, the diocesan who advised with the Archbishop of Canterbury, William Laud. Because of the severity of the matter, there was "a solemne, pious, and grave forme of *Penance* prescribed for admitting him againe into the Christian Church." The Archbishop called on William Gouge to preach the formal message at the penitent's reinstatement into the Church. Gouge writes, "At the performance whereof this duty of preaching the Word was enjoyned to mee: Which in obedience to *Authority*, and with hope in Gods assistance I have undertaken."[2] His text of choice was the story of the Prodigal Son in Luke 15, of whom it says, "He was lost, and is found."

In his published sermon from that occasion titled, *A Recovery from Apostacy*, Gouge teaches that persecution and temptation to deny the faith come from an unseen and invisible spiritual war.[3] As Haman,

---

1. William Gouge, *A Recovery from Apostacy: Set out in a sermon preached in Stepny Church neere London at the receiving of a penitent renegado into the Church, Octob. 21. 1638. By William Gouge D.D. and min. in Black-Friers London Herein is the history of the surprizall and admirable escape of the said penitent* (London: George Miller, 1639), 5.

2. Ibid., 6.

3. Gouge brought the sermon into publication as quickly as possible, concerned that one with the skill of brachiography would print the sermon and not get its

the anti-Jewish villain in the Old Testament book of Esther, sought to destroy the Jewish people, so does the devil seek to destroy Christianity by causing Christians to renounce their faith, says Gouge. When genuine Christians renounce their faith, they are stricken with a terrorized conscience. However, when the Christian endures suffering and hardship to the point of death, Christianity is not ultimately injured but instead it flourishes. "So while Satans instruments sought to make an end of Christians, they increased the more." Quoting Tertullian's famous dictum found in his *The Apology*, Gouge continues, "For, *the blood of the Martyrs is the seed of the Church*."[4] Therefore, the devil is disappointed by the constancy of Christian martyrs and pleased when they, like Jukes, deny their faith.

When understood within the backdrop of spiritual warfare, Vincent Jukes' story highlights the urgency that exists for every Christian to be furnished with the spiritual armor of God. "Without this armour wee are naked," says Gouge, "and lye open to every dart and shot of our spiritual enemies: and are no more able to free our selves from the power of the Divel, then a poore silly Lambe or Kid from a roaring Lion or ravenous Bear."[5] Carrying this concern for his church in Blackfriars, Gouge preached nearly one hundred sermons expounding and applying the contents of Ephesians 6:10–20, the principal biblical passage on the armor of God. Gouge wanted to influence a wider audience with the contents of his exposition by reworking and preparing the message series for print. In the preface addressed to his congregation in the 1616 edition of his work *Whole Armour of God*, his pastoral concerns

---

contents correct. He writes in his preface, "Many have beene much wronged hereby: and that by the *Short-writers* omissions, additions, mis-placings, mistakings.... I have heard living Authors much complaine hereof. The wrong done to Authors deceased is the greater, because no redresse can be made thereof." Furthermore, Gouge's public sermon was shorter in length than his published one where he added a lengthy discussion on the torturing of martyrs in times past and the testimonies that came from those who faithfully endured. Gouge, *Recovery*, A3–A4.

4. Ibid., 55. Tertullian says to the persecutors of the church, "The oftener we are mown down by you, the more in number we grow; the blood of Christians is seed." Tertullian, *The Apology* 50 in *The Ante-Nicene Fathers*, vol. 3, ed. A. Roberts, J. Donaldson, and A. C. Coxe, trans. S. Thelwall (Buffalo, NY: Christian Literature Company, 1885), 55.

5. William Gouge, *The Whole Armour of God. Or, A Christians spirituall furniture, to keep him safe frō all the assaults of Satan*, 5th ed. (London: I. Beale, 1639), 33.

for the spiritual wellbeing and battle preparation of the church bleeds through his words. He writes to them, concerning this present and dangerous war,

> For the time of our life being a time of war, a time wherein our spiritual enemies (who are many, mighty, malicious, sedulous, and subtle) put forth there strength, and bestirre themselues to the uttermost that possibly they can; Seeking whom to deuoure, what can be more behoofull, then to discouer their cunning strategems and wyles, to declare wherein their strength lieth, to furnish Christs souldiers with compleat armour and sufficient defence and to show how our enemies may bee disappointed of their hopes, and we stand fast against all their assaults? This is the scope of this treatise.[6]

Gouge states that the apostle Paul presents the armor of God last in his epistle to the Ephesians introduced with the word, "finally," not as an addendum to his letter, but as a final necessary point to be delivered before concluding his exhortation. A failure to heed this final exhortation of being properly furnished with the armor of God would render Paul's preceding instruction of doctrines of the faith and precepts of life useless. Using a simile to drive this point home, Gouge writes, "In hearing we must well heed it: after we have heard it, we must well keep it, and not let it slip like water put into colinder or riven dish."[7]

The book would be republished six times in English and once in French by 1643. The second English edition was published in 1619 with several differences. Most notably different is that 1616 edition contains the Greek ΠΑΝΟΠΛΙΑ ΤΟΥ ΘΕΟΥ (Armor of God) preceding the English *Whole-Armor of God*. The 1619 edition does not retain the Greek (although later editions do).

The 1619 and 1627 editions have a fascinating title page decorated by a frontispiece portraying the spiritual battle along with a descriptive

---

6. William Gouge, *Panoplia tou theou. The whole-armor of God, or, The spiritvall fvrnitvre which God hath prouided to keepe safe euery Christian sovldier from all the assaults of Satan* (London: Iohn Beale, 1616), A9.

7. Gouge, *Whole Armour of God*, 3.

poem explaining the image.[8] The drawing pits the "constant complete" soldier up against the failing world, the infecting flesh pictured as a wealthy dressed lewd woman smoking a pipe with a horned goat on her lap, and the devil dressed in Jesuit garb with a halo over his head. The vigilant soldier is furnished with the armor of God standing on a cornerstone of prayer depicting Elijah praying for rain. A hand coming out of heaven reaches for the soldier carrying a wreath with the words, "The reward of the righteous" above it. Opposite the faithful Christian is the Roman Emperor Julian (c. 331–363), known as "The Apostate." He received this nickname from Christians for reinstituting paganism into the Roman Empire after Constantine had begun to eradicate it. He is pictured standing in hell on the buttress of a pillar with the word "desperation" beneath it. Julian carries a flag with the inscribed words, "Thou hast overcome, O Galilean." The fifth-century church historian, Theodoret, attributed these to Julian as his last words where he conceded his failure to root out Christianity and its founder, Jesus of Nazareth in Galilee.[9] The foundation of the buttress upon which he stands has an image on it depicting King Saul falling on his sword. Julian, symbolizing apostasy as a whole, is driven by fear and his reward is pictured as a snasre, sword, fire, and brimstone.

A third and more substantive difference with the 1619 publication is that Gouge expanded his section on the "too-much-neglected duty of fasting" at the request of his readers. A fourth difference in the 1619 publication is that Gouge annexed a treatise on the *Sin against the Holy Spirit*, further developing statements he makes in the *Whole Armour of God* that one should not pray for those who have sinned in this way. Because he does not want to trouble weak consciences by his admonition, he extends this section to clarify his position.[10] Lastly, in addition to the structural outline of Ephesians 6:10–20 that begins

---

8. The 1619 and 1627 editions appear to be the only publications of the *Whole Armour of God* with this addition.

9. Theodoret of Cyrus, "The Ecclesiastical History of Theodoret," in *Theodoret, Jerome, Gennadius, Rufinus: Historical Writings, Etc.*, ed. Philip Schaff and Henry Wace, trans. Blomfield Jackson, vol. 3, *A Select Library of the Nicene and Post-Nicene Fathers of the Christian Church*, Second Series (New York: Christian Literature Company, 1892), 106.

10. Gouge, *Whole Armour of God*, A2–3.

his first edition, he adds in its second publication a ten-page table of headings summarizing the thematic progression of the work at its outset. Gouge's third edition does not appear to be extant as there are no records of it in the most important archives, libraries, databases, and rare book collections. In 1627, a fourth edition of *Whole Armour of God* was combined with his *Domestical Duties* and published together as "The Workes of William Gouge." The advertisement to reader and discussion of changes to the publication are no different in the fourth edition from that of the second edition, leading to the conclusion that the content of the third edition is the same as the second and fourth. In 1639, he released a fifth edition to the *Whole Armour of God* with Gouge's eighth edition of his *A Brief Method of Catechizing* added before the index.

In 1643, Gouge's work traveled to mainland Europe, published by the Genevan printer Jacques Chouet in French, *L'Armure Complette de Dieu* for which David LeClerc (1591-1654), the Swiss Protestant theologian, wrote the foreword. Gouge's sixth and final English republishing in 1647 is identical to the fifth edition. The finished 1639/1647 product, from which this chapter primarily draws, contains over 575 pages of a detailed biblical theology of spiritual warfare. Gouge references scores of passages that add color and texture to each piece of armor and provide a thicker description of the spiritual battle. Equally robust is Gouge's application of these spiritual matters to the personal lives of his readers. William Gurnall (1617-1679), the Puritan rector of St. Peter's and St. Paul's Church, Lavenham, in his *The Christian in Complete Armour* (1662-1665), briefly expresses an appreciation of Gouge's work. In his exposition of the Christian soldier's feet shod with the gospel of peace, he writes,

> As for the grace held forth by this 'preparation of the gospel of peace,' I find great variety in the apprehensions of the learned, and indeed variety rather than contrariety. I shall therefore spare the mentioning of them—many of which you may find in a bunch collected by the Rev. Dr. Gouge upon the place, with his thoughts upon them—and crave the boldness to lay down, with

due respect to others, the apprehensions I have had thereon,
which, I conceive, will rather amplify than thwart their sense.[11]

Although this is Gurnall's only direct reference to Gouge in his work
on the armor of God, this statement tells us that Gurnall not only read
Gouge, but also possessed a high respect for him, even to the extent
to which he would refer his readers to Gouge's discussion on this
particular piece of armor.[12]

This present chapter focuses on major themes of Gouge's theology
of spiritual warfare, including the Christian knowing his enemy, his
reliance on God in the battle, and God's provision of the armor. Special
attention is given to Gouge's practical theology primarily as it relates to
the assurance of salvation in the midst of the spiritual battle.

KNOWING YOUR ENEMY

"Is there not just cause to be very watchful against such an enemy?"
Gouge asks, concerning the devil. The rhetorical nature of the question begs for a response of "yes, there is just cause to be very watchful
against him." The vigilant Christian will do well to understand first,
the One against whom Satan fights. Gouge insists that the Christian
must understand that Satan's primary agenda is to fight against heavenly priorities. All that is heavenly pertains to God and his glory before
anything. Satan and his devils desire that God would not receive glory,
and therefore, wage war against God. Furthermore, they endeavor to
thwart the salvation of sinners, which is a heavenly priority. When
sinners repent and trust in God, they are given a new longing for heaven
and will ultimately live there in happiness. Satan, who opposes joy,

---

11. William Gurnall, *The Christian in Complete Armour* (Edinburgh: Banner of
Truth Trust, 1983), 1:559.

12. In summary, Gouge provides six different understandings to what is meant
by the preparation of the gospel of peace, two of which he believes are nearest to
the sense. Those two are that it refers to knowledge of the gospel and the other,
peace of conscience. He believes this is the sense because the soul cannot be settled
without knowledge of the gospel. Furthermore, the knowledge of the gospel creates
within the Christian a peace of conscience. In reference to the "preparation" of this
"gospel of peace," Gouge understands it as a matter of patience. Thus, the gospel
of peace prepares the Christian to endure patiently through difficulties. Gouge,
Whole Armour of God, 161–62.

desires to prevent such happiness. He fights against heavenly priorities not because he desires to attain them, says Gouge, but because he desires to spoil them. Each Christian is confronted with a choice in the battle, "whether we wil serve our Heavenly Father, or the hellish feene: whether we will let goe, or fast hold that heavenly treasure which Christ hath purchased for us, all those heavenly things whereby God is honored, and our soules are saved."[13] Such are the stakes of the spiritual warfare.

Christians must neither underestimate nor overestimate the power of the devil. A proper understanding of the extent and restraint of his might is necessary if the Christian is to be victorious in the spiritual conflict. Gouge argues that Satan is the driving influence in every temptation. To believe otherwise is to fail to recognize the extent of the devil's evil machinations and to be guilty of thinking too highly of one's own strength to overcome temptation. Gouge gives the examples of Satan tempting Eve in the Garden of Eden, of Jesus rebuking Peter because he had become a stumbling block used by Satan, and of Ananias and Sapphira whom Satan tricked into lying about land they had sold.[14] On his own, the Christian cannot withstand the attacks of the enemy and to underestimate his power in temptation is dangerous. If physical skirmishes with flesh and blood can wear down any man or woman and pose a threat of danger, how much more so with spiritual attacks of demonic principalities and powers? "It is the Divell," says Gouge,

> which bloweth vp in vs the fire of lust, pride, covetousnesse, and all other vices he layeth before vs evill baites agreeable to our nature, and so seduceth vs, he inrageth persecutors, hee blindeth idolaters, he seduceth heretikes, etc. If this were well weighed it would make vs pitie *flesh and blood* when it fighteth against vs rather than envie it: it would keepe vs from snarling like a dogge at the stone which is flong.[15]

While Gouge places a high degree of responsibility in temptation upon satanic influence and emphasizes it over the weakness of man's

---

13. Ibid., 92.
14. Ibid., 56–57.
15. Ibid., 57.

sinful flesh, it is not appropriate to understand his emphasis to be at the neglect of understanding the spiritual weakness of humanity. It is best to understand his emphasis within the "know your enemy" framework. The great danger within the Christian life is to underestimate Satan's demonic working, a mistake Gouge intends on not making. With this perspective, people are not the enemy, but rather Satan who uses them to accomplish his evil purposes. Thus, when spiritual attacks confront the Christian at the hands of men, those tempters, such as those who captured Vincent Jukes, should be pitied because they are instruments in the hand of the devil.

Satan is an enemy who is powerful, malicious, subtle, and constant.[16] His diverse tactics are effective when the Christian lets his guard down. According to Gouge, Satan often begins with small temptations, as with the question he posed to Eve (Gen 3:1), "Did God actually say, 'You shall not eat of any tree in the garden'?" He attempts to make some people see sin as a small matter while making others believe their sin is unforgiveable. "If he cannot seduce men by moving them to make light account of sin, he will perswade them that every sinne is most heinous, that their sins are unpardonable. If he cannot make them superstitious, he will strive to make them prophane: and thus help one temptation with another."[17] When Puritans like Gouge instruct Christians to reflect on their own sin, the purpose is not to lead them to believe their sins are beyond God's hand of mercy, but instead to take those sins to God's grace where they find forgiveness and comfort for their afflicted conscience. A kind of cataloguing of sins that leads to deepened anxiety is not consistent with Gouge's teaching. In fact, he bemoans how in his own day the enemy used the Papists, Anabaptists, Separatists, and all other sects to influence the weak, when the enemy was unable to move magistrates and ministers, who were strong. Also common in his day were groups who encouraged the damaging recounting of things to be sin that are not sin and called certain spiritual acts necessary spiritual duties, which are not necessary. Unfortunately, Gouge does not provide examples of specific groups that he has in mind with this statement. However, in

---

16. Ibid., 38.

17. Gouge, *Whole Armour of God*, 40–41.

his preceding point, he tells of the Catholic Church's failure to see how Satan has "ambushed" their work for the Lord with a temptation to the conceit of merit and pride. If it is the Roman Catholic Church and its leaders that Gouge has in mind when referring to the counting of things to be sin that are not and the calling of things to be necessary duties which are not necessary, one will find numerous examples in Gouge's writings of how this applies to Catholic life and worship, which he calls carnal and pompous.

In his Hebrews commentary, Gouge writes about having a "carnal disposition in worshipping God," which happens, in part, when someone calls things to be necessary that are not necessary. He adds, "Papists exceed herein. Their religion is merely carnal. It consisteth in outward rites: as in erecting curious images and manifold altars, in arraying priests with glorious copes, in pompous processions, in melodious music, in abundance of tapers, in sprinkling water, in magical crossings, in numeral prayers, in mimical gestures, and a thousand others."[18]

As it pertains to calling things to be sin which are not sinful, Gouge laments the Pope's instructions that withhold "sacramental wine to the people," "the liberty of marriage in sundry times of the year," "the free use of sundry meats on sundry days of every week and all Lent long, and other privileges."[19] Gouge, like other reformed Protestants of his day, understands the Church of Rome to be in Satan's grasp, ambushed by his tactics, and deceived by his schemes.[20] Gouge is concerned with this kind of improper and misinformed reflection and consideration of sin, because it ultimately causes the Christian to stumble in his or

---

18. Gouge offers no critique of the Church of England in these instances. While he did not agree with some elements of the Church of England's practices, the Catholic Church was in an altogether different category. This is why he was able to remain within the Church of England with a clear conscience as a non-conformist. Gouge, *Commentary on Hebrews*, 514.

19. Ibid., 642.

20. Gouge's critiques of hypocrisy and inaccurate understandings of sin are not exclusively leveled at the Papists, but also Protestants within the reformed fold, "many professors of the true reformed religion," says Gouge, "will be found of carnal dispositions, in that they content themselves with a carnal serving of God, and observing Christian ordinances carnally ... as men content themselves with a mere outward performing of them [i.e., ordinances] they are made carnal." Gouge, *Commentary on Hebrews*, 514.

her faith.[21] These examples remind us of how Gouge sees Satan's tactics at work to create snares for stumbling and deceive people, further emphasizing the importance of knowing your enemy.

Gouge observes Satan's cunning in other ways: in good things, he makes men separate the means from the end, and in evil things, he makes them separate the end from the means. The former scheme leads to a spiritual farsightedness, where the righteous goal is desired but the means to that goal is blurred and replaced with something sinful and destructive. The latter refers to spiritual nearsightedness where the distant consequences of sin are blurred so that the pleasures of sin in the moment are enjoyed. Or as Gouge states it, Satan tricks men to "looke for the good and happy end of righteousnesse, and yet be backward in walking that way that leadeth thereto: and contrariwise, eagerly and swiftly to runne in the way of sinne and yet not feare the wages of sinne, and the issue of that course."[22] Gouge's description of Satan's schemes are not mere rhetoric, but sobering reminders to Christians that their enemy has calculated ways to blur the lines of sin and withhold clarity from their spiritual eyesight. This examination of Satan's tactics heightens the intensity with which the Christian must view the spiritual battle.

Gouge paints a picture of Satan that can be disconcerting to the weary soul that feels the persistence of temptation and the realities of sin in nearly every moment. He has made it clear that Christians have an enemy who is relentless in tempting and destructive in his ways. However, awareness rather than despair is the goal of Gouge's vivid description of the devil. When consoling the weary Christian, Gouge intends to help the Christian first see the spiritual dynamics of their struggle, not in order to legitimize sin, but to affirm them in the fight and thus motivate them to personal holiness. Gouge's approach would cause his readers to take serious the battle in which they find themselves rather than sit passively waiting for temptation and trials to pass. Before the pendulum swings too far and his readers begin to live in fear of Satan, Gouge provides a balanced corrective. Because

---

21. Gouge, *Whole Armour of God*, 42–43.
22. Ibid., 36.

his aim is to provide spiritual direction to the battle-weary Christian, Gouge proceeds in making sure that his readers do not have an uneven view of Satan.

While there is great spiritual danger when one underestimates Satan's power, there is equally great danger when his tactics and might are overestimated producing undue fear and despair. Every trace of authority that Satan possesses is due to God's permission as one way he justly judges and punishes the wicked.[23] Because Satan's power has been permitted by God, it is limited in its extent. He cannot do whatsoever he will, for only God is infinite in power. Satan is also not able to do anything against the will of God that God has ordained in creation. Gouge concludes, therefore, that the devil cannot work miracles, force the will of man, know the secrets of a man's heart, nor can he foretell things to come, "for all these are eyther above, or against the course of nature."[24] The combined emphasis upon both the power and impotency of Satan leads the Christian to gain an accurate theological framework for the practical life trials they experience.

While his discussion is far from complete, knowledge of the Christian enemy is an insightful place to begin addressing the spiritual battle. Gouge's observations on the source of Christian warfare give way to the important solution to Christian warfare, namely, reliance upon God.

RELIANCE UPON GOD

The Christian must have a proper perspective of Satan, neither making light of his power nor dreading him too much. When the enemy is understood in his proper context the necessity of reliance upon God and protection through God's provided armor rise to the surface. Because Gouge wants his readers to live victoriously, he knits into his exposition the assurance of faith that is grounded in God and not the frail follower of Jesus. "This sure ground, and safe rocke is onely the *Lord*. Strong he is in himself, and can both strengthen us, and weaken our enemies.... Thus may we be sure of victorie: *Through God we are more*

---

23. Ibid., 62.
24. Ibid., 66.

then conquerours," says Gouge.[25] The reader can hear in these words
Gouge's pastoral tone. It is important to note that from the outset of
his writing, Gouge is less concerned about practical steps to overcome
temptation as he is with giving his readers a theological framework
for the battle. He in no way wants his readers to grow self-confident in
their methods of overcoming temptation, but instead to be confident
in God to provide victory over temptation.

> Indeed, if the ground of our assurance rested in, and on our
> selves, it might iustly be counted presumption; but the *Lord, and
> the power of his might* being the ground thereof, they either know
> not what is the might of his power, or else too too lightly esteeme
> it, who account assured confidence thereon, presumption.[26]

The repetition, "too too," is original to Gouge's writing and is more
than a mere typo. We know this because the wording is preserved
in each of his printed editions. It seems that Gouge is emphasizing
the grievous nature of self-confidence over God-confidence in the
Christian life. These statements are significant because they under-
line what Gouge expresses throughout his *Whole Armour of God*, that
the Christian's primary ground for assured faith and confidence in the
spiritual battle is the power of God and not the works or efforts of the
Christian. Gouge demonstrates a view of the assurance of a believer's
salvation that rests not on one's devotional practices or ability to root
out sin from one's life, but the sure ground that is Jesus.

Demonstrating his concern for practical application of theology,
Gouge uses similes and metaphors to describe God's power and spur
the believer to a greater dedication to God.

> According to God's greatnesse is his power infinite, incompre-
> hensible, inutterable, unconceivable: as a mighty winde which
> driveth all before it: as a swift and strong stream against which
> none can swimme: as a burning flaming fire which consumeth
> and devoureth all: so is Gods power, Whatsoever standeth before
> it, and is opposed against it, is but as chaffe before a strong winde

---

25. Ibid., 11.
26. Ibid., 15.

or bulrushes before a swift current, or stubble before a flaming fire; for all adverse power, though to our weaknesse it seeme never so mightie, yet can it be but finite, being the power of creatures, and so a limited power, yea, a dependant power, sub-ordinate to this *power of might*, of *his* might, who is Almightie, and so no proportion betwixt them.[27]

As Gouge expounds upon the various pieces of the armor of God, he is careful to tell his readers that victory does not come in one's ability to put on the armor or wield its weapon, but rather in the God who pro-vides the armor for the battle. Therefore, assurance and confidence in spiritual warfare rests upon God's omnipotence.

Still, this confidence in God does not relinquish the responsibilities that the believer has in the midst of the battle. In Gouge's approach, it actually does the opposite. Christians must be diligent in faith and stand alert. Not only is the Christian dead in sin until God "quickens" him, but it is also God who sustains him beyond his conversion. "Yea, after we are quickened, we are stil supported by God's grace, which worketh in us: yet being quickened we must do our indevor, because of that order which the Lord hath in wisdo[m] appointed to bring us to glory."[28] The Christian's "indevor" involves circumspection over his own soul. Gouge goes so far as to say, in his notes on Hebrews 3:12, that one necessary component for preventing apostasy is keeping vigilant watch over one's life as it pertains to sin, Satan, self and to God who gives man over to sin when he is insistent upon rebellion.[29] "Hereby we may take information of one special reason of men's failing and falling away from God, namely, their want of circumspection; they do not take heed which they should. If men that are circumspect be not-withstanding oft overtaken, how is it possible that they who are secure and careless should stand firm and stable?"[30]

Gouge desires that his readers properly balance between assur-ance in God and the believer's responsibility to persevere in faith,

---

27. Ibid., 13.
28. Ibid., 30.
29. Hebrews 3:12 says, "Take care, brothers, lest there be in any of you an evil, unbelieving heart, leading you to fall away from the living God."
30. Gouge, *Commentary on Hebrews*, 262–63.

avoiding the errors of the Roman Catholics and Libertines. Concerning the errors of the Roman Catholic Church, he refers to the teaching of his contemporary Robert Bellarmine (1542–1621), the Jesuit scholar of the Counter Reformation. Gouge understands the monergistic beginnings of Catholic soteriology but critiques its synergistic development which ultimately attributes salvation and assurance to the efforts of the Christian. He writes,

> The Papists establish their owne power and strength, hold and teach, that after the first motion and stirring of the heart, which they acknowledge to be of God only, a man absolutely by his free will may doe well if he will. But Christ saith of the branches which were in the vine, whose hearts were stirred up, *Without mee yee can doe nothing.*[31]

On the opposite side of Gouge's spectrum are the Libertines, who neither trust God for victory over sin, nor make efforts toward obedience, but rather who carelessly live their lives without giving attention to their personal spiritual responsibilities. These people "pamper their flesh, and pursue their carnall delights" because God is able to forgive and save them. They abuse God's grace and therefore mock his power. In their pursuit of comfort, some Christians advocate that when they strive to be furnished with the armor spiritual attacks are heightened, and conclude that it is best not to have the armor. Gouge has a solemn message for such people, "I easily believe it: but what is the reason? Because the Divell hath them in his power, he needeth not eagerly pursue them."[32] Satan's grasp is evident in those who love darkness (i.e., evil deeds), produce unfruitful works, and oppose God's Word and the proclamation of it. Such persons are in "slavish bondage" and in need of spiritual deliverance.[33] Gouge urges his readers to avoid both extremes of the Roman Catholic Church and Libertines and instead to chart their own *via media* and lean upon the truth of God's grace lest

---

31. Gouge, *Whole Armour of God*, 30.
32. Ibid., 34.
33. Ibid., 77–78.

they develop a theology of works righteousness, and to persevere diligently in faith and holiness, lest they neglect God's work in their lives.[34]

As this section began, the primary focus of Satan's attack is heavenly, which is to say that he opposes God's glory and the salvation of the lost, endeavoring to spoil the Christian's joy, which is found in Christ. Although lengthy, the following statement summarizes well the urgency and pastoral concern Gouge has for both the glory of God and the perseverance of the believer.

> It is no small matter that we fight for, but a matter of the greatest weight and consequence that can be ... I [say] to the Lords souldiers, It is the Lord of Heaven whose battels ye fight, his honour is ingaged therin, it is your souls salvation, and heavenly happinesse, which is in hazard: your enemies seeke to spoil you of the precious grace of Gods sanctifying Spirit, and to deprive you of that rich & glorious inheritance, which Christ by no lesse price then his owne blood hath purchased for you: if ye yield to your enemies, all these yee lose, and become vassals unto your mortall and malicio[u]s enemie the Divell, ye are even fire-brands of Hell. Be strong therefore, and of a valiant courage: fear not, but fight and stand it out to the uttermost; so shall ye be more then conquerors.[35]

---

34. Ibid., 31. These errors of the Roman Catholics and Libertines magnify the need to be furnished with the girdle of truth. The girdle of truth covers a broad range of ways to be truthful. Gouge understands truth to refer holistically to the truth of judgment, heart, speech, and action. Truth of judgment concerns matters of doctrine and theological soundness. Truth of heart refers to uprightness of heart. Truth of speech pertains to the truthfulness of words that are spoken. Truth of action has to do with one's lifestyle and purity with which one lives. Each of these ideas of truth must be included in the belt of truth, says Gouge. The whole "lump" of a man, his opinion, affections, communication, and conversations must be "leavened" with truth. When the enemies of truth cannot overthrow it, they will then seek to adulterate it, as the "Popish Jesuites, Priests, and Fryers" did in Gouge's estimation, when they seek to "dispossesse us of the Truth of Religion." On the other hand, the "prophane worldlings" seek to make the pursuers of truth appear foolish for not yielding to their way of life (*Whole Armour of God*, 122–23, 135).

35. Ibid., 94.

In pastoral form, Gouge warns, corrects, and directs the faithful to keep watch because the failure to do so carries grave spiritual consequences. This quotation provides two important insights.

First, the readers of Gouge do well to note an important emphasis in his treatise, namely, the idea that addressing the "how" of facing temptation victoriously (i.e., how the Christian overcomes temptation to lust, fits of anger, jealousy, etc.) is secondary to the more important question of "why" we should battle against temptation. His answer is, namely, to bring God glory. A major part of Gouge's pastoral strategy for comforting the afflicted in the midst of the feverish spiritual war is calling them to rely entirely on God, reminding them of who they are in Christ, and calling to mind that it is for the glory of God that they pursue a life of victory.

Second, Gouge's choice of words in this quotation, "spoil," "deprive," "lose," and "hell" create a tension. While it is true that Christians make war for the glory of God, and that God has equipped his children in the fight, and that their salvation is secure because of the finished work of Christ, there remains a true warning that all of the benefits of Christ can be lost if one yields to the enemy. How these matters fit together will become clearer in the following section.

GOD'S PROVISION OF ARMOR

The whole armor of God consists of six pieces, all of which are defensive except the sword of the Spirit. The other five pieces are the girdle of truth, the breastplate of righteousness, the shoes of patience (readiness), the shield of faith, and the helmet of hope (salvation). No piece of armor is for the back of the soldier because "wee should always stand against our enemies face to face," never yielding to him. However, if the Christian does yield to the devil, he must not think that the skirmish is over for "it is not the glory of conquest that he seeketh, so much as our destruction."[36]

The whole armor is complete and the soldier is in no need of additional covering. Gouge expresses his aggravation at how the Roman Catholic Church say it believes in the perfection of the Word of God

---

36. Ibid., 119.

and at the same time adds to the armor of God thereby compromising its power and ultimately producing "paper armour." What makes their armor paper is their reliance on human traditions, seeking the help of saints, and adding works to faith for the justification of the sinner.[37] These comments demonstrate how Gouge desires to remove works righteousness and human dependence from the Christian's understanding of faith and instead cultivate complete reliance upon God for justification and perseverance through the armor he provides.

Although much can be said about each piece of armor, one piece in particular rises to the surface as most pertinent for this discussion. When the apostle Paul writes, "Above all, taking the shield of faith," he urges faith "above" any other piece of armor because faith is the mother of all graces.[38] Each of the saving graces represented in the armor of God (e.g., truth, righteousness, patience) are essential. They are like links in a chain where one broken link compromises the whole chain. In the same way, each link of saving grace is essential for the salvation of the believer. However, some links are put to greater stress than others. In the spiritual battle, faith is the grace that bears "the greatest brunts, and in that respect may be counted most excellent, and most necessary; even as the shield of all other parts of armour is the most needful."[39]

In this section, Gouge's theology of the nature of faith establishes his position on the assurance of a believer and the many important questions such as, how are we to understand the word "faith"? What kind of faith is in order in Ephesians 6:16? How might the Christian test the genuineness of his faith? Can a Christian be certain that he or she has saving faith? Can the follower of Jesus lose genuine faith? In order to understand his theology, Gouge's teaching on saving/justifying faith will now be discussed.

In order for Christians to understand the shield of faith, it is essential for them to know the kind of faith of which the apostle speaks. Gouge presents five different "kindes" of faith, one of which is in view in Ephesians 6:16. First, there is extraordinary or miraculous faith. This kind of faith is a "beleef that some extraordinary and miraculous

---

37. Ibid., 120.
38. Ibid., 195, 202.
39. Ibid., 199.

thing shall fall out." A person might possess this kind of faith because of a special promise in the Scriptures or a personal revelation given by the Spirit of God not only for the recipient of the revelation, but for the good of others. Second, there is ordinary or historical faith. People possess this kind of faith when they give assent to the truthfulness of the Word of God. This kind of faith gives credence to the historical nature of God's Word and can therefore be possessed by the reprobate and the believer. Temporary faith is a third kind of faith that is seen in the person whose mind is given to the gracious promises in the gospel for only a season, but fails to endure. Oftentimes, trials and persecution cause this kind of faith to fade away underlining the temporary and inadequate nature of it. A fourth kind of faith is what Gouge calls hypocritical faith whereby people either intentionally (because they seek their own glory) or unintentionally (because of ignorance) deceive others into thinking they possess genuine faith. The fifth kind of faith is the faith the Apostle has in mind in Ephesians 6:16, which Gouge calls saving or justifying faith.[40]

At this point, Gouge may have been influenced by the works of William Perkins. While Gouge does not note Perkins as a reference, we know that he had read Perkins and that Gouge's and Perkins' expositions of faith are strikingly similar.[41] For instance, "there be three kinds of faith," says Perkins, "historical, temporarie, and saving faith." Perkins continues,

> In Historical faith is knowledge of the Word of God with assent unto it. In temporary faith are 3 things; knowledge of the Word, Assent, and Approbation also, with some joy. In Saving faith there are foure things: Knowledge, Assent, Approbation, and Apprehension: that is in applying of the promises of God unto mans selfe; whence proceedeth joy.[42]

---

40. Ibid., 208–10.

41. For specifically noted instances where Gouge refers to the work of William Perkins, see Kenneth Allen East, "William Gouge: Preacher and Scholar" (PhD diss., University of Chicago, 1991), 389.

42. Perkins's prose oddly alternates between the spellings "temporarie" and "temporary" along with providing the numerical value "3" in one instance while spelling "foure" in the next. William Perkins, "Exposition or Commentarie Vpon

While Perkins lists three kinds of faith where Gouge listed four (Perkins not including "extraordinary faith" as Gouge does), the names and descriptions of the remaining three kinds of faith, historical, temporary, and saving are very similar. William Gurnall uses the identical categories and similar descriptions as Gouge in 1662, when he speaks of historical, temporary, miraculous, and justifying faith.[43] We should not see this as Gouge and Gurnall being strictly dependent on Perkins here, but rather, that these distinctions in defining faith were part of a broader reformed description of faith.[44]

Most pertinent for this study is saving or justifying faith, where Gouge, like Perkins and Gurnall, believes that the one who possesses such faith, cannot fall away. Gouge defines saving or justifying faith in his *Whole Armour of God* as he does in his catechism, "a beliefe of the Gospel, whereby Christ and all his benefits offered therein, are received."[45] The first part of the definition, namely, a belief of the gospel, is something that is affirmed by the other kinds of faith

---

the Three First Chapters of the Revelation" in *The Workes of that Famous and Worthy Minister of Christ in the Universitie of Cambridge, Mr. William Perkins*, 3 vols. (London: Iohn Haviland, 1631), 271.

43. William Gurnall, *The Christian in Complete Armour* (Edinburgh: Banner of Truth Trust, 1983), 2:2.

44. Calvin laments the ways in which professors of theology incorrectly present faith as merely assent. He writes, "In fact, when faith is discussed in the schools, they call God simply the object of faith, and by fleeting speculations, as we have elsewhere stated, lead miserable souls astray rather than direct them to a definite goal." John Calvin, *Institutes of the Christian Religion* 3.2.1, ed. John T. McNeill, trans. Ford Lewis Battles, 2 vols. (Philadelphia: Westminster, 1960), 1:543. Jeffrey Mallinson demonstrates how Beza, who closely resembles Calvin in this matter, held to a tripartite understanding of faith where there is knowledge (historical faith), assent, and trust (application of the facts to one's self). Mallinson writes, "Beza employs this definition when discussing the knowledge of Scripture. He holds that while the unregenerate may know Scripture according to the first and second aspects, they cannot arrive at the third aspect, for this is only available to minds illumined by the Spirit. Hence, they do not have true faith" (219). Therefore, Perkins, Gouge, and Gurnall are not inventing a new discussion with new descriptions but follow from their reformation predecessor, Calvin and his successor, Beza. See Jeffrey Mallinson, *Faith, Reason, and Revelation in Theodore Beza (1519-1605)* (Oxford: Oxford University Press, 2003), 214-34.

45. William Gouge, *A briefe method of catechizing wherein are briefely handled the fundamentall principles of Christian religion, needfull to be knowne by all Christians before they be admitted to the Lords Table. Whereunto are added sundry prayers, with thanksgivings before and after meale*, 8th ed. (London: John Beale, 1637), 6.

previously mentioned, but is insufficient to provide salvation. The second part of Gouge's definition, "whereby Christ and all his benefits offered therein, are received," is what differentiates justifying faith from the rest. At this juncture, Gouge inserts a rare clarifying footnote. Gouge uses this lengthy note in order to demonstrate to his readers that his definition is considerate of and in agreement with the many definitions of other godly teachers as well as the various definitions found in the Scriptures. Without giving the names of specific individuals, he says that definitions of faith from sound teachers may vary in form but are essentially the same in substance. Similarly, the Bible itself might use various phrases to define faith, all of which are the same in essence. By including this footnote, Gouge exhibits his pastoral concern for his readers, because he desires that they would not be bogged down by unnecessary controversies surrounding the nuances of definitions that are ultimately the same in substance.[46] Furthermore, he also addresses any accusation of novelty by demonstrating the consistency between his definition and those of other church leaders before him.

Gouge's definition falls in line with the Puritan distinction between the direct act of faith and the reflex act of faith.[47] For Puritans such as Cornelius Burgess (1589-1665), Thomas Goodwin (1600-1680), and John Flavel (1627-1691), the direct act of faith refers to those acts of the soul "whereby it is carried out immediately to some object."[48] In Gouge's definition, he begins with a belief in the gospel, where the gospel (and the God of the gospel) is the direct object upon which faith is placed. The reflex act of faith is where the soul takes notice of the acts with which it has done. As Beeke states, "It's as if the eye were turned inward to see itself."[49] For Gouge, this reflex act is seen by the words, "are received" with reference to the benefits of Christ because it reflects the action or response of the Christian not only to have direct faith in the gospel, but also to respond to that faith by receiving the benefits therein.

---

46. Gouge, *Whole Armour of God*, 210–12.
47. For more on "faith" according to the Reformers and Puritans, see chapter 1.
48. Joel R. Beeke, *The Quest for Full Assurance: The Legacy of Calvin and His Successors* (Carlisle, PA: Banner of Truth, 2000), 132.
49. Ibid.

Gouge further demonstrates the direct and reflex acts of faith in stating two particulars of saving faith. First, the one who possesses such faith "giveth full assent in his mind to the truth of the Gospell" (direct act) and second, "with the assent of the mind, there goeth a consent of the will" (reflex act). Continuing on, he places an emphasis on the joy that is received through the reflex act of faith, just as Perkins noted. He writes: "so as what the believer conceiveth in his understanding to be true, lie embraceth in his will to be good, and so in his heart joyfully receiveth that favour which God freely offereth unto him, namely Christ Jesus, and in, and with him all things needful to salvation."[50]

Gouge proceeds by dividing his definition of saving faith into five different parts. First, it is a "belief" because without giving assent to something, there is no faith at all. Second, saving faith is a belief "of the gospel" because it is the gospel in particular which moves and affects the heart of a believer. In its simplest form, the gospel for Gouge is the "good message" that Jesus Christ came to bring full redemption to all who are in the "woeful estate" of sin.[51] The third component to Gouge's definitions revolves around Jesus, "whereby Christ and all his benefits." In this, Gouge seeks to communicate that "Christ Iesus is the subject matter, and very substance of the Gospel, and so the proper and pecular object of justifying faith."[52] The benefits of Jesus, namely, wisdom, righteousness, sanctification, and redemption, are fourthly, "offered" to the believer through saving faith. The fifth element, "therein are received," demonstrates how saving faith responds to the aforementioned offer

---

50. Gouge, *Whole Armour of God*, 213–14. Without using the expressions "direct act" and "reflex act," Gurnall brings these descriptions, as does Gouge, into his definition of justifying faith. He writes, "Assent to the truth of the word is but an act of the understanding which reprobates and devils may exercise; but justifying faith is a compounded habit, and hath its seat both in the understanding and will ... as the promise is true, so it calls for an act of assent from the understanding; and as it is good as well as true, so it calls for an act of the will to embrace and receive it. Therefore, he which only notionally knows the promises, and speculatively assents to the truth of it, without clinging to it, and embracing of it, doth not believe savingly, and can have no more benefit from the promise, than nourishment from the food he sees and acknoweldgeth to be wholesome, but eats none of." Gurnall. *Christian in Complete Armour*, 2:3.

51. Gouge, *Whole Armour of God*, 165–66. For a full description of Gouge's understanding of the gospel, see chapter 2.

52. Ibid., 212.

and involves the human will. If the offer of Christ and the benefits found in him are not received, then he is in effect being rejected. Every true believer possess saving faith, having given full assent in his mind to the truth of the gospel along with full consent in his will to receive God's favor freely offered to him.[53]

God has given the gift of faith strictly out of his own kindness for the primary purpose of bringing glory to himself and derivatively to save sinners. "The end which God aimeth at in working this grace is principally in respect of himself, the setting forth of his owne glory ... but secondarily the salvation of mankind."[54] The sinner honors God only when he turns away from sin possessing this God-given justifying or saving faith in Jesus. God is glorified in the justification of sinners because through saving faith, they acknowledge that God is holy and that they are defiled with sin and in need of Christ's purging blood and righteousness. Through their saving faith, God is also glorified for his wisdom, since they acknowledge that God knows what is best for them. God is glorified for his truth, since they believe God is faithful to fulfill his promises. God is glorified for his power, since they affirm that nothing is impossible with God. God is glorified for his mercy, since they confess that God has pardoned their sin. Lastly, God is glorified for his justice, since they believe that God has expiated sin and satisfied his wrath in Jesus and "will not exact that of them."[55]

Gouge gives pastoral words of assurance when he explains the relationship between faith and God's justice in the life of the believer. The Christian understands that even his best works are polluted and imperfect and do not stand a chance in the face of God's justice. However, in the same breath, Gouge writes, "but yet in confidence of the All-sufficient sacrifice of Christ Iesus, they may appeal to God's justice: For God is not unjust to require a debt that is paid." The believer is both justified and spiritually preserved because of God's justice in satisfying his wrath and expiating the believer's sin through the cross of Christ. Gouge then explains that when the believer's faith increases in strength, so also is glory given to God increased. Still, Gouge's assuring words of

---

53. Ibid., 213–14.
54. Ibid., 217.
55. Ibid., 200–201.

confidence in the sufficiency of Jesus' atoning work to justify the sinner who has saving faith are not celebrated without a warning attached. The antithesis of faithfulness is infidelity, which dishonors God and by deduction, calls God unholy, unwise, untrue, powerless, merciless, and without justice.[56]

Gouge understood that the "popish" opponents of reformed Christianity fear that this kind of emphasis upon justifying faith and the assurance of faith apart from good works becomes a hindrance to and diminishes the need for right living. He counters stating that such a mindset is true only of those who have been blinded by Satan. "The truth is, that no other doctrine can make men more conscionable in performing all duty to God and man then the doctrine of faith. From Faith proceed all good works."[57] Gouge teaches that the believer is compelled to do good works foremost by God's love. He writes,

> He that indeed beleeveth that God so loved him as he spared not his only begotten Sonne, but gave him a price of redemption; that God in his Sonne hath vouchsafed to bee reconciled to him, to give him pardon of all his sinnes, freedome from hell and damnation, and to bestow on him all things pertaining to life and happiness, hee that is thus perswaded of GODS love to him, cannot but have his heart enlarged to doe what may be pleasing and acceptable to God. No hope of reward, no feare of revenge can so provoke a man to all good works, as love which Faith worketh.[58]

Gouge places God at focal point of the believer's good works with the emphatic motivation being "GODS love."

What one sees at this point in Gouge's teaching is that assurance of salvation comes through justifying faith, which God gives strictly as a gift of his grace. This saving faith does not allow good works to lay dormant in the believer's life, but instead compels such works to flow out of faith. In other words, Gouge is teaching the practical syllogism as a ground for discerning whether an individual possesses justifying

---

56. At this point, Gouge does not discuss what the consequence of such spiritual infidelity is for the believer.

57. Ibid., 206.

58. Ibid., 206–7.

faith. The practical syllogism was based upon sanctification, emphasizing "the believer's life of obedience that confirmed his experience
of grace."[59]

If Gouge's goal in defining justifying faith was strictly descriptive he
could have ended his discussion with the definition of terms. However,
because Gouge is a pastor with practical concerns he guides his readers
beyond the description of saving faith into the very real question of
how one might demonstrate genuine faith and its relation to the full
assurance of faith. Although the practical syllogism plays an important role in discerning saving faith, in the next section it will be seen
that it still is not the primary ground for the Christian's assurance,
according to Gouge.

FULL ASSURANCE OF FAITH

Gouge asserts that the believer can be certain of possessing saving faith
and should not be content with speaking of a "good hope" of salvation
that lacks of certainty. "The true believer may know that hee hath a true
and sound Faith."[60] At the same time, he differentiates between those
who seem to have faith and those who truly have it. The only way one
might be able to prove his faith is by testing it.

Doubt is an enemy that at one time or another plagues the faith of
every follower of Jesus. Yet, the presence of doubt does not denote the
absence of faith. Even King David, says Gouge, though he displayed
many evidences of the assurance of salvation, himself doubted. So
what does one make of the reality of doubting one's faith? One must
remember that doubt does not arise out of faith but out of the weakness of human flesh and will remain so long as one is alive. Just as the
believer must strive to subdue the flesh, he must in like manner strive to
dispel doubting lest the presence of doubt destroy faith, for "they stand
together as two implacable & irreconcileable enemies. The combate
must cost one of their lives."[61]

As he frequently does in his writings, Gouge sets up his exposition
with an imaginary interlocutor who raises objections that demand

---

59. Beeke, *Quest for Full Assurance*, 132.
60. Gouge, *Whole Armour of God*, 235.
61. Ibid., 237.

further explanation of a given subject matter. The inquisitor asks, with "full persuasion" being part of Gouge's definition of faith, how is it that faith and doubt are able to stand together? Is full assurance, then, of the essence of faith or not? Gouge reminds his readers that definitions are meant to be what something should be like (prescriptive), but not necessarily the way that things are (descriptive). Full assurance is of the essence of faith in faith's perfected definition, but may not be the reality of the believer in a fallen world. "They who know that the excellencie of Faith consisteth in assurance, will the more endeavour to get assurance, and not sooth themselves in their wauerings and doubtings." He continues: "Definitions must be made according to the *forme* of the things defined, and not according to the condition of the subject in which they are. Now *doubting* is not *formally* in faith, as Faith is considered *in it selfe* though it be *materially* in the subject, that is, in the party which beleeveth."[62] Thus, the presence of doubt does not demonstrate the lack of genuine faith in a person, but reveals the frailty of the human condition even as it pertains to one who possesses saving faith.[63]

Gouge recognizes that some oppose defining assurance as of the essence of faith. Rather than remove assurance from faith, Gouge prefers to speak of degrees of assurance, which can be found in even the weakest of faiths. He writes, "There be degrees of assurance answerable to the degrees of Faith. Where Faith is weak, assurance is small; Where Faith is strong assurance is stedfast. So much faith as there is, so much assurance there is. Thus may some assurance be in the weakest Faith. These degrees of assurance are not duely considered of them, who so much inveigh against those Divines that make assurance a Property of Faith."[64]

---

62. Ibid., 238.

63. Gouge is consistent with Calvin in his seemingly paradoxical description of faith as certain belief that is tinged with doubt. Gouge parses out this paradox differentiating between faith as it ought to be and faith as it is in reality. Likewise, Calvin defines faith as "a firm and certain knowledge of God's benevolence" but adds, "Surely, while we teach that faith ought to be certain and assured, we cannot imagine any certainty that is not tinged with doubt, or any assurance that is not assailed by some anxiety." Calvin, *Institutes* 3.2.17.

64. Gouge, *Whole Armour of God*, 238.

Genuine faith is proven or demonstrated by considering how faith is brought about along with the kind of faith it produces. If one strictly looks at the fruit of faith, but not its origin, one could be deceived by hypocritical faith supposing it to be genuine. The origin of faith must be the experiential grief that comes from the recognition of one's misery apart from God because of sin followed by a true desire for, and trust in, Christ. It is God, through man's misery, who stirs the heart to "desire and embrace the sweete promises and consolations of the Gospell."[65] Again, he marvels in the power of the gospel, "It is the Gospell, and nothing but it, that can worke in mans heart a true desire of Christ: because by it alo[n]e is Christ reuealed and offered."[66] This beginning of justifying faith then gives way to the fruit of faith. Thus, one ground for assurance of faith is the fruit of faith in the life of the Christian.

"Every sanctifying grace is a fruit of faith," says Gouge, evidenced in a quiet and clear conscience. A quiet and clear conscience is possible because of a holy security of mind grounded in the confidence that his salvation is secured in God. "They onely who by Faith have received Christ, and have their consciences quieted through his blood, can thus securely cast themselves upon God."[67] He continues to explain that the fruit of joy in the believer has as its sure ground Christ who is apprehended by a "true and lively Faith."[68] Some whose faith is temporary or hypocritical, may possess a kind of joy, but it is not true, sound, or solid joy, "but a mere shadow and shew thereof." Temporary faith is evident, according to Gouge, from the quickness by which it sprouts up and vanishes away. Genuine faith remains, even through the trials of life. Speaking metaphorically, Gouge explains that temptation and sorrow can obscure true faith as a cloud obscures the sun, but it is not ultimately vanished because Jesus is the foundation of the believer's faith and subsequent joy.

When testing one's faith, this inevitable and penetrating question must be addressed: "What if a man cannot find in him these effects of Faith, as peace of conscience, security of minde, ioy of heart, hath he

---

65. Ibid., 241.
66. Ibid., 244.
67. Ibid., 249.
68. Ibid., 251.

then no true faith at all?"[69] There are times in the Christian life where one's faith is like a tree in winter, struggling to bear fruit, says Gouge. For this reason, it is important to search for evidences and proofs of faith in one's life. Gouge helps the reader see that one, although not the primary, ground for assurance of salvation is the fruit of a life changed by God. Again, this amounts to the practical syllogism. When most fruitful, the Christian life should be characterized by peace, security, and joy. However, even in its lowest common denominator, the fruit of a changed life is reflected in a love for God, love for others, and a desire and attempt to please God.

It is significant to observe the locations of assurance in Gouge's theology of faith. The practical syllogism is one ground for assurance, but Gouge's primary emphasis is not in that particular ground. Most emphasized in Gouge's theology of assurance is a ground rooted not in man, but in the power and promises of God himself. Saving faith is proven to be genuine when the sinner is confronted with his sin and God enables him to surrender entirely to Jesus by believing the promises of God in the gospel. Consider the assurance fashioned in the believer because of the promises of God in the gospel applied to himself in this informative paragraph concerning the desire for God's mercy preceding saving faith,

> They which have this desire wrought in them, wil give no rest to their soules, till they have some sweet feeling of Gods love to them in Christ, and some assurance that Christ is theirs: whereupon God who hath offered to satisfie the hungry and thirsty, and to satisfie the desire of such as pant and long after him, by his Spirit worketh in such as are so prepared, such an inward assent of mind and credence unto the promises of the Gospell that particularly they apply them unto themselves, and gladly accept the free offer of God, and so receive Christ with all his benefits.[70]

---

69. Ibid.
70. Ibid., 223.

Through the enabling of the Holy Spirit, the sinner is able to possess faith, holding fast to the promises of God applying them to himself and receiving all the benefits that are found in Christ.[71]

Included in the promises of the gospel, Gouge's primary ground for assurance, are the promises of expiation of sin and reconciliation with God. Gouge again demonstrates this assurance when he comments on the shoes of the preparation of the gospel of peace in Ephesians 6:15. He writes, "the Gospel of Peace which assureth us of our reconciliation with God, and of the remission of our sinne, assureth us also that nothing can hurt us because the sting of every thing, which is sinne, is pulled out."[72] Rather than casting doubt on our assurance, the believer must remember that even his sin will be used for God's divine plan, much like an apothecary takes poison and uses it for medicinal purposes.[73]

While the shoes of the gospel of peace produce patience, not every child of God enjoys this fruit because of a lack of perseverance. Therefore, Gouge admonishes the reader to labor for and pursue the patience that stems from the gospel of peace, "As we desire true patience, so labour wee that it be rightly grounded in us. For this end we must acquaint our selves with this Gospell of peace, and labour for true, saving, sanctifying knowledge thereof." At first glance, Gouge's admonition might lead a reader to conclude that he is carelessly promoting a merit-oriented understanding of salvation. However, lest one think he is advocating that the gospel is received through one's efforts, he clarifies in the next breath, "The promises of God in his word are to be observed, especially such as concerne our reconciliation with God, and his favour towards us, as *David* did. Without knowledge of Gods

---

71. Concerning the certainty of Christian hope, Gouge similarly says, "For the ground of our Hope is the promise of God, who is faithfull and true: we may well waite for that which he hath promised, whatsoever it be. In this respect this true hope is termed, *The Hope of the Gospell*: that is, a hope which waiteth for those things which in the Gospel are promised." *Whole Armour of God*, 297.

72. Ibid., 171.

73. Gouge knew the practices of skilled apothecaries at first hand. Historian Anthony P. House recounts how William Delaune, a Huguenot minister and physician, secured a site at the end of the sixteenth century that became an Apothecary Hall in Blackfriars in Gouge's day. A. P. House, "The City of London and the Problem of the Liberties, c1540–c1640" (PhD diss., Oxford University, 2006), 151.

promises there can be no sound confidence."[74] When understood in context, Gouge is saying that the believer must labor to grow in one's understanding and confidence in the gospel of peace in order to be better grounded in the promises of God apart from which there is no confidence.

When it comes to testing the genuineness of one's faith, two extremes must be avoided. The first extreme is overconfidence and the second is a childish fear of losing faith. Some Christians enjoy a confidence in the promises of God based on orthodox teachings of Scripture, but then become prideful and fail to cherish this faith and persevere in it. The great danger is that their faith may not be genuine, but simply temporary and lacking persevering authenticity. Gouge references seven different New Testament texts, which warn against falling away from the faith, because the Holy Spirit "well knoweth how prone we are to fall away from grace.... We are to decay in grace, if we bee not watchfull over our selves and carefull to use all good means for nourishing and increasing thereof."[75] Overconfidence relinquishes persevering responsibilities from the Christian.

Conversely, others live in fear of losing their faith, "Though true Faith cannot totally and finally fall away yet it may to their feeling be so farre gone." Those who live in this kind of fear are keenly aware of their fleshly weaknesses. In those times of doubt and fear, the Christian must remember that God uses this uncertainty to call them to repentance and further cast their trust in him. He writes, "our assurance is not in our selves, but in Christ our head; as we lay hold of him, so he fast holdeth us: for there is a double bond whereby we are knit into Christ, one on Christs part, the other on ours."[76] By first pointing the Christian to find assurance in Jesus, Gouge points the Christian to the gospel. For, as stated earlier, the gospel is the "good message" that Jesus Christ came to redeem sinners. Gouge carefully walks the line between the Christian's full assurance being squarely upon Jesus, in whom are found the promises of God in the gospel, while retaining the Christian's

---

74. Gouge, *Whole Armour of God*, 173.

75. 1 Cor 10:12; Rom 11:20; Heb 3:12; 4:1; 10:38; 12:15; Matt 26:41. Gouge, *Whole Armour of God*, 260–61.

76. Gouge, *Whole Armour of God*, 258–60.

own responsibility to "lay hold of him." The remedy for a weak and fearful faith is not a self-confident faith, but an unshakeable trust in Jesus who, through God's gospel guarantees, keeps those who are his. Thus, to say that the primary ground of assurance is the gospel, is to say that the Christian's full assurance is found in the person and atoning work of Jesus Christ.

One interesting observation exists when comparing the grounds of assurance previously discussed with what we find in Gouge's Hebrews commentary. While all that has been previously discussed in this chapter finds no revision, what we might find is a "higher" ground of assurance even above the promises of God in the gospel in his exposition of Hebrews 3:12. Gouge mentions six grounds for assurance in this order: first, "The stability of God's decree"; second, "The faithfulness of God's promises"; third, "God's constant care over them"; fourth, "Their insition into Christ, and union with him"; fifth, "Christ's continual and effectual intercession;" and sixth, "The abode of the Spirit in them." It seems that grounds two through five are various expressions or implications of the Gospel which therefore amount to the primary ground of the "promises of God in the gospel" as seen in his work on the armor of God. His sixth ground, amounting to the inward testimony of the Holy Spirit.[77] Noteworthy is the triune emphasis in these six grounds, which Gouge says prevent man from boasting in self and "returneth all the glory to the blessed Trinity."[78] Also noteworthy in his Hebrews commentary is that there is no explicit ground testifying to the believer's response in faith (reflex act). However, this makes sense according to the particular emphasis at this point of the Hebrews commentary. What Gouge desires to show is that the triune God is ultimately the one in whom the grounds of assurance are found.

The most important difference is the stated highest ground of assurance in his Hebrews exposition, namely, the decree of God. Christians can be assured of salvation based upon God's electing them, "so as God

---

77. As discussed in Chapter 1, the inward testimony of the Holy Spirit was an important ground for assurance within reformed and Puritan writers. Gouge does not differ in this regard from his reformed predecessors.

78. Gouge, *Commentary on Hebrews*, 269.

will bring his elect to glory. Therefore they cannot finally fall."[79] A similar ground is appealed to in Gouge's *A Treatise of the Sinne Against the Holy Ghost*. When engaging the question of whether a believer can finally fall away, he appeals to the Christian's election as the ground for assurance. The sins of the elect are venial, says Gouge, because they are elected to life. "All that are elected, are elected to eternall life: and being elected thereto, they shall assuredly be made partakers thereof. God's purpose and decree remaineth firme and stable, and cannot be made frustrate. They are not therfore in danger of eternall damnation: and so cannot fall into that sinne [against the Holy Ghost]."[80]

How are we to understand this potential difference in the primary ground for assurance in Gouge's writings? Rather than seeing a difference, it seems best, however, not to see God's decree as a separate ground for assurance, but one that is in line with God's promises in the gospel. Accordingly, grounds one through five in his Hebrews commentary collectively amount to the promises of God in the Gospel. Again, the primary emphasis in his six stated grounds for assurance in his Hebrews 3:12 exposition lies in the fact that each are found in the triune God himself. If this is true in Gouge's writing, it would demonstrate the consistency of his theology with that of those prominent French Reformers, John Calvin and his Genevan successor and contemporary of Gouge, Theodore Beza (1519–1605) before him. Without explicitly naming either at this juncture, Gouge saw election and the finished work of Christ as an inseparably linked primary ground of assurance as they did. Gouge's triune emphasis in assurance reflects a similar theme in Calvin's writings where the Father's election, the Son's atoning work and imputed righteousness, and the Spirit's inward testimony assure faith and conquer doubt.[81] Theodore Beza followed Calvin's theological lead. "Faith in Jesus," said Beza, "is a sure witness of our election." Elsewhere he adds, "We receive assurance of election from Christ himself rather than from the secondary causes of salvation."[82] Gouge's twin

79. Ibid.

80. William Gouge, *Treattise of the Sinne Against the Holy Ghost* (London: I. Beale, 1639), 642.

81. Beeke, *Quest for Full Assurance*, 55–65.

82. Ibid., 76.

emphasis on God's decree and the finished work of Christ amount to assurance rooted in the promises of God found in the gospel.

Why, then, does Gouge not state God's eternal decree in his thorough discussion on assurance in the *Whole Armour of God*? The probable answer to this important question is twofold. first, Gouge provides pastoral insight into God's decree, when he warns against presumption. A person can mistakenly think he is elect when indeed he is not. "If he be deceived and mistake markes of his election, then he is not exempted from this sin [against the Holy Ghost], and the fearefull issue thereof." So while the decree is sure in the sight of God, it can be confused in the eyes of man. This is not to say that election is a cause for lost assurance, but that it has its pastoral limitations, which leads to the second reason for the difference. In *Whole Armour of God* Gouge is writing what largely amounts to a work of practical divinity whereas his Hebrews *magnum opus* is predominantly a commentary on Scripture. The priority of the former is to write as a physician of the soul whereas the priority of the latter is biblical exposition and instruction. In conclusion, the difference may be one of theology versus one of practical theology. The two do not stand in opposition but the presentation of the two does differ. Theologically, the decree of God is sure and secure as it pertains to the effectual calling of Christians by God. Pastorally, the believer comes to understand he or she is elect through faith in Jesus thereby receiving the promises found in Him. Confidence in one's election, thus, can be produced when holding fast to the finished work of Christ on man's behalf. For this reason, the promises of God in the gospel are presented as the primary ground of assurance in Gouge's practical divinity.

Returning to genuine faith, no spiritual attack in this war can extinguish the light of faith in the believer any more than the creatures of earth can put out the light of the sun. Just as the sun is far beyond humanity and out of extinguishing reach, so also is Christ beyond the reach of the diabolical enemies of faith. "Christ must be plucked out of Heaven, if true faith utterly fall away."[83]

Still, Christians face frequent attacks on their faith, which the apostle Paul likens not simply to arrows, but "fiery" arrows. The shield

---

83. Gouge, *Whole Armour of God*, 262.

metaphor, then, takes on a double meaning, observes Gouge. First, the shield protects from arrows as faith protects the Christian from Satanic temptations. Second, the shield extinguishes the flames of these arrows as faith cures the hurt done by spiritual temptations if they pierce through and wound one's soul. Gouge is not content to remain in the realm of observation and exposition, but pastorally moves into practical application.

Two questions arise from his exposition of the metaphor. First, how then does faith protect against temptation? Second, how does faith cure the hurt done by temptations? Faith alone can protect against temptation because "faith alone giveth us assurance of God's love" and "by it we so rest and repose our selves on the favour of God in Christ, as nothing can make us doubt of it, or separate us from it."[84] When the Christian is assured of God's love, spiritual attacks do not cause him to despair because he understands that his loving God is in control, just as Job was able to confess, "Though he slay me, yet will I trust in him."[85] The Christian must therefore remain steadfast in the faith, resist the devil, and trust in God. Indeed, faith is a shield through which the believer need not despair.

There are times in the Christian life when the fiery darts of Satan pierce the soul. When one gives in to the darts of temptations to sin, they are tormented by their sin and the anguish brought to the soul, if not cured, will soak out the very life of a person. Gouge urged Jukes, in his reinstatement sermon,

> If therefore thy conscience shall hereafter be over much troubled with doubtings, and feares, and despaire of pardon of thine Apostacy, account it a temptation of Satan, and yeald not unto it, but resist it; and say to thy soule, *Why are thou cast downe, O my soule? Why art thou disquieted in me? Hope in God: He is thy God*, reconciled unto thee: He hath discharged thee: who then shall lay this sinne to thy charge? By exercising thy faith after this manner thou wilt bring much peace to thy conscience.[86]

---

84. Ibid., 281–82.
85. Ibid., 282.
86. Gouge, *Recovery*, 89.

Persuading his readers with an *a fortiori* argument, Gouge reminds them of David's own vexation after his sin, when he cries out in Psalms 6 and 31, "My bones are vexed: my soule is also sore vexed" and "I am in trouble, mine eye, my soule and my belly are consumed with grief." If David, a mighty man of faith, a man after God's own heart, is so battered by temptation and sin, how can one with lesser faith extinguish the burning sensation of sin? "The onely meanes to coole this scorching heate, and to asswage this burning, is the blood of Christ: and Faith onely is the meanes to apply the efficacy of Christs blood to our soules: by Faith therefore, and by nothing else, may the *fiery* Darts be quenched." Gouge continues, "so Faith, which applieth the vertue of Christs sacrifice to a perplexed and troubled soule, dispelleth the inward anguish thereof."[87]

Vincent Jukes knew firsthand the emotionally destructive nature of the fiery darts of Satan. He experienced its burning anguish and the guilt and shame that it produced from giving into the temptation of the sin of apostasy. He also understood the forgiveness and renewed faith that comes through repentance. His reinstatement into fellowship with the church displays the guarantee of salvation that belongs to every child of God, because genuine faith produces the fruit of faith, repentance and restoration. Gouge urges the apostate, "O, be not more ashamed of confessing your sinne, then you were of committing it ... that which now thou dost openly with thy tongue and body before us children of men doe it *ex amino, do it heartily as to the Lord* the Searcher of hearts."[88] When the fallen Christian turns from sin, it can be said that he who was lost is now found.

Like Jukes, every child of God finds himself in the thick of the spiritual battle, according to Gouge. Satan has warred against the children of God since the beginning of time, therefore his tactics are many and his tempting experience unparalleled. This enemy of the soul is a mighty foe before whom none can stand on his own strength. "Having seene

---

87. Gouge, *Whole Armour of God*, 283.

88. Gouge, *Recovery*, 83. In confessing to God the Searcher of Hearts, Gouge elsewhere admonishes Christians to do their own searching in order to not fall into the traps of apostasy, "great circumspection must be used for preventing apostasy, yea, and other sins also." Gouge, *Commentary on Hebrews*, 262.

our owne weaknesse, and thereupon renounced all confidence in our-selves, our care must be to flye to a sure ground, and rest thereon: so shall we be safe and sure, yea so may be quiet and secure. This sure ground, and safe rocke is onely the Lord."[89] The only way the Christian can stand is by the strength of God's might and being furnished with the full armor that God provides. Of the six pieces of armor, Gouge argues that the shield of faith is most important because faith is the mother of all graces.

Saving faith, as understood by Gouge, is "a beliefe of the Gospel, whereby Christ and all his benefits offered therein, are received."[90] In his definition, Gouge presents a traditional Puritan approach to faith, which demonstrates the direct act of faith where the Christian belief is set squarely upon God and the reflex act of faith where the benefits of faith are believed to be applied to one's self. Without directly using the term "practical syllogism" Gouge affirms that genuine faith when fully enjoyed by the Christian produces spiritual fruit such as peace, security, joy, love for God, and love for others. This genuine faith within the believer cannot be lost, because it is established by the shed blood of Jesus, and not by the efforts of the Christian.[91] Just as saving faith produces assurance of salvation, it also produces fruit in the life of the believer, where he resists the attacks of the enemy, brings God glory through obedience, and finds consolation and healing when he fails.

When reading Gouge's exposition on spiritual warfare, one will find a pastor-theologian who cares deeply about the truths of the Scriptures as well as the spiritual lives of the people under his care. He desires to see his flock come to justifying faith and not be fooled by what appears to be authentic, but is only temporary or even hypocritical. Just as faith is wrought strictly through God's grace, so also is perseverance in the faith an outcome of God's grace. When temptations and spiritual attacks mount up, the follower of Jesus can prevail as he relies upon the strength of the Lord. Gouge provides this metaphor from Isaiah 61,

---

89. Gouge, *Whole Armour of God*, 10–11.

90. Ibid., 210.

91. "No true sanctifying, saving grace can be totally lost.... They who are effectually called, and endued with such grace, cannot finally fall away." Gouge, *Commentary on Hebrews*, 269.

"We must therefore be like sound Oaken trees, which the more they are shaken, the deeper root they get in the earth." He concludes with these words of encouragement, "and [we must] know for our comfort, the Divel can raise no greater stormes then God in wisedome permitteth him. God in the end will turne al to our good, as he dealt with *Iob* so that if we believe, we shall surely be established. Faith maketh men secure in perils."[92]

---

92. Gouge, *Whole Armour of God*, 293.

4

Humiliation, Suffering, Death, and the Practice of Piety

Every human is faced with the certainty of impending hardship in life. Christians are no exception. "Many troubles and crosses must bee undergone in this World, before we can come to enjoy the rest and happinesse in Heaven ... experience of all ages [i.e., generations] doth verifie the truth of those Scriptures" that refer to the sufferings of the people of God.[1] As Gouge writes, "In a word, it is as possible for sheepe to live quiet among wolves without hurt, as for the Church in this world without trouble and persecution."[2]

With every difficult experience, suffering drives Christians to ask a variety of important questions such as: why must pain, suffering, and death be inevitable human experiences? Why are Christians not exempt from such hardships? Is suffering evidence of the presence of sin in one's life? Is suffering always the consequence of someone's sin? What purpose does suffering serve? Do all afflictions come from the hand of God? What assurances do Christians possess amidst hardship and the realities of suffering and death? In this chapter, I will first unpack Gouge's theology of divine providence, which functions as a foundational component to his practical divinity in general and theology of suffering in particular. Then, I will explore Gouge's teachings on suffering and the various ways he seeks to comfort afflicted saints through the scriptures.

---

1. William Gouge, *The Whole Armour of God. Or, A Christians spirituall furniture, to keep him safe frō all the assaults of Satan*, 5th ed. (London: I. Beale, 1639), 175.
2. Gouge, *Whole Armour of God*, 175.

SUFFERING AND DIVINE PROVIDENCE

It was about 3:00 pm in Blackfriars, London on Sunday, October 26, 1623[3] that the quietness of the Lord's Day was interrupted with the crackling sounds of breaking beams, a collapsing floor, crashing stones, and the shrieks of over two hundred terrified people. At least ninety-one of those panic-stricken congregants would plummet to their deaths that afternoon. What would follow in the weeks and months after this terrible occasion was an array of religious polemical treatises directed between Protestants and Catholics proclaiming God's providential hand in favor of one group and not the other.[4]

The two hundred people gathered that afternoon were present to hear a prominent Catholic priest and Jesuit by the name of Robert Drurie. It was a mixed group consisting of Protestants, Catholics, scholars, and others assembled in the upper floors of a tall edifice, which was the residence of the French ambassador in the lower chamber of the mansion. Drurie arrived with an assistant and began the service with quiet prayers before continuing with a Scripture reading from Matthew 18:22–35. He followed the reading with an exposition of three points, "the debt we owe God," "the mercy of God in forgiving it," and "mans unmercifulnesse to his brother." About half an hour through his message, the floor suddenly gave way, taking the lives of Drurie, his assistant, and at least eighty-nine others.[5]

Being in Blackfriars, Gouge was able to give a firsthand account of what occurred, "I was an eye-witnesse of many of the things therein related, and heard, from the mouth of such as were present at the sermon."[6] Gouge assembled carpenters to survey the wreckage, met with the coroner for further observation, and listened to the testimonies of five individuals present at the tragedy, four of whom actually fell to the ground. Gouge relates the turmoil of that Lord's Day when discussing

---

3. This date is according to the Julian calendar, while it is November 5 in the late-Gregorian calendar.

4. William Gouge, *Extent of God's Providence, set out in a sermon, preached in Black-Fryers Church, V. Nov. 1623. On occasion of the downe-fall of papists in a chamber at the said Black-Fryers, 1623. Oct. 27* (London: George Miller for Edward Brewster, 1631), 393.

5. Ibid., 396.

6. Ibid., 393.

the wreckage. Of the ninety-one dead that day, only sixty-three bodies remained the following morning. Gouge suspects family members carried their loved ones off to provide a proper burial for them. That Monday morning, two mass pits became graves for the remaining corpses, one pit eighteen feet long by twelve feet wide and the other twelve feet by eight feet. Gouge recounts,

> Their manner of burial seemed almost (if not altogether) as dismall, as the heape of them when they lay on the floore whereupon they last fell. No obsequies or funeral rites were used at their burial. Onely on the day after, a blacke crosse of wood was set upon each grave. But soone was it by the authority commanded to be taken downe.[7]

For Gouge, these events were not coincidental, but a direct byproduct of the gathering's occasion, namely, to hear the sermon of a papist. He interpreted these events as God's judgment upon those who would mislead and misinform the church.

Alexandra Walsham has compiled a listing of dozens of accounts surrounding this momentous event.[8] She laboriously sorts through the polemical material discussing the competing claims to divine providence from both Protestants and Catholics. This providentialism led to both verbal aggression and physical assault. Walsham argues that just as anti-Catholicism was a unifying factor among post-Reformation Protestants, providentialism also functioned to unite Protestants against the papists. She takes her claim a step further when she writes, "Providentialism was possibly one more respect in which Protestantism, far from smothering and eradicating 'superstition,' helped in fact to sustain and intensify it, and to reinforce key elements of an older cosmology."[9] Artists, publishers, and pastors like Gouge were guilty of this sort of providentialism, says Walsham.

Although Walsham acknowledges that providentialism fit into a theological framework and post-Reformation predestinarianism, a

---

7. Ibid., 399.
8. Alexandra Walsham. "'The Fatall Vesper': Providentialism and Anti-Popery in Late Jacobean London," *Past and Present* 144 (August 1994): 36–87.
9. Ibid., 143.

more nuanced approach to William Gouge's understanding of divine providence is in order. Thus, this chapter asks in what ways did Gouge understand and expound the doctrine of divine providence and what implications did this doctrine have on his instruction on suffering and living the Christian life?

Five of Gouge's works are particularly relevant when seeking to investigate this question. Most relevant is the sermon delivered on the Sunday following the "downe-fall of the papists" titled *The Extent of God's Providence* (preached in 1623, published in 1631). Other important treatises include his treatise delivered before the House of Lords, *The Progresse of Divine Providence* (1645); his treatise discerning God's providential hand in bringing famine, plague, and sword titled *God's Three Arrows* (1631); *The Saints Sacrifice* (1632) calling for gratitude for God's hand of mercy upon the nation; and his sermonic reflection upon Queen Elizabeth I coming to power following Mary's reign in *Mercies Memorial* (1644, published 1645).[10] Other relevant portions of Gouge's works will be considered alongside these mentioned.

As stated above, the doctrine of divine providence in William Gouge's theology directs much of his thought and outlook on life in general and his theology of suffering in particular. A careful reading of Gouge demonstrates that his exegesis of the Scriptures, his theological framework, and his view of the unfolding of history inform his thinking. It is the aim of this section to unpack these dimensions and present a nuanced perspective of Gouge's doctrine of divine providence.

---

10. William Gouge, *Extent of God's Providence; Gods three arrovves: plagve, famine, svvord, in three treatises* (London: Edward Brewster, 1631); *The Progresse of Divine Providence, set out in a sermon preached in the Abbey Church of Westminster before the House of Peers, on the 24th of September, 1645, being the day of their monethly fast* (London: I. Kirton, 1645); *The Saints Sacrifice: Or, A Commentarie On the CXVI. Psalme. Which is, A Gratulatory Psalme, for Deliverance from deadly Distresse* (London: Edward Brewster, 1632); *Mercies Memorial, set out in a sermon preached in Paul's church, Novemb. 17, 1644, in memoriall of the great deliverance which England had from antichristian bondage by Queen Elizabeths attaining the crowne* (London: Ioshua Kirton, 1645).

DIVINE PROVIDENCE AND THE EXEGESIS OF SCRIPTURE

William Gouge produced at least seventeen published works in his career, spanning over five thousand pages.[11] As a learned pastor, the study and exposition of the biblical text represent Gouge's greatest strengths. Thus, one should not be surprised to learn that his most pointed and thorough explanations of divine providence are found in his exposition of the Bible. Matthew 10:29–31 is his primary text in *The Extent of God's Providence* and Ezekiel 36:11 in *The Progresse of Divine Providence*. This section will consider these treatises in search of understanding the relationship between Scripture and Gouge's doctrine of divine providence.

Prior to discussing the fatal disaster in Blackfriars in his reworked treatise of the Sunday morning sermon the week after the event, Gouge opens with an exposition of Matthew 10:29–31 that is nineteen pages in length. In this treatise, the biblical text is the clear starting point. Stemming from his primary text, his aim is to show how divine providence is applied to every area of life. The text states, *"Are not two sparrows sold for a farthing? And one of them shall not fall to the ground without your Father. But the hairs of your head are all numbered. Fear ye not therefore: ye are of more value then many sparrows."* Gouge declares that every word and phrase in these verses present the extent of God's providence. Here Jesus uses a *kal vachomer* (*a fortiori*) argument, making a lesser to greater comparison. A bird is a rather small animal. And a sparrow is among the smallest of birds. Likewise, a farthing is a small denomination of money. The diminutive nature of these two words expresses the minutia of the matter at hand. Furthermore, argues Gouge, the phrase "not one of them" includes all creatures of little prominence. In Gouge's estimation, what follows is the proof that the most casual things are ordered by divine providence, namely, that this little sparrow cannot fall to the ground without God knowing. Gouge writes, "Hitherto, Christ hath set out one instance of the divine *Providence*, taken from one of the least

---

11. Two of his works were published posthumously: *An Exposition on the VVhole Fifth Chapter of S. Iohns Gospell: also notes on other choice places of Scripture, taken by a reuerend diuine, now with God, and found in his study after his death, written with his owne hand* (London: Iohn Bartlett, 1630); and *A learned and very vsefvl commentary on the whole Epistle to the Hebrewes* (London: J. Kirton, 1655).

of unreasonable creatures."[12] Even one's hairs, as Jesus states in verse 31, are included in the providential workings of God. If these matters of seeming insignificance are under the auspices of God's providential hand, then one can infer this general point, that "divine providence extendeth it selfe to all things," even suffering and hardship.[13]

Gouge states that the one who rejects divine providence is left with the grievous alternative of chance, fortune, and luck.[14] He calls fortune "fiction," a mere category of thought created to turn people away from God. Here lies Gouge's greatest opposition to fortune, namely, that "God is robbed of much honour."[15] He concludes that this concept of fortune is thus an idol. It is given supremacy over the course of one's life and detracts attention off the true God onto itself.

While the subject matter of *The Progresse of Divine Providence* is similar to that of the treatise discussed above, its occasion, audience, and time period differs significantly. This sermon was delivered, not at Blackfriars but at Westminster Abbey before the House of Lords, September 24, 1645.[16] Gouge's text is Ezekiel 36:11, "*I will do better unto you then at your beginnings.*"[17] This sermon differs from the one discussed above in that his exposition of Ezekiel 36:11 itself is shorter followed by lengthy theological and practical application of the principles drawn from the text. Throughout the treatise, the words "*I will do better unto you then at your beginnings*" weave in and out of his discussion. After a presentation of Ezekiel's historical context as a prophet to the people of Israel in Babylonian captivity, he sets out to explain the text.

In his explanation, he notes five particular observations from this verse. First, the words "*I will*" tell the reader of the Author of these

---

12. Gouge, *The Extent of God's Providence*, 375.

13. Ibid., 377.

14. Gouge understands these terms to be synonymous.

15. Gouge, *The Extent of God's Providence*, 380. Margo Todd, in her article, "Providence, Chance and the New Science in Early Stuart Cambridge," *The Historical Journal*, 29, no. 3 (September, 1986): 697–711, argues that certain streams of Puritan providentialism led to an increased interest in scientific speculation, which in turn led to "increased puritan participation in empirical science" (p. 700).

16. This is two years after his selection by parliament to serve as part of the Westminster Assembly.

17. His translation of the Hebrew is rendered, "*I will doe good above your beginnings.*"

words. The preceding context going back to v.7 and the proceeding context clearly express that the Lord God ("Jehovah") is the one who speaks. The corresponding theological principle is that "The Lord is the foundation of all good." Second, the act that will take place is that of doing good, "*do better,*" which is stated to be efficient because of the hiphil stem of the Hebrew verb. Thus, "God causeth his goodnesse to flow forth." Third, the word "*then*" is a comparative word in Hebrew, which is to say, "God's goodnesse ever increaseth." Fourth, the recipient of these words from the Lord God, or the object, is "*unto you.*" Understood principally, these words are directed not to Israel, but to the church with whom is "the proper object of God's goodnesse." Fifth, the timing of God's "doing better" is in contrast to the beginnings, which is to say in the later times. From this phrase is the principle born that directs the remainder of his treatise. Namely, "the best things are reserved for the last times," in which his present audience found themselves.[18]

Gouge then explores how it is that God has reserved better things for the later times in his providential ways. In *The Extent of God's Providence,* Gouge had stated that, "He that wrought six dayes in creating all things, worketh to this very day, and so will do all the dayes of this world, in and by his *Providence.*"[19] His 1623 reference to the six days of creation and seventh day of rest is here unpacked in his 1645 *The Progresse of Divine Providence.* Gouge develops and explains this approach in attempting to convey that the Lord "*will do better unto you then at your beginnings.*" Just as God created the earth in six days and rested on the seventh, so can the unfolding of history be divided into six days with the seventh day representing eternal rest. Gouge divides the six days according to important transitional moments in biblical history.[20]

Day one covers the span from Adam to Noah. This first day is marked by the hope of redemption declared in the words of Genesis 3:15, that the seed of Adam would bruise the head of the serpent while only the heel of Adam's seed would be struck. As interpreters before and after him, Gouge understands this text as a reference to Jesus Christ's victory over Satan.

18. Gouge, *The Progresse of Divine Providence,* 2–6.
19. Gouge, *The Extent of God's Providence,* 386.
20. Gouge, *The Progresse of Divine Providence,* 12–16.

Day two begins with Noah bringing the first day to close and leads up to Abraham. Noah is Gouge's selection for the second day based upon the great deliverance found in the ark. The ark serves as a type of God's deliverance as Peter picks up on in 1 Peter 3:21 corresponding to baptism.

Day three begins with Abraham from whom all nations are blessed, and ends with David. "In this day," says Gouge, "the Tabernacle, with the many other types of Christ, his offices and benefits to his Church were first ordained, and Israel settled in the land of Canaan, a type of their heavenly rest. Thus did this third day farre exceed the former in glory."[21]

Day four goes from David to the Babylonian captivity. The royal kingdom, temple, and prophetic office represent various types of Christ. These types, according to Gouge, make day four more glorious than day three.

Day five extends from the Babylonian captivity to the time of Christ's ascension. Certainly, this day surpasses the four before it. The deliverance of Israel from Babylonian captivity is the fullest picture of the redemption found in Christ. John the Baptist declared the arrival of the Christ, who would bring redemption to sinners. As stated before, day five surpassed the glory and greatness of day four.

Day six begins with Christ's ascension and will conclude at the time of his second coming to judge the world. Gouge calls this day a day of "cleare and full revelation of all the glorious mysteries that were hidden from the beginning of the world till then."[22] Because this day has yet to see its culmination, better things are still to come.

Gouge maintains that this division presents the continuance of the present world and world to come as one progressive unveiling of God's providential hand in the times and seasons of humanity. This biblical historical progression in the development of Gouge's doctrine of divine providence is significant. The doctrine of divine providence is not simply a polemical tool nor is it rooted in any sense of superstition. It is, in part, a result of reflection upon the historical unfolding of Scripture and God's plan of redemption. Because the sixth day in his timeline has

---

21. Ibid., 14.
22. Ibid., 15.

yet to reach its conclusion, contemporary events should be considered within this grid. Although not mentioned in this treatise, the collapse of the multi-leveled edifice in Blackfriars is no exception. For Gouge, it belongs to the sixth day just as the building of Solomon's temple does in day four or the confusion of languages at the tower of Babel in day two. The ending of each day appears to be better off then the beginning of each day (within the progress of providence). While Israel's exit from captivity was the fullest type or picture of Christ's redemption, the redemption at the cross is not a type but the real redemption itself. Thus, in day five, the latter was far greater than the former parts of it. The same is true with day six, which is the most privileged and blessed of all because God has promised to do better in the later times then "*at your beginnings.*"

DIVINE PROVIDENCE: A THEOLOGICAL OUTLOOK

"What is the chief end of man?" asks the first question of the Westminster Shorter Catechism. The answer, "Man's chief end is to glorify God and enjoy him forever."[23] William Gouge was among the Westminster divines who crafted these words over twenty years after he wrote his treatise, *The Extent of God's Providence.* As one who maintained the theological convictions of Reformed Protestantism, Gouge, in this treatise, recognizes the glory of God to be the central goal of all things, especially divine providential workings. He writes, "God thus extends his Providence to all things that he may bring them to such ends as him-selfe hath appointed. Which owne in generall, 1. His own glory. 2. His childrens good. God's glory is the most principall and supreme end of all."[24] In the margin of this text, he quotes the church father Jerome's (c. 347–420) comments on Ezekiel 10:1 in Latin for historical support of this proposition, "The glory of God is in the knowledge of much: and then is manifested, when all matters of providence are manifested: this happens neither by chance, nor by someone speaking."[25]

---

23. *Westminster Shorter Catechism* (Glasgow: Free Presbyterian, 1958), 287.

24. Gouge, *The Extent of God's Providence*, 378.

25. Gouge, *The Extent of God's Providence*, margin, 378. "Gloria Dei sedet in scientia multitudine: & tunc manifestatur, quando cuncta rei providentia manifestantur:

He anticipates the objector who submits that the things of this earth are so base that they would impeach and bury God's majesty. Gouge answers this objection in a twofold manner. First, he quotes Joseph Hall, Bishop of Exeter's *Meditations and Vows*, which state that there can be no greater honor to God than to extend his providence to the smallest of matters.[26] Second, he refers to Psalm 113:5–6 and notes that who better to providentially order the great and the base things than he who created them.

God supremely works all things for his glory, and subordinately, for the good of his children. By appealing to Romans 8:28, Gouge affirms that God even turns the evil practices of men for the good of his children. Gouge concludes that if God did not "meddle with the things here below," then the magnification of his glory and the bringing about good for his children would not be accomplished so well.[27]

With reference to futuristic culminations of God's providential ordering, Gouge is unconvinced that God has set apart in his providence a future millennial reign of Jesus Christ. Rather, he maintains that in this sixth day, the greatest of blessings are reserved for those who live in it. The words of Revelation 21:10–21 are in reference to the "glorious estate of the Church of Christ under the gospel yet to come, and that before his last comming to judgement."[28] Along with this glorious state of the church yet realized, there is for him an anticipation of a mass conversion of the Jews. Rather than understanding promises made to the Jews in relation to their exodus from the Babylonian captivity, he sees these promises in relation to the latter parts of the sixth day. To express further this belief, he published what became a controversial work of Sir Henry Finch, *The Calling of the Jewes*, which presents Gouge's position.[29] Gouge was imprisoned for nine weeks by King James I for

nec fortuito quid fieri, nec dicere quempiam." The source of this reference is difficult to track down. It is likely that he has Jerome's Ezekiel commentary in mind.

26. See Joseph Hall, *Meditations and Vows Divine and Moral*, ed. Charles Saye (New York: E.P Dutton, 1901), 129. Hall's work was originally published in 1605.

27. Gouge, *The Extent of God's Providence*, 379.

28. Gouge, *The Progresse of Divine Providence*, 29.

29. Henry Finch, *The calling of the Ievves: A present to Iudah and the children of Israel that ioyned with him, and to Ioseph (the valiant tribe of Ephraim) and all the house of Israel that ioyned with him. The Lord giue them grace, that they may returne and*

publishing this text because the king viewed it as a threat to the nation. Gouge cleared himself of the offense and was released after reassuring the king of his allegiance to him.[30]

Up to this point, Gouge's doctrine of divine providence has been shown to be more than a polemical tool; it is also a doctrine that stems from serious thought and exegesis of biblical texts. He understands the biblical text to teach that God's hand providentially orders all courses of life, great and small, in both the Old and New Testaments. Furthermore, there can be seen a providentially guided continuity between the two testaments when one reflects upon the progressive nature of divine providence beginning in the Garden of Eden, culminating at the return of Jesus Christ, leading into eternal rest. He also affirms the doctrine of divine providence through theological reflection. If the chief end of all natural and human events is that God might be glorified, and subordinately that God would bring good to his people, then one must believe that God's hand providentially guides everything.

Within Gouge's structure of viewing all of human history as seven days, the present era represents the latter portion of the sixth day until Jesus Christ returns. As a Christian living in the sixth day, which Gouge determined to be the most blessed day from Ezekiel 36:1 ("I will do better unto you then at your beginnings"), how does the Christian view the recent past and the present day? Gouge's answer would likely be, "providentially and discerningly." He writes:

> It is without question a point of prudence to eye the divine *Providence* in all things. For by it without all contradiction are all things thorowout the whole world governed and disposed: especially affairs of his Church on which sometimes the light of his favour brightly shineth: other-times haile-stones of indignation are showred downe. By a due observation hereof, may our disposition to God be so ordered, as that, which God expecteth,

---

seeke *Iehovah their God, and Dauid their King, in these latter dayes. There is prefixed an epistle vnto them, written for their sake in the Hebrue tongue, and translated into English,* (London: William Bladen, 1621).

30. See J. A. De Jong, *As the Waters Cover the Sea: Millennial Expectations in the Rise of Anglo-American Missions, 1640–1810* (Kampen: Kok, 1970), 48–51; Iain Murray, *The Puritan Hope* (London: Banner of Truth, 1971), 44–45.

be effected: namely *Gratulation* for his *Favours*: *Humiliation* for his *judgements*.[31]

Elsewhere he writes, "God is to be beheld in all our affairs. If a sparrow fall not to the ground without him, what do we, what can we do without him? And if his hand be in all that we do or can do, ought we not to take notice thereof, to behold it, well to observe it, and marke whereto it tends?"[32] Gouge leads by example putting his words into action through interpreting natural occurrences, political and ecclesiological changes in England, and physical ailments and death through a providential lens.

GOD'S PROVIDENCE AND SUFFERING AMIDST NATURAL OCCURRENCES

Two of Gouge's treatises are a result of interpreting through a providentialist lens the plague and famine that began in 1625 and lasted until 1631. Those treatises are *God's Three Arrowes* (1631) and *The Saints Sacrifice* (1632). Gouge says this plague began in the first year of Charles I, which places the initial outbreak of this plague in 1625. Also, in his 1631 treatise, *God's Three Arrowes*, he writes, "we have felt the bitternesse of the plague within these six years more then in many hundred yeares before in this land." He adds elsewhere, "In the yeare 1630 the plague began againe to increase, as another great plague was feared. It hovered over the city all Sommer and Autmne of that yeare."[33] At least 1,317 people died in the London and its surrounding parishes. The cost of corn soared and there was a great loss of jobs, cattle, servants, and children.[34]

Given his theological convictions and his view of the present state of England, Gouge sought to understand why God had chosen to afflict England so severely. Was it a "hailstone of indignation" or a testing of the righteous to be faithful? Gouge decided to turn his attention "to such Scriptures as afforded fit remedies for removing the fore-said judgements."[35] The fruit of Gouge's work is the treatise *God's Three Arrowes*.

---

31. William Gouge, *Gods Three Arrowes*, A3.
32. Gouge, *The Extent of God's Providence*, 386.
33. Gouge, *The Saints Sacrifice*, A9.
34. Ibid., A5–A6.
35. Ibid., A6.

The three arrows of God's judgment are famine, plague, and sword. Numbers 16:44–50 was Gouge's text to address the plague. He determines that God brings plagues upon a people who are in sin and rebellion.

Gouge lists no less than a dozen kinds of sins that invoke God's judgment such as idolatry (the thick clouds of "popery" are again forming in England); profaning holy things and times (prayer, preaching, the Sabbath and sacraments are neglected or carelessly observed); polluted professors who provide justification to their adversaries because of their own lewdness; vilifying God's mercies (some do so by wishing the days of Queen Mary would return); magistrates abusing their authority (by taking bribes, perverting justice, oppressing the innocent, and using power for their own advance); ministers who pervert their function (by discouraging the upright and favoring profane people); trampling on those who have spiritually fallen; conspiracy to and consent in sin; obstinacy in sin (i.e., sinners are not responding in repentance in the midst of this plague); infidelity to God (the faithful ministry of the Gospel has no effect on their hearts); and impenitency (no true fruit of repentance can be found because people are settled in their own sin. Men would rather grow worse and worse and let their hearts grow harder as did Pharaoh's) and apostasy, that is, abandoning the faith. "If these, and other like provocations of Gods wrath among us be duly weighed, we shall see cause enough to confesse that God's wrath is justly gone out against us, and that we have deservedly pulled this Plague upon our owne pates."[36]

Thus, the remedy, or as he says, "plaister" for the plague is turning to God in prayer and fasting with a heart of repentance. These involve seven characteristics: godly sorrow; true confession; loathing the sin, resolve to never return; solemnly promise and covenant to follow through on your resolve to not return; sense the weight of the covenant you made; and seek God's remission of sins and reconciliation with him.[37] Gouge tells his readers that it was the second of July, 1625, when the first public fast was called as a response to the death of 405

---

36. Gouge, *God's Three Arrowes*, 82.
37. Ibid., 8.

people of the plague that week. The primary purpose of these public fasts was to seek God's grace and favor through personal humiliation.[38]

If God providentially orders even natural occurrences to execute judgment upon sin, what does one make of the righteous people who suffer under such a judgment? Gouge maintains that the righteous, in so many ways, are exempt from God's judgments. On the one hand, he realizes that righteous people suffer under such judgments, but on the other hand God's judgment is not directed to the righteous and he uses these judgments upon saints for his glory or for the good of his people. Some die in the present but are spared of the evil to come, thus are recipients of God's mercy and goodness. Some are able to do greater good for God through a trial than they could otherwise. For this point, Gouge refers to Ezekiel who was taken away to captivity in Babylon and did a great work for God, which could not have happened if he remained in Israel. Others are granted great favor in the midst of trial and are able to do the church great good, as in the case of Daniel, Mordecai, and Esther. Still others are removed from this present life with all of its suffering and brought into heaven through an act of mercy.[39] Through these observations, Gouge concludes that those who suffer under the plague are not necessarily those whom God is punishing.

From a practical standpoint, Gouge's teachings at this point remind Christians who suffer that their suffering has a purpose that involves a greater providentially ordered good. Here we see the pastoral value of Gouge's decision to craft a biblically grounded theology of suffering. The suffering Christians in his parish who wondered why they experienced the plague needed answers that were informed by their faith. The need for this kind of pastoral direction is only magnified in light of varying opinions about the reasons for suffering that circulated in London. Without giving any names, Gouge speaks of those who maintain that someone's dying of the plague is evidence of their unbelief. Gouge says that to believe that all who die of the plague go to hell is not only uncharitable, but also incorrect. Rather, while it is true that the wicked die of the plague, it is equally true that even believers die of the

---

38. Ibid., 9–10.
39. Ibid., 19–20.

plague and then are gathered to God. In the same way, one thief on the cross died in his wickedness, while the other was gathered into glory.[40]

In addition to comforting distraught Christians who suffer, Gouge also wanted to stir the hearts of his non-Christian audience to come to the realization through his writing that they are indeed not Christians. He desired that these would begin to feel the weight of their sin and the judgment due to them. In his attempt to comfort even these afflicted unbelieving souls amidst their suffering, Gouge had to help them understand the gravity of their sin and the magnitude of God's mercy to all who repent.

> Poore penitent sinners, whose hearts are broken with sight and sence of their sinnes, may hence, and will hence receive much comfort, that there is meanes of attonement and reconciliation betwixt God and them ... true penitents that are pierced with sence of their sinnes, know that while there remains enmity betwixt God and them, they are in no better estate then the Devils. They find by the heavy burden of sinne oppressing their soules, and by their deepe apprehension of Gods wrath thereupon, that Gods favour is more sweet then life itself, and infinitely to be preferred before all contents and delights that this world can afford.

Gouge then switches from talking about the sinner's predicament to addressing the sinner himself. He writes,

> Take notice therefore, O ye poore in Spirit, take notice of this soveraigne ground of comfort, *There is meanes of reconciliation betwixt you and your God.* An attonement is made. Comfort your soules herewith. It is sufficient, and in stead of all righteousnesse, to have him alone, against whom alone I have sinned, propitious and gracious in pardoning sinne.[41]

With pastoral courage and sensitivity, Gouge not only reveals the sinner's gloomy situation, but also provides the hope of gracious reconciliation. "An attonement is made," Gouge declares, by Jesus himself,

---

40. Ibid., 21–22.
41. Ibid., 56–57.

because of his human and divine natures was able to satisfy the wrath of God directed toward man because of sin. "Thus as God-man is Christ the meanes of attonement betwixt God and man."[42] While God's providential hand is seen even through the suffering that comes in the midst of plagues, God has a plan to execute judgment on the wicked, work a greater good among his people, and call sinners to repentance.[43]

This great plague and famine in the land lasted until the autumn, 1631. Gouge calls this removal of the plague "extraordinary and admirable (if not miraculous)." He continues, "While the judgements lay heavy on us and others, instant and earnest prayer was made for the removal thereof. Now that our prayers are heard, should we not returne what he requires that hath granted our desires?"[44] What else does God require but praise of him? From this statement stems Gouge's 293-page exposition of Psalm 116, titled *The Saints Sacrifice,* which he subtitles, *A Gratulatory Psalme, for Deliverance from deadly Distresse* (1632). Gouge has two purposes for writing this treatise, both of which reflect his pastoral concerns for people who are suffering and those who are not. First, "to stirre up mine owne soule, and the soules of others to endeavour with our uttermost power to render to him who hath beene so gracious to us, that which is most due, all possible praise." Second, he aims at stirring believers to continue in humble and sincere devotion to God.[45] These two goals can be summed up with the words prayer and praise. For Gouge, these two responses to God's goodness (even amidst suffering) are distinct, yet inseparable. "Prayer and praise are like two twinnes, which though they have each of them their severall and distinct members, yet by navell are from their birth knit together, and so grow together, as if you force them asunder, you kill them both: one

---

42. Ibid., 54.

43. For this reason, Gouge takes issue with the Catholic teaching that a Christian should pray for the dead. Opportunity for repentance is only given to those who live. "Life is the time of receiving all needfull grace," says Gouge. "How foolish, how impious, how sacrilegious are they that spend this sweet incense of prayer in vaine: as all they do, that offer it up for the dead." Gouge, *God's Three Arrowes,* 108.

44. Gouge, *The Saints Sacrifice,* A5.

45. Ibid., A5–A6.

without the other cannot live."[46] This call to prayer and praise reflects Gouge's understanding that God's providential working brought the plague in 1625 and removed the plague in 1631. For during the time of the plague, the appropriate response was repentance, prayer, and fasting. So after the removal of the plague, praise and adoration were the appropriate responses.

Ronald E. McFarland highlights the importance of gratitude in response to God's mercy in seventeenth-century Puritan and Anglican teaching. In his study, he observes that preachers agree that full requital for God's mercy is impossible and that expressions of gratitude flow from a thankful heart. For ministers like Nathaniel Hardy (1618–1670), who preached a message of thanksgiving after his own recovery from a fever, "the culmination of thanksgiving of the soul and voice is the thankful life, the life of practical piety. While good works do not prompt the gift of grace, cannot lead to justification, they are the proper fruit of grace."[47] The same can be observed of Gouge's teaching. Gouge defines thanksgiving as a "gratefull acknowledgement of a kindesse received." While this would include God's removal of plague and famine from the land, it can also include gratitude for what the plague and famine accomplished. Though illness and suffering may be seen as evil results from the fall of man, they are not without their purpose and reasons for thanksgiving. "God doth always so dispose of the estate of the Saints," says Gouge, "that he maketh the decaying of the outward man to be renewing of the inner man. In these respects it is a virtue proper to Christians, to give thankes to God for such things as seeme evill."[48] Thus, thanksgiving to God is owed in all circumstances, because he uses trials to accomplish his self-glorifying and good purposes in creation as a whole and the lives of his children in particular.

---

46. Ibid., 177.

47. Ronald E. McFarland, "The Response to Grace: Seventeenth-Century Sermons and the Idea of Thanksgiving," *Church History* 44, no. 2 (1975): 199–203.

48. Gouge, *Whole Armour of God*, 399, 417.

GOD'S PROVIDENCE AND SUFFERING AMIDST
POLITICAL AND ECCLESIOLOGICAL CHANGES

As one who went to Cambridge at the time of Queen Elizabeth I, and became a pastor during the reign of King James I, and now wrote in the time of King Charles I, Gouge ministered during a time of relative peace. He was not ignorant, however, of England's history and the trials the church faced under heavy-handed leaders when he wrote his *The Extent of God's Providence* in 1631.[49] By 1645, when he wrote *The Progresse of Divine Providence*, he had come to experience some of England's past heartache in present expressions, being three years into their civil war at that time. In both works, Gouge provides a brief survey of God's providential workings in England's history under the rubric of four landmarks dating back to the time of John Wycliffe in 1371 leading to the present time. Separating the political and the ecclesiological is not found in Gouge's survey. The overarching and unifying theme of his survey is God's providential deliverance of England from the "dismall and damnable darknesse of Popery," which is closely knit to England's monarchy.[50]

In the late fourteenth century, during the reign of Edward III (r. 1327–1377), John Wycliffe (c. 1330–1384) held out the light of the gospel in the midst of this Catholic darkness. He advocated first that the Lord's Supper is only a figure of the body of Christ and not the very body of Christ. Second, Rome is not the head of all churches nor has Peter special authority over the other apostles. Third, the Pope has no particular access to the keys of the church than any other priest. Fourth, the gospel is sufficient to guide in living. Fifth, any additions of rules and observances do not perfect or even add to the gospel.[51] As bright as Wycliffe's light shone, the Roman church sought to extinguish it.

A second landmark is found in the reign of Henry VIII. The *Act of Parliament* early in Henry VIII reign withdrew the Pope's authority in England and gave it to the king. Henry VIII in turn removed images, had the Bible read in English and preached in pulpits, and catechized

---

49. One wonders if he could have foreseen the civil war that would break out less than a decade later.

50. Gouge, *The Extent of God's Providence*, 390.

51. Gouge, *The Progresse of Divine Providence*, 33.

children only to see these advances halt six years later. At that time, Parliament enacted six articles, reflecting the Pope's teaching, which came to be known by the faithful as the "scourge with six strings" that brought back an "Egyptian darkness" to the church.[52] These six articles were: (1) transubstantiation reestablished, (2) communion in both kinds excluded, (3) the marriage of priests prohibited, (4) vows of chastity warranted, (5) private masses allowed, and (6) auricular confession justified.[53]

A third landmark is Edward VI's coming to the royal throne in 1546. Edward VI would bring about great reforms by removing the six afore-mentioned articles.[54] However, Edward VI's reign was short lived. He was succeeded by Queen Mary I only six years after becoming king at the age of nine. Of her reign, Gouge says that she brought back the dark clouds of Popery as in the days of Henry VIII, which overshadowed the land, "Then instead of heavenly light of the Gospell, an hellish light of burning fire brake out to the destruction of many." She would terror-ize those seeking reformation for five years and receive the nickname, Bloody Mary, or as Gouge calls her, "a popish bloody Queen."[55] "Many hundreds were burnt then for the Gospell sake," says Gouge, "many more were forced to fly their country, and exile themselves."[56] In the treatises presently being discussed, unlike what is seen elsewhere in Gouge's writings, he does not address whether faithful saints who suffer under the hand of Mary I do so because of sin and punishment or because of persecution and need to endure. However, we know from his other writings his belief that Christians do suffer as part of God's plan to bring himself glory and work for the good of his people. Indeed, this is what Gouge observes took place. He says that the gospel shone brightly during the days of Edward VI, "yet for a surer setling of it, [God] suffers it to be sealed by the blood of many worthy martyrs in

---

52. Often referred to as the "scourge of six strings," says Gouge. *The Progresse of Divine Providence*, 34; *The Extent of God's Providence*, 391.

53. Gouge, *The Extent of God's Providence*, 391.

54. See Diarmaid MacCulloch, *The Boy King: Edward VI and the Protestant Reformation* (Berkeley: University of California Press, 2002), 57–104.

55. Gouge, *The Extent of God's Providence*, 391–92. Gouge, *The Progresse of Divine Providence*, 34.

56. Gouge, *God's Three Arrowes*, 366.

Queen Maries daies."[57] Furthermore, if one applies his discussion of the plague in *God's Three Arrowes* mentioned above to this situation, it would seem that he would call all to pray, fast, and repent because everyone has sin in his or her heart. He would follow that with a call to remain faithful and endure suffering in a Christ-like manner.

The reign of Queen Elizabeth I marks the fourth landmark in Gouge's providential historical survey. While maintaining Puritan convictions, Gouge affirmed the soundness of doctrine established by Elizabeth I throughout England and declared that England was restored to such gospel integrity and truth as never witnessed since the time of the apostles.[58] Gouge's regard for Elizabeth I's reign could hardly be overstated. He proudly preached a sermon celebrating the eighty-sixth year of her coming to power.[59] He also dedicates five pages discussing "Englands Deliverances, since Queen Elizabeth began her raigne" in "The Churches Conquest over the Sword" in *God's Three Arrowes*.[60]

Concerning these four landmark deliverances in the days of Edward III, Henry VIII, Edward VI, and Elizabeth I, Gouge says, "These have been very speciall deliverances, which have apparently beene wrought by the divine Providence. They ought oft to be thought on: that our hearts may be more inflamed to give the glory of them to God."[61] Thus, with both the sufferings and deliverances experienced in the midst of political and ecclesiological change, Gouge reminds Christians that God is in control. His providential touch is over all of these circumstances, which is a source of comfort on the one hand and should enliven their hearts with God-glorifying praise on the other hand.

GOD'S PROVIDENCE AMIDST LIFE'S SUFFERINGS AND DEATH

Gouge's personal résumé of suffering function as a "badge of honor" that add substance and passion to his teaching. These trials include physical

---

57. Gouge, *God's Three Arrowes*, 367.

58. Collinson discusses the challenges many early Presbyterians, of whom Gouge was not one, faced with reference to Elizabeth I's Church of England. Patrick Collinson, *The Elizabethan Puritan Movement* (Oxford: Clarendon Paperbacks, 1990), 132–33.

59. Gouge's 1645 sermon was titled *Mercies Memorial*.

60. Gouge, *God's Three Arrowes*, 353–59

61. Gouge, *The Extent of God's Providence*, 392.

ailments, sudden financial loss, imprisonment, and the untimely deaths of those closest to him.[62]

Gouge battled asthma and suffered kidney stones much of his adult life in addition to a "very dangerous disease" that gripped him in August 1630. The disease returned in November of that same year and again in February 1631. He laments the fact that his ailments kept him from his congregation for the better part of a year saying, "great has been the weakenesse of my body." He assures his congregation that he remained vigilant in his studies, for their benefit, during that time. Gouge writes, "I endeavoured to spend that cessation which I had from publike imployments, in my priuate studies, so as some fruit thereof might redound to you and others. By this my true and just *apology*, I hope the fore-mentioned *seeming neglect* of you, appears to be but *seeming*."[63]

Gouge was also acquainted with suffering that came in the form of religious persecution. He spent nine weeks in an English prison at the hands of King James I of England, having experienced the King's ire after publishing Sir Henry Finch's work *The Calling of the Iewes*. It was the second of Finch's works that Gouge published. The first being *An exposition of the Song of Solomon: called Canticles. Together with profitable observations, collected out of the same* in 1615.[64] He would go on to publish Finch's work on the restoration of the Jewish people in 1621. At that time, Gouge was a budding Puritan pastor having begun his service at St. Anne's parish in 1608. Gouge and Finch were both skilled Hebraists with a common love for the Old Testament Scriptures. When writing his foreword for *The Calling of the Iewes* (1621) Gouge commented on Finch's proficiency with the Hebrew text, "The worke it self is the worke of one who hath dived deeper into that mysterie then I can doe.

---

62. Chapter 1 discusses in detail the sudden financial loss that he, Sibbes, Davenport, and Offspring experienced in 1632 when the King confiscated properties and funds they procured for the advancement of Puritan ideals within the Anglican church.

63. Gouge, *God's Three Arrowes*, A ii.

64. Henry Finch, *An exposition of the Song of Solomon: called Canticles. Together with profitable observations, collected out of the same.* (London: Iohn Beale, 1615).

His great understanding of the Hebrew tongue hath bin a great helpe to him therein."[65]

Finch not only had a love for the Hebrew Scriptures, but also for the Jewish people. He clearly addressed this work to them with affection, "To all the seed of Iacob, Farre and Wide Dispersed. Peace and Truth be multiplied vnto you. Daughter of Tzion by fleshly generation: Ierusalem which stickest close to carnall rites & ordinances, & to the legall worship: To you I bring this present, where ever you be dispersed."[66] In his dedicatory epistle, he expressed a prayer of grave concern,

> My hart shal neuer faile to pray for thy prosperitie all my days. Bowing my knees to the Father of our Lord Iesus Christ, the God of glorie, that he would hasten that which he hath spoken concerning thee by the Prophets of old, and by the Apostles sent by his sonne. Whose counsels are without repentance, his loue neuer changeth: he will not forget his promises to thy Fathers: but will graft thee in by faith into that naturall Oliue tree, from which, thorough infidelity thou art hitherto broken off.[67]

Finch was deeply grieved by the Jews' refusal to receive Christ, calling it a catastrophe. The fruit of their rejection is 1600 years as a "renegate people," without Church, commonwealth, form or face of government whether or good or bad. Not only have they as a people reaped the fruit of their rebellion, but so has their land which was once pleasant and fruitful but is now a dry and barren wilderness. However, as Finch saw it, they are not left without hope or comfort.[68]

Five biblical convictions that are interwoven throughout his work drive Finch's interpretation of the restoration of the Jews in Scripture.[69] First, the Jews have rejected Christ, but God has set apart a remnant seed (Rom 11:5). Second, God has called the Jews and will in the last days gather this remnant to himself as part of his church. Third, this great conversion of the remnant has a clear order beginning with those from

---

65. Finch, *The Calling of the Iewes* (np) "To the Reader."
66. Ibid., A.
67. Ibid., A3–A4.
68. Ibid., 1.
69. Ibid., 2–5.

the North and East quarters (according to Dan 11:44 and Isa 41:26–27) and ending with the conquest of Gog and Magog (forty-five years after their first conversions), which he believed to be the Ottoman Empire. Fourth, once this victory over Gog and Magog is obtained, their church and commonwealth will flourish together. Fifth, after their calling and return to Christ, the Gentile nations will follow in being converted.

Perhaps the most significant reason to consider Finch's work is its reception, or better yet, rejection. Finch's work was not considered blasphemous as much as it was treasonous by King James I. The King was enraged at the idea that the Jews would be reestablished in Israel with a great and mighty King before whom all nations shall bow. Consider the splendor and might of this King as Finch described him in his exposition of Isaiah 24:23:

> After the Turke once destroyed commeth the kingdome of Christ to be set up among the Iewes, as it is also certain by Ezechiel, Daniel, and the booke of the Reuelation, which is the second degree of their restoring.... The King is Iesus Christ, the Lord of Hosts, Soueraigne commander of heauen and of earth, and of the armies and powers of them both, that nothing can be lacking to those what haue such a King.... The glory of the Kingdom shall be so great, that in comparison of it the Sunne and Moone shall cast no light.... What if by the Sunne and Moone he meane here the Churches of the Gentiles, who shall blush to see their zeale and loue of piety so eclipsed by a farre more excellent shining light.[70]

Joseph Mede (1586–1639), the prolific Cambridge scholar and admirer of Finch's work, believed that Finch's words were no threat to the King and should not have been taken as such. In a personal letter to Sir Henry Stuteville, Mede writes examining a particular statement that Finch makes which troubled King James I the most:

> But the thing, which troubles His Majesty, is this point, which I will write out for you *verbatim*; "The Jews & all Israel shall return to their land & antient Seats, conquer their *foes*, have their Soil more fruitfull than ever. They shall erect a glorious

---

70. Ibid., 102–3.

Church in the Land of Judah it self & bear rule far and neare."
We need not be afraid to aver and maintain, that one day they
shall cometh to Jerusalem again; be Kings & chief Monarchs of
the Earth; sway & govern all, for the glory of Xt [Christ]; that
shall shine amongst them.[71]

The King would have been enraged by Mede's sentiments.

King James I had Finch and Gouge arrested in 1621. Both men served
nine weeks in prison until a group of examiners received a satisfactory
clarification of their position.[72] Mede's sympathy and Gouge's release
upon this clarification demonstrate the unjust nature of his nine-week
imprisonment. Although not expressed, one might imagine the emotional anguish the imprisonment created having separated Gouge from
his wife, children, friends, and church for two months.

Gouge and his wife Elizabeth were parents to thirteen children.
However, the Gouges understood the deep sorrows of losing children,
with only eight of their children reaching adulthood. In addition to
these sorrows, on October 25, 1625, Elizabeth Gouge died of dropsy,
which she had battled on-and-off for over a year, shortly after giving
birth to their thirteenth child, a son. Nicholas Guy, who delivered the
message at Elizabeth's funeral, likened William and Elizabeth to Jacob
and Rachel of the Scriptures. Of Elizabeth and Rachel, Guy writes, "In a
strange place they both fell in trauell, and in the time of their child-bed
they both departed this life." In addition to a likeness with Rachel in
death, the Gouges shared a likeness to Jacob and Rachel in life. "Rachel

---

71. Cited in Douglas J. Culver, *Albion and Ariel: British Puritanism and the Birth
of Political Zionism* (New York: Peter Lang, 1995), 136.

72. Gouge's son, Thomas, recounts the ordeal in his prefatory notes to Gouge's
Hebrews commentary, outlining Gouge's six propositional responses to the
King that secured his release ("Narrative," x; cf. Culver, *Albion and Ariel*, 115-17).
Furthermore, Peter Toon writes, "The book itself was suppressed but somehow
it was well known to Cambridge Puritans in the 1630's and Thomas Goodwin, for
example, referred to it on several occasions in his sermons on Revelation" (*Puritan
Eschatology: 1600-1660* [Cambridge: James Clarke, 1970], 32). Toon refers the reader
to Bishop Joseph Hall's description of King James' indignation recounted in Hall's
The Revelation Unrevealed (1650), 103-4.

could not be more deare to her Iaakob, then this Elizabeth was to her William," writes Guy.[73]

Gouge's life was the classroom where he studied adversity and began to major on the art of suffering. These trials not only tested his own faith, but also provided him opportunities to speak from his experiences into the lives of others who suffered. It was Gouge's *curriculum vitae* of affliction and the lessons learned under the hand of God's providential arrows that informed his practical divinity. Christians sought Gouge's counsel when afflicted by life circumstances, physical ailment, or cases of conscience. His son Thomas recounts these kinds of scenarios:

> By reason of his ability and dexterity in resolving cases of conscience, he was much sought unto for resolving many doubts and scruples of conscience, and that not only by ordinary Christians, but also by divers ministers in city and country, and that by word of mouth, and writing, being accounted the father of London divines, and oracle of his time. He was likewise a sweet comforter of troubled consciences, wherein he was exceeding skilful and dexterous, as many hundreds in the city have found time after time, being sought unto far and near by such as groaned under afflictions and temptations; many of whom, through God's blessing on his labours, were restored to joy and comfort out of unspeakable terrors and torments of conscience.[74]

Gouge's aim, according to his son, was not to cause Christians to further doubt their standing with God when afflicted, but rather to restore them to "joy and comfort." In this way, it seems that Gouge "practiced what he preached," having exhorted Christians elsewhere to come to the assistance of a brother who is struggling. He writes, "O that men

---

73. Nicholas Guy, *Pieties Pillar: or a sermon preached at the funerall of mistresse Elizabeth Govge, late wife of Mr. William Govge, of Black-friers, London* (London: George Millar, 1626), A5–6.

74. Thomas Gouge, "A Narrative of the Life and Death of Doctor Gouge," in William Gouge, *A Commentary on the Whole Epistle to the Hebrews, Being the Substance of Thirty Years' Wednesday's Lectures at Blackfriars, London* (Edinburgh: James Nichol, 1866), 1:xii.

would be watchfull one over another, to observe wherein their brother fainteth or faileth, and afford what helpe and succor they can."[75]

Gouge's reason for coming to the aid of afflicted saints is noteworthy. While we have seen that Gouge comforted afflicted consciences as part of his pastoral ministry to help Christians be assured of their faith, it was not strictly because he was a pastor that he did this. For Gouge, it is also the responsibility of all Christians to help their brothers and sisters in times of need. This kind of practical divinity was not strictly relegated to clergy, but a calling for all Christians as fruit of a life that has been truly changed by God. "By our willingnesss and readinesse to succour such as need our succour, we gaine assurance and give evidence that our corrupt nature is altered," writes Gouge. He goes on to say that this is "good evidence of their regeneration" because "a true feare of God will keepe men from such inhumanity" as neglecting their fellow man when they are afflicted.[76]

So we see three ways in which the realities of suffering relate to practical divinity and the assurance of faith in Gouge's practical divinity. First, when a non-Christian suffers, Gouge urgently pleads with them to place their faith in Jesus. Second, when Christians suffer, the goal is to comfort the afflicted conscience leading them to find joy and comfort in God. Third, it is the responsibility of Christians to demonstrate that they are regenerate and that their old self has been transformed by the gospel by lovingly caring for one another during times of need. With this fruit of the Spirit demonstrated in their lives, they could be further assured that they are truly children of God.

The trials and afflictions of this life will ultimately lead to death, and the realities of death confront every individual, whether young or old. In 1638, Gouge's friend Thomas Sheafe (1562–1639) asked him to write a foreword for his book *Vindiciae Senectutis, or, A Plea for Old-Age*.[77] Sheafe's work was dedicated to Laurence Chaderton (1536–1640) who

---

75. Gouge, *Gods Three Arrowes*, 276.
76. Ibid., 278.
77. Thomas Sheafe, *Vindiciæ senectutis, or, A plea for old-age: which is senis cujusdam cygnea cantio* (London: George Miller, 1639).

was over one hundred years old at the time of its writing.[78] In his fore-word, Gouge recognizes that both the righteous and the wicked can live long lives. However, for the Christian it is a "blessing" from God because with age comes wisdom for life. Eventually, however, all will succumb to the pains of death, whether they are young (as Gouge's children) or old (as Chaderton), or whether it is sudden (as those who died on that fatal vespers in London), or slow as is the case of those who die from illness (as did Elizabeth Gouge). In each case, the realities of impending death and reflection upon death as a whole warrant adequate consideration as to how death relates to divine providence and suffering.

In his 1973 article, "Death and Dying in Puritan New England," David E. Stannard rightfully observes that "the vision of death and the act of dying were to the Puritans profoundly religious matters. Much of the average Puritan's life was centered about and predicated on the vision of death, the afterlife, and the expected manner in which the passage from this world to the next should be made." Stannard next makes this provocative statement: "But in the Puritan scheme something was wrong, as though an improper 'fit' was made between the vision of death and the manner of encountering it."[79] Stannard argues that the Puritan's regular doubting of his assurance no longer made death a thing to be anticipated, but a frightful event which led to despair. He writes, "As death drew near for the Puritan the tension normally built into the doctrine of assurance became increasingly more intense, for now the time of decision was at hand, the time when the Puritan's sin-riddled soul would be judged and either admitted to heaven or cast into the fiery pit of hell."[80] Stannard gives several examples where New England Puritans reflected this tension within the doctrine of assurance. While it may be true that there were those within the Puritan camp who taught a kind of assurance that was no assurance at all, this cannot be said of William Gouge. Gouge's aim was to console the

---

78. Chaderton was Gouge's uncle by marriage through his mother's side of the family.

79. David E. Stannard, "Death and Dying in Puritan New England," *The American Historical Review*, 78, no. 5 (December 1973): 1305–6. For a more detailed description of Stannard's thesis, see his *The Puritan Way of Death: A Study in Religion, Culture, and Social Change* (New York: Oxford University Press, 1977).

80. Ibid., 1326.

afflicted conscience with the aim of restoring joy and providing comfort
as they reflected on the goodness and promises of God.

Few sources paint a better picture of the Christian's outlook on death
in the seventeenth century as do funeral sermons. Loved ones of the
deceased would ask their minister to perform a funeral ceremony,
which included a sermon and biographical summary of the life of the
deceased. In the case of ministers who died, they would set in order
a fellow minister or respected peer to deliver the message upon their
passing. Such was the case for Richard Sibbes. Sibbes, a close friend
of Gouge, wrote in his will that Gouge would deliver the sermon at
his funeral. Sibbes' will read as following, "To my reverend frende Dr
Gouge, I doe give as a testimony of my love, twenty schillings, desiring
him to take the paynes to preach my funeral sermon."[81] Mysteriously,
Gouge did not hand his message over to the press for print, a fact Sibbes'
biographer greatly laments. He writes, "It is vexatious that importu-
nity should have got printed this large-thoughted mans funeral sermons, for a 'Mrs Margaret Ducke!' ... and secured not this."[82] Indeed,
such a funeral sermon for Sibbes would be an invaluable asset for both
Sibbes and Gouge studies, not to mention Puritan studies as a whole.
Nonetheless, as Sibbes' biographer noted, Gouge's funeral sermon for
Mrs. Ducke is extant and is significant in its own right.

Arthur and Margaret Ducke were a part of Gouge's parish in
Blackfriars for many years. Upon Mrs. Ducke's death, her husband asked
Gouge to publish the message preached at her funeral. His desire is that
her "kindred and friends" and "our two children" might remember her
legacy. He also wanted others to "consider the love and affection I owe to
the Memory of a Wife so deer and deserving of me." As part of his pastoral consolation to Mr. Ducke, Gouge writes, "to gratifie your earnest
desire, I have here (as well as I could call to minde and memory) sent
you a copy of my Sermon."[83] The published work contains forewords

---

81. Alexander B. Grosart, "Memoir of Richard Sibbes, D.D.," in *The Complete
Works of Richard Sibbes, D.D.* (Edinburgh: James Nichol, 1862), cxxix.

82. Ibid., xx.

83. This comment seems to imply that Gouge either preached the message
extemporaneously or had an outline, not manuscript, from which he preached.
William Gouge, *A Fvneral Sermon Preached by Dr. Gouge of Black-friers London, in
Cheswicke Church, August 24, 1646* (London: Joshua Kirton, 1646), A1–2.

by Gouge and Mr. Ducke, Gouge's funeral sermon, and a biography of Mrs. Ducke written by an unnamed friend.

Mrs. Ducke lived in Blackfriars and sat under Gouge's teaching for several decades. All residents of Blackfriars were well acquainted with one of the parish's biggest attractions, the Blackfriars theatre, for which William Shakespeare wrote plays.[84] Pious Christians, like Mrs. Ducke, did not look favorably upon the theatre. They were in disagreement with the themes of the plays as well as the perceived waste of time play attendance demanded in that it produced "too much retiredness." Her biographer, who at this juncture refers to statements made by Gouge at Mrs. Ducke's funeral, said she had many opportunities "to see Playes, to which the neighborhood and vicinity of the Play-house there, and the frequent throngs of Gentlewomen which prest thither, might have been forcible and prevailing invitations, she could never while she lived there, nor all the time of her being in *London*, be induc'd to see any." She questioned why she should go to the playhouse to watch a tragedy if in God's house she could go and there "behold before her eyes Iesus Christ evidently set forth crucified among them."[85] When Mrs. Ducke became

---

84. For descriptions and reconstructions of the Blackfriars Theatre and Shakespearean plays, see Richard T. Thornberry, "Shakespeare and the Blackfriars Tradition" (PhD diss., The Ohio State University, 1964); Robert M. Wren, "The Blackfriars Theatre and Its Repertory, 1600-1608" (PhD diss., Princeton University, 1965).

85. Gouge, *A Fvneral Sermon*, 26-27. Allan Pritchard comments, "The view of the theater attributed here to Margaret Duck[e] is not surprising in a follower of William Gouge, the eminent and popular Puritan preacher of St. Anne's, Blackfriars. Gouge had headed the list of signatures on a petition to have the Blackfriars theater closed in 1619 and had come into conflict with Laud for his refusal to read the Book of Sports from his pulpit." Pritchard says that it is "not surprising" that Gouge headed a petition to have the theater closed in 1619, but does not clearly state why it is "not surprising." What is implied is that Gouge opposed the theater because of its content, which is likely true. However, Anthony Paul House has shown that in addition to concerns regarding the kinds of people the theatre attracted and the controversial themes of the play, was the problem of traffic. A resolution in 1631 drafted by the residents of Blackfriars seeking to regulate "the access of wheeled traffic to the playhouse ... the true nuisance of the playhouse proved to be the disruption caused by the carriages of the great and the good attending the theatre." Allan Pritchard, "Puritans and the Blackfriars Theater: The Cases of Mistresses Duck and Drake," *Shakespeare Quarterly*, 45, no. 1 (Spring 1994): 92-95. Anthony Paul House, "The City of London and the Problem of Liberties, c. 1540-c. 1640" (PhD diss., University of Oxford, 2006), 130.

ill, her faith in and devotion to Jesus is what brought her comfort in her affliction. Her biographer notes how she committed herself, among other things, to "reading books of Piety and Devotion most willingly of Dr. Gouges, by which means she made her heart *Bibliothecam Christi*, a Library of Christ."[86] Margaret Ducke died on August 15, 1646, and William Gouge delivered her funeral message nine days later.

Gouge's sermon emphasized the importance of considering divine providence not only when suffering, but also on the occasion of death. "God hath his hand" over sickness, hurt, pain at the hands of man, and seemingly accidental occasions. "The supream Soveraignty of God, his almighty power, his unsearchable wisdom, and other like excellencies, plainly shew that his hand is in all things," says Gouge, with this end goal in mind, "that all things may be disposed to his own glory and to the good of his chosen children."[87] Such providential thinking raises questions concerning divine sovereignty and the free will of man, especially as it relates to the question, "Who is responsible when someone suffers?" It is in questions such as these that life and theology meet. Gouge, with his practical divinity, is prepared to respond to such questions. He says that the line of thinking that chooses to "blame God" fails to consider the unsearchable judgments of God. Thus, in cases of suffering and death, Christians are called to submit themselves to God's wisdom even in the midst of "losses that befall us."[88] This however is not a kind of emotionless submission. Gouge contends that submitting to God's providential hand even in times of great loss is the means for comfort in sorrow. Consider his pastoral tone when he writes,

> We may well comfort our selves on this ground, in the losse of any friend. For what God doth, he doth seasonably: and thereupon we may infer, that the time wherein a friend is taken away, is the most fit and seasonablest time for a friend to be taken away,

---

86. Gouge, *A Fvneral Sermon*, 29. Although one might expect a biographer to represent kindly a loved one after her death, these details nonetheless remind us of the social context of Gouge's ministry and the "worldly" temptations and spiritual adversity with which Christians were regularly confronted.

87. Ibid., 10.

88. Ibid., 11.

God hath appointed to everyone his work, and allotted the time wherein he should do it.[89]

For Gouge, when a Christian considers and submits to divine providence in the face of the loss of a loved one, he find grounds for comfort as he trusts God.

Although Margaret Ducke's death was a slow death at the hands of "a long and tedious sickness," Gouge takes the occasion to discuss the question why the righteous die sudden and seemingly inexplicable deaths.[90] Just as Ezekiel's wife, the "delight of his eyes" was swiftly taken from him, what should a Christian make of circumstances where the righteous die untimely deaths? Gouge urges his readers to remember that "Gods waies are unsearcheable." Sympathizing with the questions the grieving individual has, he continues, "There is scarce any thing, wherein Gods waies more seem to be past finding out then in this." Rather than attempting to interpret the meaning behind the manner of one's death, and judging the genuineness of their conversion by it, Gouge recommends considering the life that person lived instead. It is foolish to judge a person by the occasion of their death, says Gouge. "It becomes us rather to observe a mans conversation while he lived on earth, and the evidences which he hath given of a true and sound faith, and answerably to judge of his estate, whatsoever his manner of death hath been."[91] In other words, the authenticity of a Christian's faith cannot be discerned by the nature and occasion of his death.

Reflecting upon death can have a sanctifying effect on Christians. Because of its inevitability and prospect of its potential suddenness, wise Christians prepare for death by expecting it in all places and at all times. Gouge, therefore, recommends that death should be considered upon going to bed, rising in the morning, going on a journey, or participating in any other kind of work. While this instruction can be perceived as having a pessimistic outlook on life, Gouge's expressed aim is altogether different. "For nothing will more keep a man from sinne,

---

89. Ibid., 11.
90. Ibid., 31.
91. Ibid., 16–17.

then continuall meditation of death near approaching."[92] Ultimately, according to Gouge, constant consideration of one's impending death has a purifying effect on the Christian life.

If death should be continually considered each day of one's life, how much more so when gravely ill? Such was Gouge's counsel for a Native American who was baptized as a Christian and given the name Mary.[93] Mary was one of about twelve Native Americans who traveled with Pocahontas aboard the English ship the *Treasurer* in 1616, brought by the English with the goal of demonstrating how "savages" might be civilized. While in London, Mary grew severely ill living in the residence of Gouge's uncle William Whitaker. In 1620, Whitaker brought Mary to Gouge's home where she could receive more adequate care.[94] Gouge said he strove to comfort her "both in soul and in body." Historian Camilla Townsend questions, however, the successfulness of Gouge's efforts. She writes, "whether his zealous style was actually comforting is doubtful, for he spoke openly of her upcoming death."[95] Whether or

---

92. Ibid., 17–18.

93. Camilla Townsend provides a captivating retelling of Pocahontas and the Jamestown settlement. Camilla Townsend, *Pocahontas and the Powhatan Dilemma* (New York: Hill and Wang, 2004).

94. Perhaps Gouge's known connection with the society of the apothecaries afforded him the resources to tend to Mary's physical needs. Furthermore, his wife Elizabeth was still alive at that time. See Kenneth Allen East, "William Gouge: Preacher and Scholar" (PhD diss., University of Chicago, 1991), 206–7. Also noteworthy is that the Virginia Company paid Gouge twenty schillings to assist with her care. The Company record reads: "The Court, takinge notice from Sr William Throgmorton yt one of the maides wch Sr Thomas Dale brought from Virginia a native of yt Country who some times dwelt a servant wth a Mercer in Cheapside is now verie weake of a Consumpcon att mr Gough in the Black Friers, who hath greate care and taketh great paines to comforte her both in soule and bodie whervppon for her recoverie the Company are agreed to be att the charge of xxs [twenty schillings] a weeke for this two monneths, if itt please god shee be not before the expiracon therof restored to health or dy in the meane season for ye administring of Phisick and Cordial for her health and that the first paymt begin this day seaven-night because mr Threr for this yeare reported his Accompts were shutt vp, Sr Wm Throgmorton outt of his pryvate purse for the same purpose hath promised to give xls: all wch monney is ordered to be paide to mr Gough through the good affiance ye Comp: hath of his Carefull menaginge therof." Susan M. Kingsbury, ed., *The Records of the Virginia Company of London* (Washington, DC: Government Printing Office, 1906), I, 338–39.

95. Townsend, *Pocahontas and the Powhatan Dilemma*, 166.

not Mary was comforted by Gouge's words is historically not available to us. However, it is not necessary to conclude that speaking of one's impending death is devoid of comfort. Certainly for Gouge, the thought of death was a source of joy for the Christian that would provide strength to endure when afflicted. Mary had professed the Christian faith, evidenced by her adult baptism. With this understanding, and as we have seen with Gouge's encouragement to the afflicted, it seems possible that Gouge sought to give Mary the precious reminder that something greater lays ahead beyond her suffering while consoling her "both in soul and in body."[96]

In these various examples, we have seen that Gouge's understanding of death, contra Stannard's examples, was not such that warranted uncertainty for Christians. Fear of death is an attitude consistent with the "natural man" for "fear is a disturbed passion, arising from the expectation of some evil which he would shun … if men could, they would flee from and avoid death." Christians, on the other hand, have experienced liberty from not only death, but also the fear of death. "Christ therefore thought it not enough to satisfy God's justice and pacify his wrath; but he would also vanquish that implacable enemy [i.e., Satan who uses the fear of death as his tool], and so deliver us out of his hands." Therefore, Christians are found to be united with Christ and delivered from the fear of death. For this reason, Gouge breaks into a prayer of thanksgiving in the middle of his commentary on Hebrews 2:15 declaring, "Thanks, therefore, to thee, O Saviour, that hast destroyed so mighty an adversary of ours by thine own death."[97]

GOD'S PROVIDENCE, SUFFERING, AND THE ASSURANCE OF SALVATION

There is no question that in Gouge's thought, God providentially orders all occurrences of history. Not only can one see his hand within the narrative of biblical history or even ancient history, but in recent history up to the present. For this reason, even a current tragedy such as the one in Blackfriars involving the Catholics in 1623 must be recognized within the scope of providence and, in this particular scenario, an act

---

96. Ibid., 166.
97. Gouge, *Hebrews Commentary*, 170.

of divine judgment upon false teachers. Gouge concludes, "If this be not an evidence of the eye and hand of the divine Providence, both seeing and ordering things below, what evidence can be given thereof." And again, "Shall these and such like judgements overtake men in the very act of their sinning, and yet be accounted no judgements, no evidences of divine providence, no signes of his indignation? Then let all things be ordered by chance: or rather let there be no order at all."[98]

Reflection upon the doctrine of divine providence must lead to personal piety. It cannot be detached from Christian living and the development of personal character especially because of one's present place in the scope of history, the sixth day—the most blessed day. Thus, there is a call to rejoice. "God hath made an abundant recompense unto us, who live in these later dayes, for putting off our time of living in this world so long. It is to our unspeakable advantage and benefit; and shall not God have the praise thereof?"[99] Furthermore, there is an inherent call to excel and abound in knowledge, in faith, in hope, in zeal for God's glory, in conforming to God's will, in charity to those in need, in using one's talents, and in patience in suffering.[100]

Gouge's understanding of divine providence was neither a strictly polemical tool nor mere superstition. Rather, Gouge's doctrine had biblical, theological, and historical foundations which when applied to suffering Christians, offer insight into present daily life. Although superstition may have been the result of some who held to similar providential views, it certainly was not true of Gouge himself, nor should it have been true of those who, like Margaret Ducke, sat under his teaching.

It is wise to exercise great caution when attempting to interpret the hand of God in contemporary occurrences. Walsham's article clearly represents these dangers. In the final analysis, one cannot know the mind of God. Still, as Gouge has shown, a safe and prudent lens to interpret divine providence is in God's primary and subordinate purpose in all things, the magnification of his glory and the good of his children.

---

98. Gouge, *The Extent of God's Providence*, 401.
99. Gouge, *The Progresse of Divine Providence*, 36.
100. Ibid., 37–38.

With his providential framework in place, we have seen that Gouge seeks to provide joy and comfort to afflicted saints by reminding them of God's sovereign control over their lives. Because God is good and works for his glory and the good of his people, Christians can submit to his wise will and trust that what God has ordained is best, even when they might not be able to discern the particulars of the question "why?" (as is the case when a Christian dies suddenly). When Christians live their lives through the lens of divine providence, they can resist the temptation to despair when suffering, and instead find reason for rejoicing, knowing that though they outwardly are decaying, they are inwardly being renewed in their faith.

In his instruction, Gouge also tells Christians that the nature and form of their suffering (especially when severe) does not provide grounds for questioning one's standing with God. Both saints and sinners may suffer identical trials and similar kinds of death. Christians' lives should not be judged by what kind of death they died but rather what kind of life they lived. In this way, Gouge calls Christians to consider the kinds of fruit the Spirit of God bears in their lives. For example, a Christian who refuses to show love to his brother or sister, especially when they are in a time of need, is not bearing fruit consistent with someone who is regenerate. Thus, by implication, those who bear this kind of fruit can be assured of their salvation on the grounds that the Spirit of God is actively working in their lives. We can conclude that there are times when Gouge believed counseling afflicted Christians involved an emphasis on the promises of God in the gospel where believers are comforted when they are reminded of God's good, wise, and caring hand in their lives. At other times, Gouge believed wise counsel called for Christians, who are themselves suffering or see others suffering around them, to examine their lives and be sure that their lives are producing fruit in keeping with their conversion.

5

Prayer and the Christian Home

Two separate yet often-related topics in Christian living are prayer and the Christian home. William Gouge wrote extensively on both, and at different junctures unites them, especially in his catechism and work on household living. Peering into these windows of Gouge's pastoral theology yields a picturesque sight of his practical divinity, which aimed at giving Christians concrete instructions for life.

A GUIDE TO GOE TO GOD: THE LORD'S PRAYER

Identifying an agreed upon prayer book and guide for worship was important for English Puritans. According to Horton Davies, the first "entirely Puritan-prayer book" printed was that of John Knox in 1556 titled, *The Forme of Prayers and Ministrations of the Sacraments, etc., used in the English Congregation at Geneva: and approved by the famous and godly learned man, Iohn Caluyn.*[1] This prayer book functioned as a guide for public worship in England and remained a staple fixture in Puritan churches until the Parliament Directory of Public Worship in 1645. The prayer book included a variety of elements for public worship including prayers of confession, Scripture readings, a sermon, singing psalms, the Apostles' Creed, Eucharistic prayers, and the Lord's Prayer. The prayer book gave theological and practical instruction for each element of public worship. For instance, with celebrating the Lord's Supper, the prayer book called for a Eucharistic prayer that emphasized gratitude for God's creation and redeeming work, it warned against cheapening God's grace at the table by partaking of the elements unrepentantly, and it encouraged the spiritually sick and needy to take of the bread and the cup.[2]

---

1. Horton Davies, *The Worship of the English Puritans* (London: Dacre, 1948), 116–17.
2. Horton Davies, *Worship and Theology in England* (Princeton: Princeton University Press, 1970), 275. For examples of Eucharistic Prayers of John Knox and

By the end of the sixteenth century, Puritans had produced a variety of treatises and guides to prayer in addition to the prayer book for public worship. These treatises gave direction on various matters of prayer. William Gouge's 1626 work, *A Guide to Goe to God*, was no exception. Unlike Knox's prayer book, which was used to order and guide corporate public worship, Gouge's prayer guide aimed at teaching people about prayer itself, and how to come to God in private prayer. Gouge used the Lord's Prayer as his focal point because in his estimation, it is as the subtitle to his work suggests, "the perfect patterne of prayer" providing in itself "all the distinct kinds of Prayer: as *Request* for good things, *Deprecation* against evill, *Intercession* for others, and *Thanksgiving*."[3]

Gouge dedicated his guide to Sir James Fullerton (1563–1630) and Fullerton's wife Lady Magdalene Bruce (1575–1631), Baroness of Kinloss. Fullerton was a Scotsman by birth, who later became a schoolmaster in Ireland (under whose teaching James Ussher sat) and later served King James VI and Charles I as Groom of the Stool.[4] Lady Bruce was a friend of Gouge and his wife, Elizabeth, before her untimely death. His dedicatory expresses gratitude for the baroness's sincere love for his wife and her respect for his ministry. In addition to these remarks Gouge states that Lady Bruce was undergoing a "long weaknesse of bodie" that caused her pain and discomfort. Gouge reminds Lady Bruce that these divinely appointed ailments serve a prayerful purpose, namely, "it worketh in us an hearty and earnest desire of going to God." Gouge recognizes the timeliness of the publication of his prayer guide in Lady Bruce's life. In his endeavor to encourage her, he writes, "For direction wherein, Behold here an helpe, A GVIDE TO GOE TO GOD, which desireth as an Handmaid to attend your Ladiship, and to bee entertained by you, that shee may be the more ready at hand to Guide you in your way to God."[5]

Richard Baxter, see Louis Boyer, *Eucharist: Theology and Spirituality of Eucharistic Prayer* (Notre Dame: University of Notre Dame Press, 1968), 420–24.

3. William Gouge, *A Guide to Goe to God or, an Explanation of the Perfect Patterne of Prayer, the Lords Prayer* (London: G.M. and R.B., 1626), 2.

4. The Groom of the Stool was one of the king's intimate servants who tended to the king in the performance of the bodily functions of excretion and washing.

5. Gouge, *Guide to Goe to God*, iii–iv.

Significant in this statement is Gouge's close linkage between Lady Bruce's suffering, God's purpose in pain that leads the Christian back to him in prayer, and the pastoral purposes of Gouge's present work. This treatise on the Lord's Prayer is, therefore, no mere biblical commentary strictly concerned with the fine points of theology, grammar, and exegesis, but a pastoral lifeline to the suffering saint, downtrodden disciple and committed Christian.

The importance of prayer in the Christian life can hardly be overstated, according to Gouge. In prayer, lowly man comes before his glorious God and is given the privilege of personal and intimate communication with him. Concerning the wonders of God and of prayer, Gouge writes,

> *God* is the highest, and chiefest *Good*, below which we may not remaine, beyond which we cannot attaine. To place our rest in any thing before we come to God is dangerous To attaine to any rest beyond God is impossible. This therefore is that *proper place* whether the soule well enlightened and rectified aspireth, as all hot light things aspire to the high hot region. The meanes whereby wee *men on earth* have accesse to *God in Heaven*, is Prayer. By Prayer we enter to the *Court* where God sitteth in his Maiestie, and wee present our selves before him speaking unto him as it were face to face. That therefore which instructeth us to pray aright, directeth us to God.[6]

The face-to-face nature of prayer allows the Christian to find rest in God and is therefore the proper "place" the redeemed Christian should seek. For Gouge, what is most needed for the spiritually tired and emotionally exhausted Christian is not necessarily more sleep or time away from various duties, but above all more prayer. Rest without God is not possible. The above quotation is consistent with Gouge's stated emphasis, that his intention is not to add to the Lord's Prayer or make its instruction better in any way, but rather to help the pilgrim Christian arrive at his destination by travelling on the correct path.

---

6. Ibid., vi–vii.

The Lord's Prayer is often divided into seven petitions. By his own admission, Gouge breaks from writers such as Augustine, some Roman Catholics and "later divines" by dividing the Lord's Prayer into six rather than seven requests.[7] The first three relate to God and his glory signified by the pronoun "thy," while the latter three relate to human beings signified by the first person plural pronouns "our/us." A brief summary of Gouge's understanding of each petition will provide insight into his theology of prayer as well as further understanding of the practical directives he gives that flow from his interpretations.

Before a petition is spoken, Jesus begins his prayer with a direct address to God the Father. The words "our Father which art in heaven" call to mind the character and attributes of God and teach the Christian how to prepare himself for coming to God in prayer. Gouge likens this God-focused address to the honor given to a king by his subject. When one recognizes the majesty of the king he is about to address, he will do so with the right degree of humility. "Yea he that cometh to God in Prayer, and doth not duely weigh that surpassing excellencie before which he approacheth, doth vnawares dishonor the diuine Maiestie with vnmeete and vnseemely suites."[8] However, in this particular prayer, the acknowledgment of God himself not only calls to mind his majesty, but also his fatherhood. Gouge says that Christians can call God "father" because he has adopted them into his family through faith in Jesus and transferred them from the place of servitude to that of sonship. Thus, concludes Gouge, "Many other more magnificent titles might haue bene attributed to God, but none more pertinent to Prayer then this title *Father*" because it produces within the faithful a child-like affection for God causing them to strive to please him and seek his favor and honor. "This answerable disposition is a maine end of the relation betwixt God and vs."[9]

The first petition in the Lord's Prayer is to hallow God's name and Gouge's interpretation is as follows. The "name" of God calls to mind his nature, his triune distinction, his various titles, his attributes, his word, and his works. To "hallow" is to sanctify or set apart. Since God

---

7. Ibid., 5–6.
8. Ibid., 7.
9. Ibid., 11–13.

is already holy by virtue of his attributes, then to hallow his name is not to make or declare him to be holy, but to esteem him as such. That God would delight in the hallowing of his name from the lips of his sinful creatures is an expression of his "admirable goodness." In pastoral fashion, Gouge wants his readers to understand the thrust of this petition in such a way that moves them to pray for themselves and for others. In prayer, Christians thus ought to request that God would make every part of their being "fit instruments of hallowing Gods name."[10] Christians do this by praying for further understanding of who God is, for their will to be submitted to God, for faith in the truths of God's word, for hearts that are entirely set on God, for speech that reverentially makes mention of God's name, and for a holy and blameless outward life.[11]

The second petition is for the coming of God's kingdom. For Gouge, the Kingdom of God has two components, the "vniuersall kingdome" and the "peculiar kingdome." The former refers to his absolute sovereignty over all of creation. The latter refers to his reign over the church in particular. Of the church, he writes, "it is a societie chosen of God, redeemed by Christ, called and sanctified by the holy Ghost, which hath bene in all ages of the world, some in heaven, others on earth spread ouer the face thereof farre and neare: in which respects it is stiled the *holy Catholicke* Church. This is properly the kingdom of Christ, in, and by whom the Father raigneth."[12] Jesus prays asking for God's kingdom to come, referring to the peculiar kingdom (i.e., the church), says Gouge. This "coming" request should be understood as metaphorical since the idea of coming implies something that has yet to arrive. This metaphorical interpretation therefore refers to degrees in which the kingdom is present. While God's kingdom is already present in the church, it is not so in its greatest degree of presence, which equates a perfect and sinless church. Thus, the request for the kingdom to come is a prayer that desires God's kingdom to progress toward the Church's perfection and full realization in glory. This petition beckons Christians to pray for local churches and the universal Church, against evils that

---

10. Ibid., 42.
11. Ibid., 42–43.
12. Ibid., 48.

come against it and for its peace and prosperity (which often comes only after adversity). Pray also for seminaries, says Gouge, for from them come ministers to preach the Gospel and properly administer the sacraments.[13]

The third petition in the Lord's Prayer is for God's will to be done on earth as it is in heaven. This request has as its aim the realization of God's secret (unknown to man) and revealed will (as seen in Scripture) on earth. Sinful humanity, says Gouge, is incapable of doing God's will according to his own efforts. This would be a point of concern for Christians were it not for God providing means for man to obey his will. Therefore, man must deny himself and call upon God "wholly depend[ing] on him for preuenting, assisting, and perfecting Grace." Only then can Christians do God's will to bring God glory.[14] Gouge draws six particular requests that should be on the lips of Christians who desire to do God's will: First, to know God's word and thereby his revealed will. Second, to readily yield one's will to God's will once it is made known to the Christian. Third, to pray for strength of memory to remember God's word as a source of consolation in the promises of God, for "things not remembered are as not knowne."[15] Fourth, to have an attentive conscience that encourages the Christian when he is obedient and corrects him when he swerves away from God's will. Fifth, to love God's word and make it one's joy and delight. Sixth, to see the Christian's life outwardly changed. In this third petition of the Lord's Prayer, we are reminded of how Gouge continues to keep life and doctrine closely knit together. As noted regarding the dedicatory words to Lady Bruce, Gouge meant this treatise to be more than an exposition of the Lord's Prayer, but something that dealt tangibly with Christian living and guides Christians in their prayer lives.

The final three petitions aim at man's good, while the first three aimed at God's glory. The fourth petition is for daily bread, which Gouge takes to refer to all temporal blessings, including but not limited to food. Thus, sleep, health, competency, children, peace, and prosperity are all meant by the word "bread." These temporal blessings are

---

13. Ibid., 59–60.
14. Ibid., 75.
15. Ibid., 86.

needed and useful for life and the lack thereof can be a hindrance to the
Christian call and works of charity, as well as a temptation to injustice,
says Gouge.[16] While every Christian should be content in his present
state, he is still wise to pray for himself and his own needs (along with
those of others).

Gouge's comments on Jesus' fifth petition, "forgive us our debts, as
also we forgive our debtors," yields rich insights into Gouge's theology
of assurance of salvation and practical divinity. It is in this portion of
Gouge's works where Bozeman accuses Puritans, like Gouge, of teaching Catholic doctrine dressed in Protestant language. As noted earlier,
Bozeman does so because Gouge and other Puritans seem to deny the
distinction between mortal and venial sins advocating that all sins are
"mortal."[17] While Bozeman is correct in recognizing Gouge's denial of
this mortal-venial distinction, readers of Gouge must understand why
he denies such a division. For Gouge, one concern of upholding this
distinction is that it fails to recognize that all sin leads to death apart
from saving faith in the atoning work of Jesus. A second grave danger
of maintaining a distinction between mortal and venial sins is that
people will fail to experience the profound sense of spiritual danger
and angst that should befall all people because of each of their sins,
not simply their "mortal" ones. For this reason Gouge taught that every
person should recognize the damning effects of every sin apart from
saving faith. Such reflection should spur a sense of genuine remorse
and repentance in the hearts of individuals. Thus, denying the distinction between mortal and venial sins is essential in order for people to
feel the weight of their sins and produce genuine faith and repentance.
Thus, when reading Gouge in his wider context, one will see that Gouge
does not teach a sort of Catholic doctrine in Protestant dress.

The "debts" mentioned in the Lord's Prayer refer to the sins of
people, thereby making sinners debtors to God owing perfect obedience to God, which they are unable to do, resulting in man's impending
physical and spiritual death. In this sense, since all sin is deserving of

---

16. Ibid., 101.

17. Theodore Dwight Bozeman, *The Precisianist Strain: Disciplinary Religion and
Antinomian Backlash in Puritanism to 1638* (Chapel Hill: University of North Carolina
Press, 2004), 149–51.

death because God's penalty for sin is death, all sins are mortal.[18] It is impossible for man to pay his debt to God; he is therefore in need of forgiveness. However, this forgiveness can only be made possible through the blood of Jesus and his perfect obedience to the Law that man could not keep. Gouge writes, "Imputation of Christs righteousness is necessary for our iustification." This fifth petition is not only a request for forgiveness, but also a reminder of the confidence the Christian has of being forgiven. With a shepherding focus, Gouge highlights the consolation these theological truths bring to believers, "This doctrine of the imputation, euen of the Active obedience of Christ, bringeth much comfort to poore sinners, who knowing that *all their righteousnesses are as filthy rags*, do thereupon tremble at the thought of the presence of the righteous Lord." Gouge further draws out pastoral reflections when he writes, "But their faith in Christ his righteousnesse imputed to them (instead of that debt of righteousnesse which they owed to God) whereby they are accounted righteous before God, maketh them with much comfort and great confidence present themselves before him."[19] The Christian's prayer life is fueled by his standing before God as one who has been imputed Christ's righteousness. Therefore, the condemnation of his own sin does not prevent him from presenting himself before God because he knows that he is forgiven. As seen in earlier chapters, Gouge's primary ground for assurance is the promises of God in the gospel. Here he highlights the promise of Christ's righteousness reckoned to the sinner through faith in Jesus (i.e., the gospel). This petition is meant not only for the sinner, but was "prescribed euen to the Disciples that were iustified."[20]

Gouge unashamedly acknowledges that his teaching here stands in stark contrast with the teachings of the Roman Catholic Church. Of their differing theology, Gouge urges his readers to "detest [their] contrarie positions," calling them "adversaries." Gouge read extensively from the Roman Catholic theologian Robert Bellarmine (who died just five years before Gouge's 1626 prayer guide) and calls him Rome's "great Champion." He laments Bellarmine's teaching that baptism cleanses

---

18. Gouge, *Guide to Goe to God*, 136.
19. Ibid., 129.
20. Ibid.

the believers from sin causing them to become, as it were, without sin, thereby denying the need for the imputation of Christ's righteousness.

In Gouge's estimation, the great travesty in this teaching, which in essence states a sinner is made sinless in baptism, is that constant awareness of one's sin is actually an ongoing impetus for seeking God in prayer and finding forgiveness. "Perfection," contends Gouge, "needs no remission. For such works then by their doctrine they need aske no pardon. O presumptuous and arrogant conceipts!"[21] To say that Gouge is repulsed by Roman Catholic theology of justification is no understatement. The great problem of humanity is the daily falling into various kinds of sins. Gouge says that sinning is as ordinary for people as drinking. When a Christian denies or rejects this understanding of the degree of his depravity, his conscience has either been seared or deceived.

In personalizing this petition in the Lord's Prayer, Gouge provides seven points of application that must be taken as a whole. The first five points are preparation for the sixth point, which is the call to pray. Among these points, Gouge makes several statements that might cause the reader to question his view of assurance of salvation (where just a few pages earlier, he spoke of the glories of the imputation of Christ's righteousness to the believer and gave a resounding affirmation of assurance). What is apparent in these seven points is that if one application point is removed from the set, the reader will almost entirely misunderstand Gouge's aim. In particular, the first four points must be read in light of points five through seven, which emphasize the propitiatory work of Christ and its meaning for the Christian life, where the first four points emphasize man's sin, God's wrath, and the need for ongoing repentance.

First, he urges Christians to set aside time every day to examine their heart and pay attention to those sins which pass from them lest they fester in their souls and "proue incurable." Second, each Christian should humble himself daily before God, being that "Gods jealousie [is] kindled by our daily sinnes, whereby he is prouoked to come out in wrath, and to take reuenge. Euery day therefore we must fall downe before him with broken spirits and humbled soules. This is a meanes

---

21. Ibid., 130.

to turne his furie to pittie." Third, Gouge makes this bold assertion, that each Christian must "renew [his] covenant with God euery day. For euery sin maketh forfeiture of the couenant." He continues, "The couenant being forfeited, with what comfort can wee apply it to our selues? with what confidence can we plead it before God?" Fourth, Gouge calls Christians to repent every day: if he sins seven times a day, then he should repent seven times a day. The reason for daily repentance is that sin invokes wrath, and repentance "maketh God to repent his wrath."[22]

These first four points of application each have aspects in which Gouge makes statements that seem to contradict his theology of justification by faith along with assurance of salvation. For instance, in what sense might unconfessed sin "proue incurable?" Is the covenant a Christian makes with God through faith in Jesus really forfeited each day with each sin? Is God's wrath truly directed at the believer beyond his conversion? Do Christians need to repent each day in order for God's fury to be removed daily? Gouge's final three application points add some clarification.

One goal of Gouge's first four points is for the Christian to gain a proper view of his own sin that invokes "godly sorrow" leading to the fifth point. Each Christian should "meditate euery day as on the *satisfaction* which the Lord Iesus once made vpon the crosse for our sinnes, so on the *intercession* which he continueth daily to make at the throne of Grace." Here Gouge emphasizes the sufficiency of Christ's atoning work to pay for the sins of all who place their faith in Jesus along with his continued intercession on their behalf. Furthermore, to put away notions of losing salvation, he continues, "This giueth good ground of assured hope of continuall pardon for our continuall sinnes. For the maine end of Christs continuall intercession is to make continuall application of his all-sufficient sacrifice to our continuall sinnes." In other words, ongoing sin is met with ongoing pardon because of Jesus' once-for-all sufficient death and continual intercession before the Father.[23]

Where point five is the theological climax to his statements, point six would be the practical one, namely, to pray every day for pardon.

---

22. Ibid., 131.
23. Ibid., 132.

Gouge says that the previous five points are all preparations for prayer. If prayer for pardon is done by faith, then forgiveness is granted each time. He wants his readers to understand that prayers of repentance that recognize one's own sin and the power of the cross of Jesus to forgive sins are vital parts of the Christian life. Lastly, Gouge urges his readers to be watchful against sin—aware of their own foolishness, sin's deceitfulness, and Satan's constant tactics. Any notion of loss of salvation in the first four points is remedied by the grand assurance of hope presented in the fifth point. The goal of points one through four was for believers to feel the weight of their sin and call Christians to glory in the redeeming work of Christ. These are the very things Gouge says the Roman Catholic Church fails to do by the practice of confessing sin once a year during Lent, as the Council of Trent decided.[24] Man's ongoing sin is an impetus for prayer that calls to mind the power of the gospel and thereby the assurance of the believer.

Historian Peter I. Kaufman has written on the Puritan reflection upon sin in prayer and concludes that Gouge's Puritan predecessors, William Perkins and Laurence Chaderton, agreed with Gouge in this matter. Perkins emphasized the Christian's reflection upon his own sin in prayer so that from that place of humility and "godly sorrow" he might find confidence in God. Like Gouge, Perkins was repulsed by the Roman Catholic approach to prayer that came across as arrogant and self-confident, making their prayers ineffective. Chaderton acknowledges the humility of some Catholics, but states that this lowliness stemmed from a faith that was wavering, driven by doubts about their election.[25] Puritans like Perkins and Chaderton, believed that confidence in their election allowed them to "examine the very bottome of [their] heartes and rippe up all the inward and secrete corners of [their] consciences."[26] Similarly, Puritans like John Freeman and Richard Rogers argued that a tool of Satan was to tempt Christians to pray little and deal lightly with their sin. Conversely, as Kaufman writes, "Godly sorrow and confidence or assurance were partners, and the partnership must

---

24. Ibid., 133.

25. Peter Iver Kaufman, "'Much in Prayer': The Inward Researches of Elizabethan Protestants," *Journal of Religion* 73, no. 2 (April 1993): 163–82.

26. William Perkins, quoted in Kaufman, "Much in Prayer," 167.

be regularly renewed." While critics of Perkins, Chaderton, Freeman, and Rogers saw this introspective practice in prayer to be gloomy and depressing, Kaufman insightfully writes, "A glance at Perkins might have helped those critics more meaningfully to draw the boundaries between disease and pious dis-ease." He continues, "Melancholy must be taken as a worldly sorrow, wherein doubts and dejection could be traced to bewilderment over the character and extent of God's mercy. Perkins confirmed that the chronically melancholic Christian badly blundered. But godly sorrow steadied the attentive Christian's course, announced God's vast mercy, and stirred prodigal petitioners to pray earnestly and often."[27] This is precisely the perspective we see here in Gouge.

Gouge anticipates the questions that might stem from his seven points and provides this objection others could have by saying, "Gods forgivenesse is full, compleate, and absolute. Whom once he acquitteth, he neuer calleth to accompt againe. His discharge is of sinnes, past, present, and to come. What need then of those daily duties?"[28] Gouge's response is helpful in understanding not only his theological convictions, but also his pastoral advice. Gouge affirms the theology of the objection, namely, the complete forgiveness of sin offered through Jesus as it relates to God's eternal decree, secret counsel, and the covenant God the Father made with his son, Jesus. Yet, it is in the matter of application that Gouge's seven points take on their significance. Gouge says that there are degrees in which one comes to understand salvation and forgiveness. Although all sins are mortal (that is to say, an offense toward God and deserving the fruit of divine justice), believers should understand that they have received a full discharge of their sins and that those sins are no longer held against them according to the divine decree and the pacification of God's just wrath through the atoning work of Jesus. However, when a believer sins and stumbles upon even those sins they once had victory over, doubt of their forgiveness begins to creep in. Indeed, "oft sinning doth much shake and weaken faith."[29] For this reason Gouge gave the seven points of application, "for

---

27. Kaufman, "Much in Prayer," 171.
28. Gouge, *Guide to Goe to God*, 132.
29. Ibid., 132–33.

strengthening our weake faith in a full pardon of all our sinnes, for new settling of it when it is shaken, for healing the wounds which are dayly made in our conscience by dayly sinnes, for preuenting the aduantage which might bee taken from our many forfeitures of couenant."[30]

Gouge's seven points of application are highly pastoral in nature, meant to comfort the afflicted Christian and bring consolation when overcome with sin. Unlike Bozeman's claim, this recalling and repenting of sin is not geared to increase doubt, but rather to settle doubt. His aim is not to cause Christians to question their assurance, but to remind them of their assured faith, because according to God's eternal decree and covenant with his son, Jesus' sacrifice was sufficient and his mediation is continual. "The free and full discharge which God giueth of sinne," says Gouge, "is a most sound and soueraigne ground of comfort to such as by faith rightly can apply the same to their owne soules." He continues, "For so freely and fully doth God remit all offence, that neither by reuenging it, doth he condemne vs: nor by vpbraiding it confound vs: nor by imputing it the lesse loue vs."[31] In these words, his theology of assurance and practical divinity are woven together expressing the comfort provided by the gospel in the life of the believer. God does not stand in the posture of vengeance or condemnation, nor does he seek to confuse or struggle in his love to Christians. Instead, they have found forgiveness through faith and thereby can be comforted in their spiritual journey, even in the midst of their battles with sin, the flesh, and Satan. This understanding of justification, assurance of salvation, and practical divinity is consistent throughout Gouge's available corpus.

This fifth petition in the Lord's Prayer emphasizes man's justification whereas the sixth petition emphasizes man's sanctification. Justification precedes sanctification as a matter of order and not of time, says Gouge. "For at that very moment that Christ pardoneth sinne, he coueigheth his Spirit into vs whereby sinne is mortified."[32] In this way, the apostle Paul places righteousness before sanctification because justification causes sanctification, and sanctification declares ones justification. According to Paul, "we are *sanctified by faith in Christ*," says

---

30. Ibid., 133.
31. Ibid., 159.
32. Ibid., 211.

Gouge, "that is, faith vniting vs to Christ, by whom we are iustified, receiueth *grace for grace*, a further grace to sanctifie vs." Just as justification theologically precedes sanctification in order, so does the prayer of faith in the fifth petition of the Lord's Prayer precede the prayer of sanctification in the sixth petition.[33]

Gouge takes the sixth and final petition in the Lord's Prayer as one petition with two parts, "lead us not into temptation, but deliver us from evil." The first part of the petition is a request asking God to prevent feared evils from confronting the believer. The second part is a prayer for recovery from evil when one has fallen into sin. The sum of this petition is that God would not deal with the Christian like a just judge, but rather like a merciful father.[34] It is a prayer for holiness to be reflected in the life of the justified Christian. Again, the application of this petition carries as much prominence as the exposition of it. By way of application, he provides no less than twenty-seven prayer requests that flow from this final petition, such as praying for sanctification in one's life, for freedom against the power of sin, for participation in the power of Christ's death and participation in the Spirit of Christ, for understanding one's own weakness, for patience under all crosses, and for preservation from a reprobate sense.[35]

Significant for this chapter is a section in this petition, which Gouge begins with the words, "There is hope of recouerie to such as are fallen." The "deliverance from" evil in this petition presupposes that a Christian can fall into evil. The prayer for recovery implies he may be delivered from that evil pit. When a soul is afflicted and conscience begins to terrorize the Christian and "feares of vtter desertion, as if God were implacable, and irreconciliable towards them that are at any time ouercome by any temptation," he must be reminded that all hope is not loss. Instead, Gouge wants the strong in faith to remind the anxious that that there is hope for recovery. He urges the strong to tell them

to not despaire, but to say as the Spirit teacheth them, *Come, let us returne vnto the Lord: for he hath torne, and he will heale vs: hee*

---

33. Ibid., 211–12, 253.
34. Ibid., 217.
35. Ibid., 259–66.

hath smitten and hew will binde us up: and withal not to continue
in Satans snares, but to do what they can to come of the same,
according to the pithie perswasion of the Lord, *Remember from
whence thou are fallen, and repent, and do the first works.*[36]

If God were not able and willing to deliver, then this petition "deliver
us from evil" would not be directed to him. The acknowledgment that
Christians fall and that there is hope for recovery because God is merciful are grounds for rejoicing for Christians. When a Christian has fallen
into sin, through prayer he can come back to God and find deliverance
and receive restoration.

In this brief summary, it has been noted that Gouge's work on the
Lord's Prayer aspired to instruct believers in their journey of prayer
by helping them understand more about the details of each of the six
petitions themselves along with their many prayerful applications and
implications for life. Sprinkled throughout the work there are lessons
on assurance and works of practical advice to guide the Christian. In
the concluding pages of his guide, he asks an all-important question,
"Q. How may we beleeue the obtaining of those things which we pray
for? A. By praying for such things as we know to be promised." Gouge's
primary ground for assurance of faith is the same ground for assurance of God hearing and responding to the prayers of his people. "God's
promises are the true and proper ground of a sound faith."[37]

PRAYING EXTRAORDINARY PRAYERS

In addition to Gouge's teaching on "ordinary" prayer in the Lord's
Prayer, he speaks in other places of "extraordinary prayer." The point
of this distinction is not to diminish the value of "ordinary" prayers, but
to highlight the necessity of "extraordinary" ones. For Gouge, extraordinary prayer includes prayer accompanied by fasting. This is the precise
kind of prayer that Gouge urges England to take part in during 1648
with the end of the civil war possibly at hand.

It had been six long years of fighting when Gouge addressed the
House of Lords on September 12, 1648. By this point in time, countless

---

36. Ibid., 250–51.
37. Ibid., 337.

houses, towns, and cities had been burned, plundered, or spoiled. Tens of thousands of people had already died by war and war-related diseases. Friends and neighbors had been divided by their allegiances to King or Parliament.[38] Many painful ills had afflicted England, when in mid-September, 1648, hope for healing was high. On September 15, 1648, three days following Gouge's address, Parliamentary commissioners arrived on the Isle of Wight to seek terms for a treaty with captured King Charles I and bring an end to the civil war. Negotiations began on September 18, 1648. In anticipation of this meeting, Parliament called for a day of public prayer and fasting for England and the seventy-three-year-old Gouge was given the task of addressing the House of Lords on that day. Gouge titled his message, *The Right Way: Or A Direction for Obtaining good Success in a weighty Enterprise*; his biblical text was, Ezra 8:21, "Then I proclaimed a fast there, at the river of Ahava, that we might afflict ourselves before our God, to seek of him a right way for us, and for our little ones, and for all our substance."[39]

Gouge's age at the time of this message is of great interest, because he was old enough to remember the effectiveness of a public fast in 1588, when he was but thirteen years old. During that time the Spanish sought to invade England with their Armada, a fleet of about 130 ships, to overthrow Queen Elizabeth I and ultimately Protestantism in England. Gouge, speaking as an elder Englishman and pastor, recalls the occasion, "I can remember a solemn fast proclaimed, and most solemnly kept in the year 1588. Upon the approach of that Spanish Armado, that carried the stile of *invincible*. Admirable was the blessing that followed upon that fast: for soon after, that proud *Armado* was strangely dissipated." In Gouge's estimation, the defeat of the Spanish Armada was directly linked to the national call to fast and pray.[40]

As an elderly and experienced pastor, Gouge, with great respect, urges the Lords to cry out to God to repair the national breach,

---

38. William Gouge, *The Right Way: or A direction for obtaining good successe in a weighty enterprise. Set out in a sermon preached on the 12th of September, 1648, before the Lords on a day of humiliation for a blessing on a treaty between His Majesties and the Parliaments commissioners* (London: A. Miller, 1648), 32–33.

39. Ezra 8:21, KJV.

40. Gouge, *Right Way*, 31. Gouge prefers the term "armado" as opposed to the more common "armada."

concluding that only the hand of God could do so through the means of prayer. "All outward endeavours of workmen will be in vain," exclaims Gouge, "unless the Creatour doe also inwardly work. Know for certain that more may be done by praiers to GOD, then by perswasions with men."[41] Thus, the proper and necessary response to national sin is two-fold, sound repentance and "hearty praier." To trust in man without God is foolishly to neglect God and invite God's wrath. When King Asa did this in Scripture and became aware of his sins, he fasted to seek God's restoration. In the same way, Ezra fasted and prayed seeking God's guidance. Using these two examples, Gouge underlines the importance of true fasting and prayer for the occasion at hand. True fasting is that fasting which is done before God and not for the praises of man. True fasting understands that God sees the secrets of the heart knowing what is sincere and what is not.[42] He says that prayer linked with fasting is beneficial because it awakens a dull and drowsy spirit, enables the Christian to continue in his devotion and not be sidetracked by preparing a meal and eating, and because it is a "visible testification of our ardent praiers and of our earnest desire to obtain that which we pray for."[43]

Gouge says that prayer and true fasting linked together produces "extraordinary" prayer. In Gouge's work, *Gods Three Arrovves* (1631), he speaks of extraordinary prayer and relates it to fervency in prayer that also exists when multiple people are gathered together praying. He says that, "mutuall assistance of Saints makes prayers much more powerfull and effectuall then otherwise they would be."[44] In his, *Whole Armour of God* (1639), Gouge broadens his definition of extraordinary

---

41. Ibid., iii.

42. Ibid., 9.

43. Ibid., 5. Gouge makes several observations for fasting and prayer as they relate to the home and children. In the case of Israel, they fasted and prayed as they set out on their journey from Babylon back to the Promised Land, in Ezra 8. The text speaks of children joining them, but as Gouge parses out the text, he comes to the conclusion that the little ones were too young to fast, barely able to walk. In such cases, the familial responsibility to the little ones was to pray for them during this time of fasting because they "could not seek their own good." Gouge, *Right Way*, 11–12.

44. William Gouge, *Gods three arrovves : plagve, famine, svvord, in three treatises* (London: George Miller, 1631), 252–53.

prayer even more to include extended times of focused prayer which would vary from hours to days and in their degree of fervency during that time. Still, even at that juncture, he says that extraordinary prayer is helped by fasting and vows.[45] He lists a variety of fasts that include physical fasts, political fasts, and religious fasts. Thus, with that same conviction, he says to the House of Lords "most of the powerfull and effectuall praiers recorded in Scripture, were poured forth on a day of fast. Christ saith of a devil, that by no other means can be cast out, that it may be cast out *by praier and fasting.*"[46] For this reason, the main idea of Gouge's message is, "*In a matter extraordinary, extraordinary means must be used.*"[47] Gouge provides three particular reasons why extraordinary prayer is needed in the Christian life. First, because believers are affected by God's dealing with them. When Christians feel the weight of their circumstances and yearn for God's favor and are grieved at the thought of his displeasure, they will proceed with extraordinary prayer. Gouge heightens the intensity of his argument so as to appeal to both heart and mind of his listeners and later readers when he likens those who refrain from extraordinary prayer to mill horses who walk in circles going about their usual path content with the ordinary. These who are content with ordinary prayers pride themselves in not being like atheists who do not pray, while overlooking the fact that they have neglected God's means for blessing in extraordinary prayer.[48]

Gouge continues his apologetic for prayer linked with fasting when he gives the second reason why Christians should take part in extraordinary prayer, namely, because extraordinary prayer is extraordinarily powerful. This can be seen in the life of King David, when he fasted and prayed for his son that came of Bathsheba when he sinned against God. Though the child died, God caused good to come through David's prayers in the form of David's prayers being pleasing to God, the deceased child receiving eternal life, and the provision of another

---

45. William Gouge, *The Whole Armour of God. Or, A Christians spirituall furniture, to keep him safe frō all the assaults of Satan*, 5th ed. (London: I. Beale, 1639), 457–60.

46. Gouge, *Right Way*, 14.

47. Ibid., 20.

48. Gouge makes gives these illustrations concerning the mill horse and atheists first in 1616 in the first edition of his *The Whole Armour of God* (p. 440) before doing it again in the *Right Way* (p. 26).

son through Bathsheba. In his *Whole Armour of God*, Gouge argues for
the potency of prayer and fasting when he says that it is necessary for
the mortification of the flesh. He calls fasting an "especiall meanes to
subdue our wanton flesh, and corrupt lusts: for a pampering our bodies
addeth strength to the olde man, so fasting mortifieth it, and keepeth
it downe."[49] These two examples of the power of extraordinary prayer
heighten the importance of fasting on the occasion of the treaty in
Gouge's day. He recognizes that an extraordinary intervention from
God is needed. After pointing out the various obstacles to achieving
the peace treaty, he says, "Now who can hope that these sundry other
difficulties can be removed for setling a good lasting peace. Yet surely
they must be removed, or a sound peace will hardly be settled. God to
whom all things are possible can do it."[50]

His third reason believers should partake in extraordinary prayer
through fasting is because it brings honor to God. Gouge writes, "By fasting and praier, which is an extraordinary humbling of our selves before
God, and an extraordinary manner of craving blessing of him, extraordinary honour is done unto him." Again he writes of national fasting,

> By the assembling of many together, men mutually stir up the
> zeal, and inflame the affection of one another: and when many
> joyn bodies and spirits in performing one and the same duty of
> piety together, that duty is the more honourable to God, and the
> more powerfull and prevalent with him. If God account him-
> self honoured by one mans calling upon him, he is the more
> honoured by many mens joyning together therein.[51]

In this statement Gouge highlights both the power of God evidenced
in fasting as well as the honor given to God in doing so. Gouge believes
in the power of prayer through fasting to God who is ready to respond.
God has responded to such extraordinary prayers throughout biblical
history, in the case of the Spanish Armada, in the case of plagues, and
in Gouge's estimation, may even do so for the present occasion. Prayer
and fasting are not mere Christian exercises for the sake of ritual or

---

49. Gouge, *Whole Armour of God*, 477.
50. Gouge, *Right Way*, 35.
51. Ibid., 28.

self-infatuation. They are vibrant parts of the Christian life. Prayer is a tool for Christians to grow in their faith, put to death the deeds of the flesh, and to remind themselves of their assured faith and redeemed identity as children of God. Prayer accompanied with fasting calls to mind the urgency of matters at hand. These extraordinary prayers are active works of faith by Christians that call on God to respond powerfully according to his providential will.

WRITTEN HOUSEHOLD PRAYERS

In opening the window to Gouge's family instructions, it is critical to see how this prominent topic of prayer intersects with Gouge's teaching on the family. This will include prayer and the family as well as instructions for the family as they relate to assurance of faith and the Christian life. Gouge provides written examples of morning, evening and mealtime prayers in his catechism and work on the family, *Of Domestical Duties*. These kinds of examples for family prayer became a staple for the Puritans. Hughes Oliphant Old surveys the makeup of daily family prayers among Puritans in terms of form and content. Families within Puritan churches would daily gather around the table in the morning and evening, sing a metrical psalm, read a chapter from the more edifying portions of the Bible, and conclude with a prayer.[52] Many Puritans likened daily family worship to the daily sacrifices of the old covenant; morning and evening prayers were as morning and evening sacrifices under the Mosaic Law. They recognized the covenantal distinction between the old and new, but also saw a precedence for morning and evening prayers in the words of the apostle Paul in 2 Timothy 1:3 when he says that he prays "night and day" for the churches. Family prayers were to continue on the Lord's Day and were never meant to take the place of the church service, nor was the church service to take the place of family prayers.[53] On the Lord's Day, there was

---

52. Hughes Oliphant Old, "Matthew Henry and the Puritan Discipline of Family Prayer," in *Calvin Studies VII: Papers Presented at a Colloquium on Calvin Studies at Davidson College and Davidson College Presbyterian Church*, ed. John H. Leith (Davidson, NC: Davidson College 1994), 69. The more tedious portions (such as Numbers and Leviticus) were thus omitted, says Old.

53. Gouge lists praying and catechizing as private duties of piety on the Sabbath in William Gouge, *Sabbath Sanctification* (London: George Miller, 1641), 6.

a greater emphasis on the reading, which included discussion of the text and even a discussion about the morning sermon and re-reading of that text. In addition, devotional literature was also often read by the Puritans, which included stories about the lives of the saints of the past and martyrologies.[54]

In like manner, Gouge gathered his own family around the table daily for family worship. His son Thomas lauded his father's example in leading his household:

> The government of his family was exemplary, another *bethel*; for he did not only make conscience of morning and evening prayers, and reading the word in his family, but also of catechizing his children and servants, wherein God gave him a singular gift; for he did not teach them by any set form, but so as he brought them that were instructed to express the principle taught them in their own words. So that his children (as Gregory Naziansen saith of his father) found him as well a spiritual as a bodily father.[55]

If Thomas's depiction of his father is accurate, Gouge put into practice those things which he taught and followed suit with other Puritans in his day. Thomas mentions morning and evening prayers, Scripture reading and catechism, with singing a metric psalm being the only element absent in Thomas' description that was present in Old's survey.

---

54. Old, "Matthew Henry," 71, 75, 77.

55. Thomas Gouge, vii. Interestingly, Gouge's son, Thomas, published his own catechism in 1680 for the families in the parish he served in Wales. Thomas' catechism is similar to his father's, taking exact wording at various points of both questions and answers. A major difference, though, is that Thomas' catechism is far more thorough and detailed than William's. For instance, where William and Thomas' catechisms both begin with the exact question, "What is every one most bound to know?" followed by the exactly same answer, "God and himself," William proceeds to the next question and Thomas provides three points of "explication" and several points of "application" before his next question. Throughout Thomas' catechism, though, the reader will find many similarities to that of his father's. This makes perfect sense since, by Thomas' own admission, his father diligently catechized his family. It is likely that Thomas did not need a copy of his father's catechism with him, but truly had committed it to memory, and could use his memory as a reference while writing his own. Thomas Gouge, *The Principles of Christian Religion Explained to the Capacity of the Meanest. With Practical Applications to each Head Whereby the Great and Necessary Duty of Family-Catechizing may with much Ease be Performed* (London: Thomas Parkhurst, 1680), 7–8.

To write, or not to write—that was the prayer question in the latter quarter of the sixteenth century. Kaufman tells of "prayer wars" that existed in England explaining how there were some in the Puritan camp, like Thomas Cartwright, who in 1572 expressed his disdain for written and memorized prayers. His concern was that prescribed prayers encouraged complacency and lifeless ritual. Conversely, Richard Hooker in his *Of Lawes of Ecclesiastical Polity* (1594–1597), was bothered by the apparent mindset of some, which implied that God only heard prayers that were new.[56] Still, others like William Gouge believed there was a place for both written and extemporaneous prayers in the life and practice of the Christian. As we have seen up to this point, much of Gouge's prayer directives point to extemporaneous prayers based on the need of the moment. As prayer relates to the family, however, Gouge also provides written prayers that suit the occasions and family members. These prayers can be found in the second and third edition of his *Of Domestical Duties* and are first appended to the second edition of his catechisms. The family prayers in *Of Domestical Duties* will first be examined before navigating the content and editions of his catechism.

In 1622 Gouge produced his second largest book, *Of Domestical Duties*, a 700-page work on the Christian household and the duties of wives, husbands, children, parents, servants and masters.[57] He would go on to publish it again in 1627 and a third time in 1634. The first two editions were identical in substance. The third edition deviates only slightly from the former two by adding a closing section on written prayers that pertain to the matters in the book. Secondary literature on this work abounds. Social historians, in particular, have noted it for its teachings on family and the ways in which it provides a glimpse into the living

---

56. Kaufman, "Much in Prayer," 164.

57. Gouge's largest work is his three-volume magnum opus, his commentary on Hebrews. It appears that he did not intend for this book to be as lengthy as it turned out to be. He writes in his foreword, "Though for such a matter as is handled in these Treatises, the worke may seeme at first sight to be too copious, yet I hope the observant Reader will not finde it too tedious. It is the variety of many, not the prolixity of few points which has made this booke to swell to that bignesse which it hath." William Gouge, *Of Domesticall Dvties: eight treatises* (London: Iohn Haviland, 1622), ii–iii.

room of seventeenth-century households in England.[58] Gouge's preface to this work is unlike his others, where he is detailed in explaining his method, the layout of the book, and provides cautions and exceptions to some of his points. Furthermore, he urges his readers to read patiently recognizing that while teachings for wives might feel difficult, when they come to the teachings on husbands, they will see that there is equal weight given to their responsibilities. The family should function like a little church, or be, as it were, a seminary for the church, whereby children are raised in the fear of the Lord and instructed in the truths and practices of the Christian. "What excellent seminaries would families be to Church and Common-wealth ... good members of a family are like to make good members of Church and common-wealth."[59]

Gouge understood that some of the matters of this work would be difficult to receive. He says that many who read will think well of themselves when they see the virtues of their own role in the family, until they see the correlating vices which will bring conviction to their souls. He cautions family members from judging others in their family by the truths taught in this book, and instead to "make aright application of every thing to themselves." In his introduction he recalls the first time he preached these truths in Blackfriars, that some of the women took exception to what they felt to be a restraining of their ability to order the "common good" for their family. Gouge clarifies that his intent is not to restrain wives in this way. Rather, he envisions households of husbands and wives sharing the burden of the home, so that the yoke would not feel more burdensome to either wife or husband. For these reasons, he affixed a prayer guide to the end of the book "for obtaining divine helpe to practice the [virtues] and avoid the [vices]."[60]

---

58. Reviewing the various interpretations of Gouge's work is beyond the purview of this work. However, Frances E. Dolan has done some of this work in *True Relations: Reading, Literature, and Evidence in Seventeenth-Century England* (Philadelphia: University of Pennsylvania Press, 2013), 154–201. See also Theresa D. Kemp and Natasha Korda's works for similar insights. Theresa D. Kemp, "The Family Is a Little Commonwealth: Teaching *Mariam* and *Othello* in a Special-Topics Course on Domestic England," *Shakespeare Quarterly* 47, no. 4 (Winter, 1996), 453–54; Natasha Korda, *Shakespeare's Domestic Economies: Gender and Property in Early Modern England* (Philadelphia: University of Pennsylvania Press, 2007).

59. Gouge, *Of Domestical Dvties*, ii.

60. Ibid., iv–vi.

The "patternes of prayers for the severall members of a family" appended to his book include "a prayer for such as intend marriage," "a prayer for husbands and wives in regard of the mutual and joint duties whereunto they are both bound," along with separate prayers for wives, husbands, children, parents, servants, and masters.[61] In every prayer, Gouge includes marginal notes linking each prayer point with a paragraph section in the book. These convenient reference guides between the principles taught and the prayers prayed make it clear that in Gouge's mind, the application of these truths could only be accomplished through prayer. God's intervention was necessary for singles, husbands, wives, parents, children, servants, and masters to perform God's call for their respective roles in the Christian household. Furthermore, learning without prayerful application—like prayer without a sufficient foundation—works against Gouge's approach to practical divinity, which requires an intersection between belief and practice.

Most pertinent for this discussion on prayer and assurance of faith are the prayers for singles and for wives. The prayer for singles intending marriage includes elements of prayer for pardon of past sins, preservation in present purity, and the provision of a spouse who is likeminded in spiritual piety.[62] The written form of these prayers allows the single person to revisit frequently the contents of the prayer and thereby God's calling for those intending on marriage. On the matter of piety, the prayer asks for single men and women to be secure in their own identity as a Christian before God provides them a mate in order that they might deal kindly with their future spouse. "Let me first have assurance of mine owne spirituall union with the Lord Iesus, that from

---

61. Ibid., 707-27.

62. The alliteration is original to Gouge: "I humbly beseech thee to *pardon* all my sinnes past, to *preserve* me from all inordinate lusts, and to *provide* for me a meet yoke-fellow" (italics added). Gouge, *Of Domestical Dvties*, 705. One might find it a bit humorous that Patrick Collinson tells of the apparent pleasure sixteenth- and seventeenth-century English writers had with the letter "p" in their writings, from which the word "Puritan" is no exception. Quoting Thomas Middleton's play *The Family of Love*, Collinson says that the "paraperopandectical doctor" was noted for "his precise, Puritanical, and peculiar punk, his potecary's drug." Patrick Collinson, "Antipuritanism," in *Cambridge Companion to Puritanism*, ed. John Coffey and Paul Lim (Cambridge: Cambridge University Press, 2008), 21.

him, as an head, I, as one of his members, may receive ability to do good to that mate which thou hast provided for me."[63] When assurance of faith is experienced in the lives of single Christians, they will be better equipped to demonstrate kindness and goodness to their future spouses. That assurance is experienced when Christians understand their union with Christ. This prayer reflects Gouge's teaching of union with Christ when he expounds the meaning of the church as Jesus' own body in Ephesians 5:30. There he says that Christians, through their participation with Jesus, receive possession of heaven, because where the head (i.e., Jesus) is, the body (i.e., the Church) follows. "This is somewhat more then hope," says Gouge of the realities of heaven for the Christian, "and serveth exceedingly to strengthen our hope, and to give us assurance of that heavenly inheritance."[64]

Husbands and wives are instructed to pray "joyntly" and separately because there are common responsibilities they share together, and unique responsibilities they must tend to separately.[65] Noteworthy in the wife's prayer is her statement of personal confidence of her salvation that is based partially on her readiness to submit to her husband. In this act and mindset of submission, she is to pray, "hereby I shall gaine assurance to my selfe, and give evidence to others that I am a true member of the true Church."[66] The wording speaks to Gouge's theology of assured faith, in that a basis for her own assurance is the fruit of the Holy Spirit giving her the ability to be subject to her husband. For a woman to live out this role properly, she must be empowered by the Spirit because it "cannot bee performed by the power of nature, it is a supernaturall worke, and so an evidence of the Spirit."[67] Concerning Gouge's theology, this written prayer provides another example of how a ground of assurance for the Christian is the fruit of the Spirit working

---

63. Gouge, *Of Domestical Dvties*, 707.

64. Ibid., 99.

65. "And, good Father, so power on us the spirit of supplication, as we always without ceasing may call upon thee the fountaine of all blessing, and in our payers be mutually mindfull of one another: and take all occasion of praying joyntly together." Gouge, *Of Domestical Dvties*, 707.

66. Ibid., 711.

67. Ibid., 351–52.

in his life (even if it is not the primary ground for assurance, as are the promises of God in the gospel).

CATECHETICAL INSTRUCTION AND FAMILY PRAYERS

Written family prayers taught Christians how to pray by providing prayer points that were deemed to be of greater importance. By committing these prayers to memory, believers were able to take the prayers with them wherever they went. These fit well with the genre of catechisms, which encouraged memorization of a series of questions and answers concerning Christian life and doctrine. Catechisms abounded in the sixteenth- and seventeenth-century English church. Ian Green has compiled a staggering list of over a thousand catechisms published in England between 1530 and 1740. He considers the years of the 1630s as "a heyday for 'godly' or Calvinist catechisms," citing Gouge as among the heyday authors.[68] When comparing the number of editions published with others before his death in 1653, we see that Gouge's catechism garnered some popularity in his own lifetime, having been published eight times between 1615 and 1639.[69] Of the eight editions, seven are extant with his fourth being the lone edition no longer available. His first edition was a mere thirteen small pages with a large font published not by Gouge himself, but by the printer John Beale (d. 1643).[70] Beale says in the introduction that "a Preacher of Gods Word" delivered these catechetical truths to the "young youths of his parish, that they might more distinctly answere him when he required an answere of

---

68. Ian Green, *The Christian's ABC: Catechisms and Catechizing in England c. 1530–1740* (Oxford: Clarendon, 1996), 580–750, 66–67.

69. In addition to the eight editions of Gouge's catechism are the at least four editions to his miniature catechism, *Briefe Answers to the Chiefe Articles of Religion*, of which only the fourth edition remains.

70. Beale's print shop was on Fetter Lane, placing it about a mile from St. Anne's Parish, Blackfriars where Gouge ministered. He says that Gouge is "well known in this Citie," adding, "if it would please him to bee made knowne." Interestingly, Beale's attestation to Gouge's popularity is significant because Gouge had only been at Blackfriars since 1608, seven years at this point and had yet to publish his first work, which would come the following year in 1616. Henry R. Plomer, *A Dictionary of the Booksellers and Printers Who Were at Work in England, Scotland, and Ireland from 1641 to 1667* (London: Blades, East and Blades, 1907), 17–18.

them."[71] The stated purpose of the catechism, then, was to instruct theologically and practically the children in his parish. Beale acknowledges the brevity of the work stating that the "Author" did more than what the catechism shows, in catechizing these youths. Beale leaves the name of the author anonymous. The following year, Beale produced a second edition of the work expanding it with two prayers by the same author. Again, he leaves out the name of preacher and keeps the work anonymous. Finally in 1621, six years after the first edition was published, Gouge takes ownership for the work. He expresses his reluctance to publish a catechism, let alone attach his name to the present one, because other "sufficient forms of Catechismes haue been published." Gouge had to look no further than his predecessor, Stephen Egerton, whose *Briefe Methode of Catechizing* was published an incredible forty-five times![72] Gouge's catechism came into being as an aid to assist the spiritual growth of the youth in his parish. He says, "by this meanes the *Printer* [John Beale] got a copie of them, & published them once & again before I yielded to father them ... & acknowledge it to be mine."[73] By the time of Gouge's fifth edition, the catechism itself continued to be "corrected and inlarged" and included a prayer to be recited before reading Scripture, a catechism prayer, morning and evening prayers, and several prayers for both before and after a meal. His prefaces remain the same from the third edition onward.

From the second edition onward, Gouge's catechism included written morning and evening prayers, which he, in puritanical fashion, calls a "morning" and "evening sacrifice." From the substance of the prayer we can determine that the prayers were written especially for the head of the household as he prayed with the family. The morning prayer specifically contains a prayer for the children, asking God to "worke in us a religious care, welto train them up." This is consistent with what we see in *Of Domestical Duties*, where parents are instructed to pray for the ability to raise their children properly by catechizing them and showing a great concern for the salvation of their souls,

---

71. William Gouge, *A Short Catechisme, wherein are briefely laid downe the Fundamentall Principles of Christian Religion* (London: Iohn Beale, 1615), A1.

72. Green, *The Christian's ABC*, 640–41.

73. Gouge, *Short Catechisme*, 3–4.

Above all, make me conscionable in training up my children unto true piety; grounding every principle that is taught them, on thy Word; exercising them to read the Scriptures, catechizing them daily, making spiritual uses of the special evide[nces] of thy providence, opening to them the mysteries of the rights of the Church, making knowne thy great workes to them, putting them to religious Schoolmasters, & being my self a patterne of piety unto the[m] lest otherwise I shew too little regard to the salvation of their soules.[74]

Both morning and evening prayers are similar in form, with words of exaltation at the outset followed by acknowledging man's sinfulness and need for grace. The prayers entrust the day or night before them to God, express thankfulness for what lies behind, present petitions for one's self and in the morning for one's family, church, and nation, and then commence with a recitation of the Lord's Prayer. Mealtime prayers are much shorter than evening and morning prayers. They consist of only a few sentences. Gouge provides three prayers before the meal and three different prayers for after the meal. The prayers range in emphasis including profound gratitude for God's provision of food, blessing on the mealtime conversations, and for strength for the activities that follow.

From his third edition onward, Gouge's catechism begins with a prayer that aims at setting the heart aright before coming to the Scriptures in study and to the catechism, which gathers principles from Scripture. The prayer has several elements, which reflect Gouge's theological convictions and pastoral priorities. The prayer runs thus:

O Father of light who hast been pleased to vouchsafe unto us poore miserable sinners, who by nature sit in darkenesse and in the shadow of death, the light of the Word to direct us thorow the darkenesse of this world, unto the light of glorie; we beseech thee for Jesus Christs sake to pardon all our sinnes, and to open the blind eyes of our understanding, that we may rightly conceiue thy Word, and withal to giue us grace rightly to apply it

---

74. Gouge, *Of Domestical Dvties*, 720.

unto our own hearts, & to yield all holy obedience thereunto, that so we may honor thee in this world, and be honoured of thee in the world to come, through Jesus Christ our Lord, and onely Sauiour, Amen.[75]

The prayer begins with words of adoration and an acknowledgment of God's attribute of being light amidst darkness.[76] What follows is the necessary humiliation of man, the product of seeing God's perfection. The prayer recognizes man's sinfulness and need for God's grace to navigate him through this life. This leads to confession of sin and a request for God's illumination of Scripture to the believer. This beginning half of the prayer reflects Gouge's theological convictions of God's glory, man's poor state, the need for God to intervene on man's behalf, and the primacy of Scripture as God's means for instruction. The latter half of the prayer reflects Gouge's practical divinity and pastoral priorities. Believers are meant to learn the truths of God's Word in order that they might be applied to life. The prayer continues asking for grace to rightly apply the Word to the Christian's heart for the purpose of producing a life of obedience ultimately leading to God receiving honor through the believer's life. The prayer closes with an eternal outlook and affirmation of the exclusive and sufficient mediation of Jesus between God and man (consistent with Gouge's theology of the gospel). The purpose of the catechism was both to affect one's understanding of the Christian faith and to produce sanctifying results in the Christian's life. Memorization of the catechism absent from the application of its truths misses the intended aim of the work as a whole.

A new prayer added to Gouge's fifth edition and those thereafter, is a prayer drawn from the principles of the catechism itself.[77] This

---

75. William Gouge, *A briefe method of catechizing wherein are briefely handled the fundamentall principles of Christian religion, needfull to be knowne by all Christians before they be admitted to the Lords Table. Whereunto are added sundry prayers, with thanksgivings before and after meale*, 8th ed. (London: John Beale, 1637), 1.

76. It is unclear if Gouge's understanding of God as light and the world as darkness refers to God's holiness amidst a sinful world, to God's truth amidst a deceitful world, or metaphorically God's provision of sight amidst a blind and lost world. The latter seems to be most consistent with the entirety of the prayer.

77. This prayer may have been in the fourth edition, were it available to us. We know for certain it is not included in the first three editions.

prayer covers redemptive history from the Garden of Eden to man's resurrection from the dead in the last days and thus includes some of Gouge's most systematized descriptions of theology proper and the gospel. The prayer expresses thankfulness for God's assistance through the study of the catechism because through its biblical truths "we attaine knowledge of thee for ourselves." He directs his gratitude and praise to God for his divine attributes and Trinitarian existence, "By it [that is, the catechism] are we taught that thou art the only true God, one in essence, but distinguished into three persons, Father, Son and holy Spirit."[78] The prayer also acknowledges man's "miserable" state apart from Christ and how Jesus provides "endlesse mercy" to deliver Christians from "endlesse misery" and displayed his "infinite power to beare that infinite burden" of man's sin. The prayer also affirms Jesus' kingly, priestly, and prophetic ministry and confesses, "all these things wee stedfastly beleeue." Confession of sin follows producing "godly sorrow" that leads to the sanctifying hope of forgiveness, "but withall, work in us faith in the pardon of sin, that thus we may daily mortifie our corruptions, and liue in true holinesse and righteousness."[79] What is evident in this written prayer is its didactic function. Not only does it instruct Christian's how to pray, but also what to believe. Gouge's written prayers are theologically robust and practically focused, teaching Christians to order their day around communion with God, to live purposefully, to keep the gospel at the forefront of their activities, and to have a thankful disposition toward God for all of his merciful provisions.

Concerning the catechism as a whole, a child or adult had to display sufficient knowledge of the catechism before partaking of the Lord's Supper. The catechism operated as a filter to evaluate who truly understood the Christian religion and the meaning of the sacraments. According to Green, children were catechized in a variety of contexts in sixteenth- and seventeenth-century England ranging from the school, to the household, or by a minister.[80] In Gouge's day, ministers

---

78. He specifically mentions God's perfection, eternality, omnipresence, omniscience, immutability, purity, wisdom, justice, faithfulness, and mercy. Gouge, *Briefe Method of Catechizing*, 14.

79. Gouge, *Briefe Method of Catechizing*, 14–15.

80. Green, *The Christian's ABC*, 170–229.

bemoaned the failure of parents to catechize their children properly. Some parents expressed a sense of being unqualified for the task, while other simply neglected the responsibility. Those who faithfully catechized their children were celebrated as exemplary parents. Funeral sermons were often the occasions for such honoring. Seeing that the mastery of the catechism was a prerequisite for participating in the Lord's Supper, some ministers, like Gouge, traveled throughout their parish and visited children in their homes in order to test whether they were fit to receive the sacrament.[81]

Although much can be said about different points and emphases in Gouge's catechism, the focus of what follows will be on what it teaches about assurance of salvation and prayer. If catechisms present the foundational beliefs for the Christian faith, then the ways in which Gouge wanted catechumens to perceive their assurance and the role of prayer in their lives need to be understood. Gouge did not number the questions in any of the editions of his catechism, but the catechism can be broken into roughly four quarters. The first quarter of the catechism deals with theology proper and the laws of God in the Ten Commandments. The second quarter pertains to the sinfulness of man and the redemption provided by Jesus, the God-man. The third quarter of the catechism teaches about the sacraments of baptism and the Lord's Supper. Finally, the catechism concludes with questions on prayer and theological truths drawn from the Lord's Prayer in particular.

In the general breakdown of the catechism above, about a quarter of Gouge's catechism is geared toward prayer in the Christian life. This indicates that Gouge wanted catechumens to receive a solid theological and practical handle on prayer for their Christian lives. In like manner entire families, who faithfully catechized their children, would also benefit from these frequent catechetical reflections on prayer. The catechism calls prayer the "right opening of the desire of the heart" which is done when the believer "directs [his heart] to God, thorow the mediation of Christ, in Truth, faith, holinesse and love." This description of prayer reveals the attitude of the Christian, who has a heart to come to God. The Christian virtues of faith, holiness, and love

---

81. Ibid., 216–20.

also express the sincerity of one praying. The catechism teaches that Christians should ask for things that either bring God glory or are for the Christian's own good.

As it relates to the content of prayer, the catechism calls Christians to pray the Lord's Prayer and provides brief descriptions of each of the six petitions of the prayer. Notable for our purposes is the answer provided to the question, "Why is this clause (*As we forgive them that trespasse against us*) added?" To which the catechism replies, "Partly to moue us to forgiue the wrongs which are offered to us, and partly to gaine assurance of Gods forgiuing us our sins." The twofold reply keeps a tension with which Gouge appears to be content, namely, the apparent conditional nature of man being forgiven by God. The catechism teaches that believers are moved to forgive because "God will not forgiue us, except we forgiue our neighbour." Gouge does not soften the words of Jesus, which seem to say that man's forgiveness from God is contingent upon his forgiving his neighbor. This answer in the catechism might cast doubt on one's assurance should a person persist in having an unforgiving heart. But, again, Gouge's answer to the question was two-fold. Where the first part stresses the conditional nature of Jesus' words, the second part communicates assurance of God's forgiveness. To the question, "How is it an assurance?," the catechism responds, "In that our forgiuing of our Brother is a fruit of coming from Gods forgiuing of us."[82] Taking these two parts together, the Christian who is forgiven by God will in turn be prepared to offer forgiveness to his brother. Or said another way, one can know that they are indeed children of God and forgiven by the way they forgive. Forgiveness, therefore, is a fruit of being forgiven and assurance is the fruit of one who forgives.

In Thomas Gouge's 1680 catechism, he takes an identical angle as his father when it comes to this clause in the fifth petition of the Lord's Prayer. He says that forgiving one's neighbor "is a reflex or fruit of God's love unto us."[83] Thomas' usage of the word "reflex" calls to mind the distinction between the direct act of faith and the reflex act of faith utilized by many Puritans when discussing the assurance of salvation.

---

82. Gouge, *Briefe Method of Catechizing*, 10.
83. Thomas Gouge, *Principles of Christian Religion*, 127.

While William Gouge does not employ that terminology as his son does at this juncture, the concept is clearly present for both of them. When a Christian catechumen memorizes these questions and answers, he will be able to be confident about his salvific standing before God because by his direct act of faith, he believes that he has been forgiven because of Christ's atoning work (forgive us our debts). Furthermore, he can also be assured about his salvation through a reflex act of faith, which recognizes the genuineness of his faith by seeing the way he can forgive his brother as a reflex of his being forgiven by God (as we forgive those who are indebted to us).

The topic of assurance was an important theme in English catechisms. Green attempts to trace the *locus* of assurance in the catechisms of his wide sampling. Broadly speaking, he says that the later sixteenth- and early seventeenth-century catechisms placed a greater emphasis on introspection and self-analysis and the catechumen's own life whereas those before and afterward tended to align with Calvin and focus on the means God has provided to increase faith in the believer.[84] This latter example is what we see in Gouge's work. While he retains some elements of introspection, his focus on assurance has more to do with the tools that God has given Christians to know that they have been justified. These tools include understanding the nature of faith and how to use it as a grid for discerning the fruit of one's justification. For instance, because Gouge defines faith as, "A beliefe of the Gospell, whereby Christ Jesus, and all his benefits offered therein are receiued," the catechumen can determine that faith provides sure access to the benefits of Christ and the hope of the Kingdom of Heaven through man's justification and sanctification.[85]

---

84. For example, John Calvin's 1538 catechism emphasized the Word of God as that tool given by God to instruct the Christian that he possesses saving faith. Calvin's catechism was translated into English and printed twelve times from 1560–1598. Concerning the question of assurance, his catechism stated for the English ear, "By [God's] owne woorde, wherin he vttereth most playnlye vnto vs, hys plentifull mercye in our sauiour Christ, & geueth vs vndoubted assurance of his louing mynd towards vs." John Calvin, *The Catechisme, or maner to teache Children the Chrisitan Religion* (London: Iohn Kyngston, 1580), 3.

85. Green, *The Christian's ABC*, 393–94. William Gouge defines a sacrament as "a diuine ordinance wherein by outward signes and rites, the promises of the Gospell are sealed vs to vs, and our faith and repentance is testified." Man's faith

In this survey of Gouge's written prayers in both his *Of Domestical Duties* and his catechism, both the written prayers and the catechetical sections serve a didactic purpose for right belief and a practical purpose for right living (orthodoxy and orthopraxy). They place a premium on prayer in the life of a Christian and operate as a tool for family instructions, even as it relates to the Christian's assurance of salvation.

PRAYER AND ASSURANCE OF SALVATION

In Gouge's estimation, the Lord's Prayer is the perfect pattern of prayer because of the contents of the six petitions and their theological focus of the glory of God and the needs of humanity. The unpacking of each petition opens the believer to an array of other prayer requests, thereby causing the Lord's Prayer to be what Gouge titled his book, a guide to go to God. Gouge's exposition seems to have in mind the spontaneous and extemporaneous expressions of prayer, whereas in *Of Domestical Duties* and the catechism we see written prayers. In all cases, for Gouge, prayer and doctrinal truths deepen Christian's understanding of God while calling them to a life of faith.

The practical priority that is clearly evident from Gouge's works on prayer is to pray. Gouge wrote on prayer not only that it might be rightly understood, but also rightly enjoyed. Through prayer, a believer is able to find many other practical benefits for their lives. In prayer, the afflicted Christian can find comfort, as in the case of Lady Bruce. In prayer, the tired Christian can find rest when communing with God face to face. In prayer, the Christian who battles wanton lusts and deceitful pleasures is able to find help in mortifying the flesh and leading a sanctified life. In prayer, combined with fasting, the Christian engages in an extraordinary work where extraordinary circumstances are brought before the throne of grace. Such circumstances, for Gouge, include personal and national sin, political uprisings, and military crises. So too, in prayer, the doubting Christian can find assurance of faith. Gouge urges Christians to pray for assurance, namely, by praying for the spiritual fruit evidenced in the life of one who has been justified. Still,

---

and repentance, his true reception of the promises of God in the gospel, are demonstrated in his receiving of the sacraments. The sacraments show outwardly what has taken place inwardly for the Christian.

Gouge maintains that assurance of salvation is primarily grounded on the promises of God in the gospel and secondarily grounded on the inward testimony of the Spirit of God through a Spirit-empowered life. As Gouge states in *A Right Way*, "praier is the most principall means of obtaining blessing, blessing from God.... That which through his grace he promiseth, upon the praiers of his Saints, he performeth."[86]

---

86. Gouge, *A Right Way*, 17–18.

6

Conclusion

Of these Examples sure I am there's need,
To back our faith, and strengthen us indeed
Against such traps and nets as now are spread
To catch Gods people in the wayes they tread.
Yet if these Worthies rather chose to dye
Than known Truths to betray, or once deny,
Then let us tread their path, which path is blest
That when we dye we may with them have rest.
(Katherine Clarke, *Lives of Ten Eminent Divines*)
Yet, Sir, your pious Labours sober men
Will prize, and praise God for your happy Pen,
Whereby that precious treasure once contain'd
In earthen vessels, now broke by deaths hand
Is for our use preserved in good part,
And we therewith enriched by your Art.
Let them who would your labours rightly prize
Endeavour to untwine these mysteries.
Candles put out, yet shining bright and fair,
Cities demolished, yet standing are;
Salt turned into dust, yet seasons much,
Uncanonized Saints, yet truely such.
(Samuel Clarke, *Lives of Ten Eminent Divines*)

Samuel (1599–1683) and Katherine Clarke (1602–1675) penned these poems for the introduction to Samuel's *A Collection of the Lives of Ten Eminent Divines famous in their Generations for Learning, Prudence, Piety, and Painfulness in the work of the Ministry*, honoring the ministers contained in the volume. William Gouge was numbered among the ten. When Gouge died in 1653, he left behind an impressive reputation, being remembered as an "eminent divine." While his name and reputation have endured within Puritan studies, his works have not persevered in the same way. One aim of this project has been to put both Gouge's name along with his works back into the picture within the frame of Puritan studies and pastoral theology.

SUMMARY OF ARGUMENT AND CONTRIBUTION

Puritan practical divinity grew through the ranks of William Perkins, Richard Greenham, and Richard Rogers before arriving at the pen of William Gouge and his contemporaries. The pastoral priorities of nurturing Christian souls and providing tools for comforting afflicted consciences are prominent themes in Gouge's works. Puritan practical divinity was concerned with right doctrine and right living addressing "'the application of redemption' in Christ to individual souls."[1] These teachings called Christians to examine themselves frequently and determine if their lives are consistent with the faith that they believed. For some Christians, this introspective activity produced anxieties that caused them to doubt the genuineness of their faith. Pastors like Gouge were not interested in seeing Christians agonize, but rather made it their aim to call the faithful to determine the authenticity of their belief through holding fast to the promises of God in the gospel and through seeing the fruit of the Spirit born out in their lives.

In this book, it has been argued that Gouge's practical divinity was indeed closely linked to his theology of assurance. Gouge was pastorally attentive to the spiritual needs of his people, seeking to address the various heart issues they experienced at the hands of sin, illness, and challenging circumstances of life. Gouge's theology of assurance was grounded primarily on the promises of God in the gospel, and secondarily on the practical syllogism, or the assurance that comes from Christians seeing the evidences of their faith born out in their lives. Saving faith is demonstrated to be genuine when sinners are confronted with their sinfulness and God enables them to surrender their lives to Jesus by believing the promises of the gospel. In this way, Gouge and

---

1. Charles E. Hambrick-Stowe, "Practical Divinity and Spirituality," in *The Cambridge Companion to Puritanism*, ed. John Coffey and Paul Lim (Cambridge: Cambridge University Press, 2008), 203.

other Puritans did not deviate from the teachings of John Calvin in substance, but further developed his ideas. To borrow language from theologian John S. Bray, Puritans like Gouge differed quantitatively from Calvin, but not qualitatively.[2] Gouge believed that assurance of salvation is of the essence of faith, but that one must properly understand that what is true theologically may not be experienced practically. For this reason, some Christians doubt their salvation and are in need of instruction on how to know that they belong to Christ. In Gouge's teaching, little faith produced little assurance, where mature faith led to steadfast assurance. Therefore, he explored practical ways to guide believers to strengthen their faith and thereby increase their assurance.

Conversely, Gouge wanted to weed out those supposed Christians who possessed a "temporary" or "hypocritical" faith that was not indeed saving faith that led to justification. Thus, for all of his readers and listeners, he believed that the starting point for both assurance of faith for the Christian and saving faith for the non-Christian was a recognition of one's sinful circumstances and need for the finished work of Jesus. For Christians, this starting point was not meant to breed fear or despair, but to ground their assurance and remind them of what Jesus had accomplished for them by imputing to them his righteousness. This reflection caused Christians to meditate upon the promises of the gospel, which justifies, sanctifies, and ultimately leads Christians into glory. For the unbeliever, this reflection upon sin should invoke a terror of God's wrath that leads to repentance and ultimately justifying faith. Although already quoted in Chapter 3, it bears repeating. Concerning unbelievers who are convicted by their sins, Gouge writes,

> They which have this desire wrought in them, wil give no rest to their soules, till they have some sweet feeling of Gods love to them in Christ, and some assurance that Christ is theirs: whereupon God who hath offered to satisfie the hungry and thirsty, and to satisfie the desire of such as pant and long after him, by his Spirit worketh in such as are so prepared, such an inward assent of mind and credence unto the promises of the Gospell

---

2. Referred to by Joel R. Beeke, *The Quest for Full Assurance: The Legacy of Calvin and His Successors* (Carlisle, PA: Banner of Truth, 2000), 3–4.

that particularly they apply them unto themselves, and gladly accept the free offer of God, and so receive Christ with all his benefits.[3]

Thus, Gouge's practical divinity aimed at deepening the faith of Christians and thereby increasing their assurance. It also aimed at pricking the hearts of unrepentant sinners appealing to them with the truth of the gospel to place their saving faith in Jesus.

In Chapter 2, it was demonstrated that Gouge's practical divinity and theology of assurance of salvation were undergirded by his understanding of the Bible, his belief in the gospel, most clearly seen in his theology of the atonement, and in his providential outlook on all of life. These theological emphases provide the basis of both his practical divinity and view of assurance. As it relates to the Bible, Gouge's dominant publishing genre is a dance between practical divinity and biblical theology. All of Gouge's works (excluding his catechism) are biblical expositions that place the biblical text at the starting point for his teaching. It is from the Scriptures that Gouge addresses cases of conscience in the Christian life. Although many of his works explain the biblical text like a commentary, they have far reaching implications for Christian living.[4]

As pertains to the gospel, Gouge has a robust theology of the atonement. His description of the atonement, as with much of his practical divinity, begins with humanity's predicament. Gouge presents human beings as in bondage from birth because their sin nature and because of the curse due to them from the Law of God, which they were unable to keep perfectly. This curse of the law invites God's wrath because his justice has been rebelled against. This bondage to sin, curse from the law, and status of deserving God's wrath will lead all of humanity to

---

3. William Gouge, *The Whole Armour of God. Or, A Christians spirituall furniture, to keep him safe frō all the assaults of Satan*, 5th ed. (London: I. Beale, 1639), 223.

4. The lone works of Gouge's that are strictly commentary are his *Commentary on Hebrews* and his *Annotations* on 1 Kings through Job. William Gouge, *A Commentary on the Whole Epistle to the Hebrews Being the Substance of Thirty Years' Wednesday's Lectures at Blackfriars, London*, Vol. I (Edinburgh: James Nichol, 1866); "First Kings through Esther" in *Annotations Upon all the Books of the Old and Nevv Testament* (London: Evan Tyler, 1657).

spiritual death, and according to Hebrews 2:14–15, emphasizes Gouge, death is a tool in the arsenal of Satan. Thus, man has a problem with his sin, the curse of the law, the wrath of God, death, and enslavement to Satan. Gouge's theology of the atonement emphasizes each of these pitiful realities, and in turns displays how Jesus' atoning work provides a remedy. Jesus' perfect life, death, and resurrection are the solution to humanity's problem when people believe in him. Gouge's atonement theology emphasizes Jesus' perfect obedience to the law, his bearing humanity's sin and his pacifying of God's wrath on the cross, and his defeat of death and Satan in his resurrection. The active obedience of Jesus makes it possible for his righteousness to be imputed to sinful people when they put their faith in him. The result for Christians is that they are given the sure hope, even the promise, of being justified before God, sanctified, and granted the hope of an eternal inheritance. These are the promises of the gospel that function as Gouge's primary ground for assurance.

Another prominent theological theme in Gouge's works is that of divine providence. Gouge encourages his readers to see God's providence in all things, from the falling of a sparrow in the forest to the collapsing of an edifice in the city. Gouge acknowledges the challenges of interpreting the meaning of God's providential workings, but nonetheless expresses that to deny God's sovereign hand over all things leaves people with chance or luck as an alternative. The salvation of men and women, and the faith that produces it, must also be seen according to God's providential workings. A Christian possesses faith because God, in his kind providence, enabled the Christian to possess faith in the gospel. "The blessing which by faith commeth to any, is obtained, not by any worth or virtue of faith as it is an act of man," says Gouge, "but merely by reason of that order which in wisdom God hath appointed for receiving from him such an such blessings." Christians are Christians because God worked faith in them. Similarly, when believers pray in faith, they are not altering God's providential plan, rather in his providence, he set apart and sanctified their prayers for his purposes. This by no means diminishes God's power, says Gouge. He writes, "Faith is not the proper, primary, and principall cause of any divine blessing, but onely a meanes subordinate to the divine providence."[5] Thus, prayer should be done in faith trusting that God will act precisely according to his providential plan. Furthermore, Christians can pray in faith, or even pray in hope, because of the assurance that is theirs, grounded in the gospel. Again Gouge states his theology of assurance of salvation clearly when discussing divine providence and prayer. He writes, "Take good notice of gods promises, and well acquaint thy selfe therewith. Gods promises are the only, true, proper ground of faith. What is promised, may and must be believed. What is believed without a promise, is not justly and duly believed. It is rather rashly and audaciously presumed."[6] Christians should pray with confidence that is based upon their assured standing before God, which, in turn, is certified by God's promises. Or said another way, God's promises give Christians grounds for assurance of faith, and from that standing of certainty, they can pray to God with confidence. It is significant to see that Gouge calls God's promises the "only, true, proper" ground of faith. This statement does not negate the existence of other grounds of assured faith, but confirms what has been argued in this book, namely, that Gouge recognizes the promises of God to be the only true and proper (i.e., the only true primary or most important) ground of faith.

In that same vein of thought concerning the promises of God and assurance, Gouge writes in his Hebrews commentary:

> If we think assurance of hope worth the having, let us do to the utmost what God enableth us to do for attaining thereunto. Let us acquaint ourselves with the grounds of hope, God's promises and properties, and frequently and seriously meditate thereon. Let us conscionably attend God's ordinances, and earnestly pray that God would add his blessing to our endeavor.[7]

Believers come to better understand the promises of God by meditating on the Scriptures, where the promises are found, by participating in the Lord's Supper, and by committing to fervent prayer. These are means

---

5. William Gouge, *Gods three arrovves : plagve, famine, svvord, in three treatises* (London: Printed by George Miller, 1631), 260.

6. Ibid., 261.

7. Quoted in Beeke, *Quest for Full Assurance*, 152.

for Christians to better understand God's promises and thus increase in assurance.[8]

Pastorally speaking, Gouge was concerned with both his own parishioners at St. Anne's, Blackfriars, as well as the wider Church in all of England and in mainland Europe. His teachings sought to address Christians within the church, unbelievers, particular individuals and even address specific circumstances. All of Gouge's books were sermons first preached at Blackfriars to his own flock. These works contain theological discussions, expository thoughts and practical divinity addressing matters such as the providence of God, spiritual warfare, prayer, means to have a godly household, suffering and even death. Through his words and works, Gouge sought to comfort those who were ill, as in the case of Lady Bruce, whom Gouge reminded that physical ailments serve a prayerful purpose, namely, that afflictions move Christians to pray. Though not recorded in Gouge's works, he also shepherded "Mary," who was a companion of Pocahontas. While he acknowledged that her illness might lead to death, it appears that he consoled her (as he did with others) by clarifying how death is not something Christians should fear. In the case of Mr. Ducke, the widower of Margaret Ducke, Gouge took into consideration his grieving and sought to console him through the truths preached at her funeral and by publishing the sermon after its delivery. When Gouge attempts to comfort people who have experienced physical ailments and emotional trials in life, he does so from the place of his own experiences. Like Mr. Ducke, Gouge was a widower and just as he counseled Mary in the face of death, he saw five of his children die before they reached adulthood. Like Lady Bruce, Gouge had his own maladies. He was stricken with frequent bouts of asthma and kidney stones along with an ailment that nearly cost him his life twenty-one years before his actual death.[9]

Gouge exhorted Vincent Jukes, the young, repentant apostate who had shipwrecked his faith under persecution. He told the penitent

---

8. Beeke, *Quest for Full Assurance*, 152.

9. Thomas Gouge, "A Narrative of the Life and Death of Doctor Gouge," in William Gouge, *A Commentary on the Whole Epistle to the Hebrews, Being the Substance of Thirty Years' Wednesday's Lectures at Blackfriars, London* (Edinburgh: James Nichol, 1866), 1:iii, xi.

Christian not to forget the sting of his rebellion but to rest in the restorative hand of God. He also reminds Christians of the intense spiritual war, in which all believers find themselves. Satan is not a foe to be forgotten, nor a fiend to be feared. When the devil is ignored, Christians easily fall into his calculated and cunning traps. However, when he is feared, Christians lose sight of God who controls all things. Gouge likens Satan's power before God as a bee flying without a stinger, but having no real potency. Instead, Gouge exhorts his readers to understand their enemy and to have utter confidence in God. God has given his children weapons and armor to fight in this battle. Of all the pieces of the armor of God, Gouge considers the shield of faith to be the most important, because it is the mother of all graces. By faith sinners are justified, Christians are sanctified, and by faith believers can deepen in their assurance of salvation.

Gouge's practical priorities included endeavoring to provide all the necessary instructions for his own parishioners to raise their children and manage their household in reverence to God. In so doing, he produced catechisms and even took it upon himself to ensure its application through home visitations.[10] The catechisms contained the substance of Gouge's theological convictions along with other practical priorities such as participating in baptism, the Lord's Supper, and devoted prayer. Indeed, prayer, whether extemporaneous or written, public or private, ordinary or extraordinary, may be the most emphasized practical priority in all of Gouge's works. He writes:

> Faithful prayer is that meanes which God him himself, the almighty and all sufficient God, the original fountaine of all blessing hath sanctified for receiving from him whatsoever he in his wisdome seeth meet to be done for, or given to any of his children. So that, it is a conduit pipe, conveying all needfull blessing from that high fountainein heaven, to us on earth.[11]

He wanted to see Christians tap into this conduit of blessing, and be moved accordingly. As noted in Chapter 5, true rest for the weary

---

10. Thomas Gouge, "Narrative," viii.
11. Gouge, *Gods Three Arrovves*, 259.

Christian can only be found in "face-to-face" communion with God in prayer.

Gouge also had an eye directed toward all of England and even beyond into mainland Europe. He leveraged the printing press to disseminate his practical divinity beyond his London parish. Although he apologizes to his parishioners for occasional absences to write (primarily in summer months), he does not appear to scale back his publishing.[12] Rather, he was grateful for his time away because it allowed for him to put on paper what he long desired to write. He says concerning his *A Guide to Goe to God*,

> Whatsoeuer is therein performed is the fruit of my affected *Retirednesse*, and suspected *Idlenesse* in the country. So many, so continuall are my imployments in the Citie, so many interupptions from my studies day after day are caused, as I neuer yet could find any leasure to set down distinctly such points as by Gods assistance were vttered out of the Pulpet. Whatsoever hath hitherto been published by me hath, in my retiring time been prepared for the Presse. This benefit of a few weeks absence in the yeare from my charge (there being in that time a good supply made by Reuerend Brethren) may gaine a sufficient dispensation with those that are not too supercilious, which I hope you, my Parishioners, will not be.[13]

He viewed publishing books as a way to speak to the Church at large, while knowing that some sacrifices, especially by his parish, needed to be made. Furthermore, it is not uncommon for Gouge to refer to various circumstances that had previously or were currently taking place in mainland Europe. For instance, in 1631 while lamenting the outbreak of plague in England, he addressed the ravages of war that the churches in Bohemia, France, and the Palatinate had experienced.[14] In his own lifetime, Gouge's actual works influenced the Church beyond his kin by crossing the English Channel into France in 1643 and, after his death, his

---

12. Thomas Gouge, "Narrative," xi.

13. William Gouge, *A Guide to Goe to God or, an Explanation of the Perfect Patterne of Prayer, the Lords Prayer* (London: G. M. and R. B., 1626), iii.

14. Gouge, *God's Three Arrovves*, vii–viii.

works crossed the North Sea into the Netherlands.[15] Thus, his publishing endeavors seemed to accomplish much of what they set out to do.

The years in which Gouge published many of his works yield important truths about his writings. Such was the case in *The Progresse of Divine Providence* after the "downfall of the papists" upon the floor collapse of a building in Blackfriars. Gouge seizes the opportunity to teach his church about the providence of God. Similarly, in his sermon *The Right Way*, we find that the September 12, 1648 publication placed Gouge's sermon in the midst of England's Civil War with Parliamentary commissioners meeting with Charles I seeking terms for peace only days after the sermons delivery. The occasional nature to many of his works tells readers that Gouge not only had his eyes in the Bible for study, but also into the culture around him. This quality was undoubtedly necessary for any pastor who wanted to provide practical instructions for their people who are affected by these various scenarios and circumstances of life.

As it relates to medieval Roman Catholicism, Hambrick-Stowe has convincingly shown that the Puritans did not invent a new kind of spirituality. They followed the trajectory of medieval Catholic spirituality, but "Protestantized" it. Indeed, there was little that was novel in practice with Gouge's Sabbath exercises, catechizing, teachings on fasting, and meditation on the Scriptures. However, what was distinct for Gouge, and other Puritans, was its Protestant accent. Puritan spirituality in practice was saturated with the Bible, had an outlook to the glory of God and his providential workings, reflected a *sola fidei* teaching, and a Christocentric thrust throughout. However, the question remains, to what extent was Gouge's practical divinity a reflection of

---

15. As noted in Chapter 1, Gouge's lone work translated into French is his *Whole Armour of God*, translated as *L'Armure Complette de Dieu* (Geneva: Jacques Chouet, 1643). Gouge's works translated into Dutch are *Sinne Against the Holy Ghost*, translated *Een Verhandeling van de sonde tegen den H. Geest* (Amsterdam: Ernestest Bach, 1659); *God's Three Arrows*, translated *De Drie Pylen Gods. Namelijk, Peste, Honger, Sweert. In drie verhandelingen, I. De plaaster voor de Peste, II. De Doot des Dieren-Tijts, III. Des Kerks overwinninge over het Sweert. In 't Engels beschreven, en in 't Nederduytsch vertaalt door Petrus Heringa* (Amsterdam: Johannes van Someren, 1666); *Progresse of Divine Providence*, translated *De Uytstrekkinge van Godts Voorsienigheyt* (Amsterdam: Johannes van Someren, 1666); and *Dignity of Chivalry*, translated *De Waerdigheyt vsn de Krijgshandel* (Amsterdam: Johannes van Someren, 1666).

Catholic doctrine? Any charge of "legalism" or "works righteousness" against Gouge only has merit if he is read with a narrow lens. However, by broadening the lens, that is, widening the context, by which we read Gouge, the charge does not hold up. Gouge's words have to be understood contextually. Some might consider it pastorally unwise for Gouge to places an occasional emphases on the secondary grounds of assurance, namely, the evidences of the Holy Spirit's working in the Christian's life, without emphasizing the primary ground in the same breath. While this accusation may have merit when he is read narrowly, it seems that Gouge tends to emphasize what the biblical text leads him to emphasize, which sometimes means placing a strong focus on the secondary grounds. Furthermore, as we saw in his *A Guide to Goe to God* and *Of Domestical Duties*, if he stresses the secondary grounds for assurance in one place in his writing, he also places an emphasis on the primary ground at other times in that same work. For this reason, the student of Gouge's theology of assurance must read each work as a whole to get a thicker description of his theology.

Still, others might say he lacks pastoral discretion when he call his readers to consider the damning effects of their sin in such a way that draws them back to the gospel. When he emphasizes man's destructive predicament he does so because he is often correcting the teachings of the Catholic church. Gouge uses the Catholic theologian Robert Bellarmine as the target for which his theological arrows are at times directed. As we saw in Gouge's *A Guide to Goe to God* he's opposing the apparent neglect of regular confession and repentance within the Roman Catholic Church. In his view, this oversight and passive dealing with sin prevents people from seeing the terrible consequences of their sins. For Gouge, this problem is grave because it is men and women's awareness of their sins that point them to God's solution, faith in Jesus. Gouge's readers will not find this neglect of man's sin in Gouge's writings. He wants his readers to be drawn regularly back to the gospel and its promises, which is the sure ground of assurance. When seen through this perspective, Gouge's polemical language against the Church of Rome makes more sense. In his estimation, the pope has lead the Roman Catholic Church to neglect the Word of God (where God's promises are found) by keeping the Scriptures in Latin, to neglect regular confession (which points people to the gospel) in favor of promoting confession strictly around Lent and Easter, and to neglect the sufficiency of Christ's work (where Christ's righteousness is imputed to Christians) by teaching that baptism removes the sins of those baptized. Gouge's conviction was that the neglectful teachings in the Roman Catholic Church rob God of his glory. "Both parts of Gods Word, the *Law* and *Gospell* doe clearley set out the glory of God. The *Law*, the glory of his *Iustice*: the *Gospell*, the glory of his *Mercy*."[16] Gouge believed that the chief end of man is to glorify God, therefore, wants people to see their sin in the mirror of God's law, and to see God's mercy in the light of the gospel.

GOUGE AND THE CHURCH IN THE PRESENT DAY

Although Gouge's voice has largely laid silent over the past three and a half centuries, it has been this book's aim to allow Gouge to speak again. The robust nature of his practical divinity has been demonstrated along with its theological and biblical foundations. Scholars of Puritan practical divinity would benefit from dialoguing with Gouge's writings more extensively in the future. Moreover, Gouge's theology of assurance is far more nuanced than the picture given by some historians. For this reason, other Puritans who were, like Gouge, accused of abandoning the promises of God as the primary ground for assurance should be studied with greater depth to discern if they have a more nuanced theology of assurance across their writings as well. Hopefully, this book will stir other scholars to rediscover the career and rich literary corpus of Gouge—a man who was eminent in his day and has become absent in ours. This reality is unfortunate. From a practical standpoint, Gouge's gospel-centered teachings on suffering, the realities of spiritual warfare, and prayer remain important topics for Christians in our own day. Especially pertinent in the present time is the call to extraordinary praying, that is, praying with fasting. When the church feels it is living in unique days and societal hardships are on the horizon, then

---

16. Gouge, *Guide to Goe to God*, 296.

at that moment it must be reminded that, *"In a matter extraordinary, extraordinary means must be used."*[17]

William Gouge above all was a pastor who committed his life to follow his Lord and to serve his people. Writing to his beloved parishioners in Blackfriars, Gouge says, "My desire is (if so it may seeme good to the divine prouidence) to spend all my daies among you and while I am among you, to helpe forward your spiritual edification. This is the maine end of my calling."[18] Indeed, he labored diligently, with a firm trust in God's providential will. He majored in pastoral care seeking the spiritual edification and nourishment of his church and readers. It appears that his son Thomas' report about his father's sentiments were true, that he wanted none other than to go from Blackfriars to heaven.

---

17. William Gouge, *The Right Way: or A direction for obtaining good successe in a weighty enterprise. Set out in a sermon preached on the 12th of September, 1648. before the Lords on a day of humiliation for a blessing on a treaty between His Majesties and the Parliaments commissioners* (London: A. Miller, 1648), 20.

18. William Gouge, *Of Domesticall Dvties: eight treatises* (London: Iohn Haviland, 1622), ii.

Bibliography

PRIMARY SOURCES

Anselm. *Cur Deus Homo: To Which is Added a Selection from His Letters*. Edinburgh: John Grant, 1909.

Bayly, Lewis. *The Practise of Pietie, Directing a Christian how to walke, that he may please God*. 9th ed. London: I. Hodgetts, 1617.

Burges, Cornelius. *The dissenting ministers vindication of themselves, from the horrid and detestable murther of King Charles the First, of glorious memory. With their names subscribed, about the 20th of January, 1648*. London, 1648. Reprint, 1704.

Calvin, John. *Calvin's Commentaries, The Epistles of Paul the Apostle to the Galatians, Ephesians, Philippians and Colossians*. Translated by T. H. L. Parker. Edited by D. W. Torrance and T. F. Torrance. Grand Rapids: Eerdmans, 1965.

———. *Calvin's Commentaries, The Epistle of Paul the Apostle to the Hebrews and the First and Second Epistles of St. Peter*. Translated by W. B. Johnston. Edited by D. W. Torrance and T. F. Torrance. Grand Rapids: Eerdmans, 1970.

———. *The Catechisme, or maner to teache Children the Chrisitan Religion*. London: Iohn Kyngston, 1580.

———. *Institutes of the Christian Religion*. Edited by John T. McNeill. Translated by Ford Lewis Battles. 2 vols. Library of Christian Classics 20–21. Philadelphia: Westminster, 1960.

Clarke, Samuel. *A Collection of the Lives of Ten Eminent Divines, Famous in Their Generation for Learning, Prudence, Piety, and Painfulness in the Work of the Ministry*. London: Samuel Gellibrand, 1662.

Dickson, David, and James Ferguson. *The Epistles of Paul to the Galatians, Ephesians, Philippians, Colossians, and Thessalonians and The Epistle to the Hebrews*. Edinburgh: Banner of Truth, 1978.

Diodore of Tarsus. *Commentary on Psalm 1–51*. Translated by R. C. Hill. Writings from the Greco-Roman World. Atlanta: SBL, 2005.

Finch, Henry. *An exposition of the Song of Solomon: called Canticles. Together with profitable observations, collected out of the same*. London: Iohn Beale, 1615.

———. *The calling of the Ievves: A present to Iudah and the children of Israel that ioyned with him, and to Ioseph (the valiant tribe of Ephraim) and all the house of Israel that ioyned with him. The Lord giue them grace, that they may returne and seeke Iehovah their God, and Dauid their King, in these latter dayes. There is prefixed an epistle vnto them, written for their sake in the Hebrue tongue, and translated into English*. London: Edvvard Griffin for William Bladen, 1621.

Gouge, Thomas. "A Narrative of the Life and Death of Doctor Gouge." In *A Commentary on the Whole Epistle to the Hebrews: Being the Substance of Thirty Years' Wednesday's Lectures at Blackfriars, London*, x–xvi. Vol. 1. Edinburgh: James Nichol, 1866.

———. *The Principles of Christian Religion Explained to the Capacity of the Meanest. With Practical Applications to each Head Whereby the Great and Necessary Duty of Family-Catechizing may with much Ease be Performed*. London: Thomas Parkhurst, 1680.

Gouge, William. *Briefe Ansvvers to the Chiefe Articles of Religion*. London: Edward Brewster, 1642.

———. *A briefe method of catechizing wherein are briefely handled the fundamentall principles of Christian religion, needfull to be knowne by all Christians before they be admitted to the Lords Table. Whereunto are added sundry prayers, with thanksgivings before and after meale*. 8th ed. London: John Beale, 1637.

———. *A Commentary on the Epistle to the Hebrews: Exegetical and Expository*. 2 vols. 1866. Reprint, Birmingham: Solid Ground Christian Books, 2006.

———. *Commentary on Hebrews*. Grand Rapids: Kregel, 1980.

———. *A Commentary on the Whole Epistle to the Hebrews: Being the Substance of Thirty Years' Wednesday's Lectures at Blackfriars, London*. 3 vols. Edinburgh: James Nichol, 1866.

———. *L'Armure Complette de Dieu*. Geneva: Jacques Chouet, 1643.

———. *Dignitie of Chivalry, set forth in a sermon, preached before the artillery company of London, June xiii, 1626*. 2nd ed. London: Edward Brewster, 1631.

———. *Of Domesticall Dvties: eight treatises*. London: William Bladen, 1622.

———. *De Drie Pylen Gods. Namelijk, Peste, Honger, Sweert. In drie verhandelingen, I. De plaaster voor de Peste, II. De Doot des Dieren-Tijts, III. Des Kerks overwinninge over het Sweert. In 't Engels beschreven, en in 't Nederduytsch vertaalt door Petrus Heringa*. Amsterdam: Johannes van Someren, 1666.

———. "To the Christian Reader." In *A commentary: or, Sermons vpon the second chapter of the first Epistle of Saint Peter : wherein method, sense, doctrine, and vse, is, with great variety of matter, profitably handled; and sundry heads of diuinity largely discussed*, i–vii. London: G. Latham, 1623.

———. "To the Christian Reader." In *A Treatise of Faith*, A9r–A12r. London: William Sheffard, 1623.

———. "Epistle to the Reader." In *Certaine devout prayers of Mr. Bolton upon solemne occasions*, A3r–A11v. London: George Miller, 1638.

———. *An Exposition on the VVhole Fifth Chapter of S. Iohns Gospell: also notes on other choice places of Scripture, taken by a reuerend diuine, now with God, and found in his study after his death, written with his owne hand*. London: Iohn Bartlett, 1630.

———. *Extent of God's Providence, set out in a sermon, preached in Black-Fryers Church, V. Nov. 1623. On occasion of the downe-fall of papists in a chamber at the said Black-Fryers, 1623. Oct. 27*. London: Edward Brewster, 1631.

———. "First Kings through Job." In *Annotations Upon all the Books of the Old and Nevv Testament: This third, above the First and Second, Edition so enlarged, as they make an entire Commentary on the Sacred Scripture: The like never before* published in English, wherein the Text is explained, Doubts resolved, Scriptures Parallel'd, and various readings observed. London: Evan Tyler, 1657.

————. A Funeral Sermon preached by Dr. Gouge of Black-Friers London, in Cheswicke Church, August 24, 1646, at the funeralls of Mrs. Margaret Ducke wife of Dr. Ducke, one of the masters of requests to his Majesty. London: Joshua Kirton, 1646.

————. A Guide to Goe to God or, an Explanation of the Perfect Patterne of Prayer, the Lords Prayer. London: G.M. and R.B., 1626.

————. Gods three arrovves : plagve, famine, svvord, in three treatises. London: Edward Brewster, 1631.

————. Gouge to Laud. 19 October 1631. National Archives. SP 16/202/3.

————. A learned and very vsefvl commentary on the whole Epistle to the Hebrewes. Wherein every word and particle in the originall is explained, and the emphasis thereof fully shewed. The sense and meaning of every verse clearly unfolded. Each chapter and verse logically, and exactly analysed. Genuine doctrines naturally raised, and applied from the severall words, and particles in the whole Epistle. The manifold types of Christ clearly, and largely unveiled. Divers cases of conscience satisfactorily resolved. Severall controversies pithily discussed. Various common-places thoroughly handled. Sundry errors and heresies substantially confuted. Very many dark and obscure places of Scripture, which occasionally occur, perspicuously opened. Being the substance of thirty years Wednesdayes lectures at Black-fryers, London. London: J. Kirton, 1655.

————. Mercies Memorial, set out in a sermon preached in Paul's church, Novemb. 17, 1644, in memoriall of the great deliverance which England had from antichristian bondage by Queen Elizabeths attaining the crowne. London: Ioshua Kirton, 1645.

————. Panoplia tou theou. The whole-armor of God, or, The spiritvall fvrnitvre which God hath prouided to keepe safe euery Christian sovldier from all the assaults of Satan. London: Iohn Beale, 1616.

————. Sabbath Sanctification. London: Joshua Kirton and Thomas Warren, 1641.

————. The Progresse of Divine Providence, set out in a sermon preached in the Abbey Church of Westminster before the House of Peers, on the 24th of September, 1645, being the day of their monethly fast. London: I. Kirton, 1645.

————. A Recovery from Apostacy: Set out in a sermon preached in Stepny Church neere London at the receiving of a penitent renegado into the Church, Octob. 21. 1638. London: Ioshua Kirton, and Thomas Warren, 1639.

————. The Right VVay: or A direction for obtaining good successe in a weighty enterprise. Set out in a sermon preached on the 12th of September, 1648. before the Lords on a day of humiliation for a blessing on a treaty between His Majesties and the Parliaments commissioners. London: Ioshua Kirton, 1648.

————. The Saints Sacrifice: Or, A Commentarie On the CXVI. Psalme. Which is, A Gratulatory Psalme, for Deliverance from deadly Distresse. London: Edward Brewster, 1632.

————. The Saints Svpport, set out in a sermon preached before the honourable House of Commons assembled in Parliament. At a publick fast, 29. June, 1642. London: J. Kirton, 1642.

———. *A Short Catechisme, Wherein are Laid Downe the Fundamentall Principles of Christian Religion.* London: Iohn Beale, 1615.

———. "To the Reader." In *A complete concordance to the Bible of the last translation. By helpe whereof any passage of Holy Scripture may bee readily turned unto. The whole reviewed, corrected, and much enlarged by Clement Cotton, And againe reuieued and corrected by H.T.*, A3r–A4v. London, 1635.

———. Treattise of the Sinne Against the Holy Ghost. London: I. Beale, 1639.

———. *De Uytstrekkinge van Godts Voorsienigheyt.* Amsterdam: Johannes van Someren, 1666.

———. *Een Verhandeling van de sonde tegen den H. Geest.* Amsterdam: Ernestest Bach, 1659.

———. *De Waerdigheyt vsn de Krijgshandel.* Amsterdam: Johannes van Someren, 1666.

———. *The Whole Armour of God. Or, A Christians spirituall furniture, to keep him safe frō all the assaults of Satan.* 5th ed. London: I. Beale, 1639.

Gouge, William, Thomas Foxley, Richard Hiller, and Henry Hickford. *To men, fathers and brethren; Henry Holland (son of the learned and laborious scholler Dr. Philemon Holland;) a citizen of London.* London, 1647.

Gurnall, William. *The Christian in Complete Armour.* 2 vols. Edinburgh: Banner of Truth, 1983.

Jenkyn, William. *A Shock of Corn Coming in its Season. A Sermon Preached at the Funeral of that Ancient and Eminent Servant of Christ William Gouge, Doctor of Divinity and Late Pastor of Black-Friers, London, December the 16th, 1653. With the Ample and Deserved Testimony that then was Given of His Life.* London: Samuel Gellibrand, 1654.

Luther, Martin. *Luther's Works.* Vol. 26, Lectures on Galatians 1535, Chapters 1–4. Edited by Jaroslav Pelikan. Saint Louis: Concordia, 1963.

———. *Luther's Works.* Vol. 27, Lectures on Galatians 1535, Chapters 5–6; Lectures on Galatians 1519, 1–6. Edited by Jaroslav Pelikan. Saint Louis: Concordia, 1964.

Mather, Increase. *Increase Mather: Two Tracts.* American Puritan Writings 22. New York: AMS, 1983.

Owen, John. *An Exposition of the Epistle to the Hebrews.* Edited by W. H. Goold. 7 vols. Edinburgh: Johnstone and Hunter, 1854.

———. *The Works of John Owen.* Vol. 20, Exposition of the Epistle to the Hebrews with Preliminary Exercitations, Vol. 3. Edited by W. H. Goold. Edinburgh: T&T Clark, 1862.

Perkins, William. *The Art of Prophesying.* Edinburgh: Banner of Truth, 2002.

———. *The Work of William Perkins.* Edited by Ian Breward. Courtenay Library of Reformation Classics. Appleford: Sutton Courtenay, 1970.

———. *The Workes of that Famous and Worthy Minister of Christ in the Universitie of Cambridge, Mr. William Perkins.* 3 vols. London, 1631.

Sheafe, Thomas, and William Gouge. *Vindiciæ senectutis, or, A plea for old-age: which is senis cujusdam cygnea cantio. And the severall points or parts of it, are laid downe at the end of the following introduction.* London, 1639.

Sibbes, Richard. *The Works of Richard Sibbes.* Edinburgh: James Nichol, 1862.

Society for the Propagation of the Gospel in New England. *Strength out of weaknesse, or, A glorious manifestation of the further progresse of the gospel among the Indians in New-England : held forth in sundry letters from divers ministers and others to the corporation established by Parliament for promoting the gospel among the heathen in New-England : and to particular members thereof since the last treatise to that effect. "To the reader" signed: William Gouge and seventeen others.* London: John Blague and Samuel Howes, 1652.

Tertullian. "The Apology." In *The Ante-Nicene Fathers*, edited by A. Roberts, J. Donaldson, and A. C. Coxe, translated by S. Thelwall, 53–140. Vol. 3. Buffalo, NY: Christian Literature Company, 1885.

Theodoret of Cyrus. "The Ecclesiastical History of Theodoret." In *A Select Library of the Nicene and Post-Nicene Fathers of the Christian Church, Second Series*. Edited by Philip Schaff and Henry Wace. Translated by Blomfield Jackson, 33–64. Vol. 3. New York: Christian Literature Company, 1892.

The confession of faith, and the larger and shorter catechisme: first agreed upon by the Assembly of Divines at Westminster, and now approved by the General Assembly of the Kirk of Scotland, to be a part of uniformitie in religion between the Kirks of Christ in the three kingdoms : together with the Solemn League and Covenant of the three kingdoms. London: Company of Stationers, 1651.

"The Westminster Confession of Faith, 1647." In *Documents of the English Reformation*, edited by Gerald Bray, 486–520. Minneapolis: Fortress, 1994.

Westminster Shorter Catechism. Glasgow: Free Presbyterian, 1988.

SECONDARY SOURCES

Augustine, John H. "Authority and Interpretation." In *A Commentary on Galatians: With Introductory Essays*, by William Perkins, xiv–xlvii. New York: Pilgrim, 1989.

Aulén, Gustaf. *Christus Victor: An Historical Study of the Three Main Types of the Idea of Atonement.* Translated by A. G. Herbert. New York: Macmillan, 1969.

Barker, William S. *Puritan Profiles.* Ross-Shire: Mentor, 1999.

Bebbington, David W. *Evangelicalism in Modern Britain: A History from the 1730s to the 1980s.* London: Unwin Hyman, 1989.

Beeke, Joel R. "Evangelicalism and the Dutch Further Reformation," in Michael A. G. Haykin and Kenneth J. Stewart, eds., *The Advent of Evangelicalism: Exploring Historical Continuities*, 146–68. Nashville: B&H Academic, 2008.

———. *The Quest for Full Assurance: The Legacy of Calvin and His Successors.* Carlisle, PA: Banner of Truth, 2000.

Beeke, Joel R., and Mark Jones. *A Puritan Theology: Doctrine for Life.* Grand Rapids: Reformation Heritage, 2012.

Beeke, Joel R., and Randall J. Pederson. *Meet the Puritans.* Grand Rapids: Reformation Heritage, 2006.

Benedict, Philip. *Christ's Churches Purely Reformed: A Social History of Calvinism.* New Haven: Yale University Press, 2002.

Billings, J. Todd. *Calvin, Participation, and the Gift: The Activity of Believers in Union with Christ.* New York: Oxford University Press, 2007.

Blacketer, Raymond. "William Perkins." In *The Pietist Theologians*, edited by Carter Lindberg, 38-51. Malden, MA: Blackwell, 2005.

Blocher, Henry. "The Atonement in John Calvin's Theology." In *The Glory of the Atonement: Essays in Honor of Roger Nicole*, edited by Charles E. Hill and Frank A. James III, 279-303. Downers Grove: InterVarsity, 2004.

Bouyer, Louis. *Eucharist: Theology and Spirituality of Eucharistic Prayer*. Notre Dame: University of Notre Dame Press, 1968.

———. *Orthodox Spirituality and Protestant and Anglican Spirituality*. History of Christian Spirituality 3. Minneapolis: Seabury, 1963.

Bozeman, Theodore D. *The Precisianist Strain: Disciplinary Religion and Antinomian Backlash in Puritanism to 1638*. Chapel Hill: University of North Carolina, 2004.

Bray, Gerald, ed. *Documents of the English Reformation*. Minneapolis: Fortress, 1994.

Bray, John S. *Theodore Beza's Doctrine of Predestination*. Nieuwkoop: DeGraaf, 1975.

Bremer, Francis J. "The Puritan Experiment in New England, 1630-1660." In *The Cambridge Companion to Puritanism*, edited by John Coffey and Paul Lim, 127-42. Cambridge: Cambridge University Press, 2008.

Brook, Benjamin. *The Lives of the Puritans: Containing a Biographical Account of Those Divines Who Distinguished Themselves in the Cause of Religious Liberty, from the Reformation under Queen Elizabeth, to the Act of Uniformity, in 1662*. Vol. 3. 1813. Reprint, Pittsburgh: Soli Deo Gloria, 1994.

Bullinger, E. W. *Figures of Speech Used in the Bible*. London: Eyre & Spottiswoode, 1898.

Burch, Brian. "The Parish of St. Anne's Blackfriars, London, to 1655." *Guildhall Miscellany* 3 (October 1969): 1-54.

Cahill, Lisa Sowle. "Nonresistance, Defense, Violence, and the Kingdom in Christian Tradition." *Interpretation* 38, no. 4 (October 1984): 380-97.

Carlson, Eric Josef, ed. *Religion and the English People 1500-1640: New Voices, New Perspectives*. Sixteenth Century Essays and Studies 45. Kirksville, MO: Thomas Jefferson University Press, 1998.

Carson, John L., and David W. Hall, eds. *To Glorify and Enjoy God*. Edinburgh: Banner of Truth, 1994.

Coffey, John. "Puritanism, Evangelicalism and the Evangelical Protestant Tradition." In *The Advent of Evangelicalism: Exploring Historical Continuities*, edited by Michael A. G. Haykin and Kenneth J. Stewart, 252-77. Nashville: B&H Academic, 2008.

Coffey, John, and Paul Lim, eds. *Cambridge Companion to Puritanism*. Cambridge: Cambridge University Press, 2008.

Cole, Graham A. *God the Peacemaker: How Atonement Brings Shalom*. New Studies in Biblical Theology. Downers Grove: InterVarsity, 2009.

Collinson, Patrick. *The Elizabethan Puritan Movement*. Oxford: Clarendon, 1990.

———. "Antipuritanism." In *Cambridge Companion to Puritanism*, edited by John Coffey and Paul Lim, 19-33. Cambridge: Cambridge University Press, 2008.

Culver, Douglas J. *Albion and Ariel: British Puritanism and the Birth of Political Zionism*. New York: Peter Lang, 1995.

Davies, Horton. *Worship and Theology in England*. Vol. 1, *From Cranmer to Baxter and Fox, 1534-1690*. Grand Rapids: Eerdmans, 1996.

————. *The Worship of the English Puritans*. London: Dacre, 1948.

De Jong, J. A. *As the Waters Cover the Sea: Millennial Expectations in the Rise of Anglo-American Missions, 1640–1810*. Kampen: Kok, 1970.

De Lubac, Henri. *Medieval Exegesis: The Four Senses of Scripture*. Vol. 1. Translated by Mark Sebanc. Grand Rapids: Eerdmans, 1998.

Dolan, Frances E. *True Relations: Reading, Literature, and Evidence in Seventeenth-Century England*. Philadelphia: University of Pennsylvania Press, 2013.

East, Kenneth Allen. "William Gouge: Preacher and Scholar." 2 vols. PhD diss., University of Chicago, 1991.

Fairbairn, Donald. "Patristic Exegesis and Theology: The Cart and the Horse." *Westminster Theological Journal* 69 (2007): 1–19.

Farmer, Craig S. *The Gospel of John in the Sixteenth Century: The Johannine Exegesis of Wolfgang Musculus*. New York: Oxford University Press, 1997.

Ferguson, Sinclair B. "Foreword." In *The Art of Prophesying*, vi–xv. Edinburgh: Banner of Truth, 2002,

Forde, Gerhard O. "Law and Gospel in Luther's Hermeneutic." *Interpretation* 37, no. 3 (July 1983): 240–52.

Fritze, Ronald H. "Impropriations, Feoffees for (1626–1633)." In *Historical Dictionary of Stuart England, 1603–1689*, edited by Ronald H. Fritze and William B. Robinson, 244–46. Westport, CT: Greenwood, 1996.

Garrett, Duane A. *An Analysis of the Hermeneutic of John Chrysostom's Commentary on Isaiah 1–8 with an English Translation*. Studies in the Bible and Early Christianity 12. Lewiston: Edwin Mellen, 1992.

George, Timothy, and Scott Manetsch, eds. *Reformation Commentary on Scripture*. 28 vols. Downers Grove: InterVarsity, 2011.

George, Timothy. "The Atonement in Martin Luther's Theology." In *The Glory of the Atonement: Essays in Honor of Roger Nicole*, edited by Charles E. Hill and Frank A. James III, 263–78. Downers Grove: InterVarsity, 2004.

Greaves, Richard L. *Society and Religion in Elizabethan England*. Minneapolis: University of Minnesota Press, 1981.

Green, Ian. *The Christian's ABC: Catechisms and Catechizing in England, c. 1530–1740*. Oxford: Clarendon, 1996.

Gribben, Crawford. *The Puritan Millennium: Literature and Theology, 1550–1682*. Colorado Springs: Paternoster, 2008.

Gritsch, Eric W. "The Cultural Context of Luther's Interpretation." *Interpretation* 37, no. 3 (July 1983): 266–76.

Grosart, Alexander B. "Memoir of Richard Sibbes, D. D." In *The Complete Works of Richard Sibbes, D.D.*, vol 1, xix–cxxxi. Edinburgh: James Nichol, 1862.

Hagen, Kenneth. "Luther, Martin." In *Dictionary of Major Biblical Interpreters*, edited by Donald K. McKim, 687–94. Downers Grove: InterVarsity, 2007.

Hall, Basil. "Calvin Against the Calvinists." In *John Calvin*, edited by G. E. Duffield, 19–37. Grand Rapids: Eerdmans, 1966.

Hall, Joseph. *Meditations and Vows Divine and Moral*. Edited by Charles Saye. New York: E. P. Dutton, 1901.

Haller, William. *The Rise of Puritanism: or, The Way to the New Jerusalem as Set Forth in Pulpit and Press from Thomas Cartwright to John Lilburne and John Milton, 1570-1643*. New York: Columbia University Press, 1938.

Hambrick-Stowe, Charles E. "Practical Divinity and Spirituality." In *Cambridge Companion to Puritanism*, edited by John Coffey and Paul Lim, 191-205. Cambridge: Cambridge University Press, 2008.

―――. *The Practice of Piety: Puritan Devotional Disciplines in Seventeenth-Century New England*. Chapel Hill: University of North Carolina Press, 1982.

Harrisville, Roy A. "Expository Articles: Galatians 5:1." *Interpretation* 37, no. 3 (July 1983): 288-93.

Haykin, Michael A. G., and Kenneth J. Stewart, eds. *The Advent of Evangelicalism: Exploring Historical Continuities*. Nashville: B&H Academic, 2008.

Helm, Paul. *Calvin and the Calvinists*. Edinburgh: Banner of Truth, 1982.

Hendrix, Scott H. "Luther Against the Background of the History of Biblical Interpretation." *Interpretation* 37, no. 3 (July 1983): 229-39.

Hill, Charles E., and Frank A. James III, eds. *The Glory of the Atonement: Essays in Honor of Roger Nicole*. Downers Grove: InterVarsity, 2004.

House, Anthony P. "The City of London and the Problem of the Liberties, c1540-c1640." PhD diss., Oxford University, 2006.

Kaufman, Peter Iver. "'Much in Prayer': The Inward Researches of Elizabethan Protestants." *Journal of Religion* 73, no. 2 (April 1993): 163-82.

Kemp, Theresa D. "The Family Is a Little Commonwealth: Teaching *Mariam* and *Othello* in a Special-Topics Course on Domestic England." *Shakespeare Quarterly* 47, no. 4 (Winter 1996): 451-60.

Kendall, R. T. *Calvin and English Calvinism to 1649*. Oxford: Oxford University Press, 1979.

Klein, William W., Craig L. Blomberg, and Robert L. Hubbard. *Introduction to Biblical Interpretation*. Nashville: Thomas Nelson, 2004.

Knapp, Henry M. "John Owen's Interpretation of Hebrews 6:4-6: Eternal Perseverance of the Saints in Puritan Exegesis." *Sixteenth Century Journal* 34, no. 1 (2003): 29-52.

Knappen, Marshall M., ed. *Two Elizabethan Puritan Diaries by Richard Rogers and Samuel Ward*. Chicago: American Society of Church History, 1933.

Korda, Natasha. *Shakespeare's Domestic Economies: Gender and Property in Early Modern England*. Philadelphia: University of Pennsylvania Press, 2007.

Krupp, Ronald A. *Shepherding the Flock: The Pastoral Theology of John Chrysostom*. New York: Peter Lang, 1991.

Lewis, Clive S. *Surprised by Joy*. Orlando: Harcourt, 1955.

Lohse, Bernhard. *Martin Luther's Theology: Its Historical and Systematic Development*. Minneapolis: Fortress, 1999.

Lualdi, Katharine Jackson, and Anne T. Thayer. "Introduction." In *Penitence in the Age of Reformations*, edited by Katharine Jackson Lualdi and Anne T. Thayer, 1-9. Burlington, VT: Ashgate, 2000.

Lualdi, Katharine Jackson, and Anne T. Thayer, eds. *Penitence in the Age of Reformations*. Burlington, VT: Ashgate, 2000.

MacCulloch, Diarmaid. *The Boy King: Edward VI and the Protestant Reformation.* Berkeley: University of California Press, 2002.

———. *The Later Reformation in England, 1547–1603.* New York: St. Martin's, 1990.

Mallinson, Jeffrey. *Faith, Reason, and Revelation in Theodore Beza (1519–1605).* Oxford: Oxford University Press, 2003.

Manetsch, Scott M. *Calvin's Company of Pastors: Pastoral Care and the Emerging Reformed Church, 1536–1609.* Oxford: Oxford University Press, 2013.

Marshall, Peter. "Britain's Reformations." In *The Oxford Illustrated History of the Reformation,* edited by Peter Marshall, 186–226. Oxford: Oxford University Press, 2015.

McFarland, Ronald E. "The Response to Grace: Seventeenth-Century Sermons and the Idea of Thanksgiving." *Church History* 44, no. 2 (June 1975): 199–203.

McGowan, A. T. B. "Evangelicalism in Scotland from Knox to Cunningham." In *The Advent of Evangelicalism: Exploring Historical Continuities,* edited by Michael A. G. Haykin and Kenneth J. Stewart, 63–83. Nashville: B&H Academic, 2008.

McGrath, Alister, ed. *The Christian Theology Reader.* 2nd ed. Oxford: Blackwell, 2001.

McKim, Donald K. "William Perkins' Use of Ramism as an Exegetical Tool." In *A Commentary on Hebrews 11 (1609 Edition),* by William Perkins. Edited by J. H. Augustine, 32–45. New York: Pilgrim, 1991.

Milton, Anthony. "Puritanism and the Continental Reformed Churches." In *Cambridge Companion to Puritanism,* edited by John Coffey and Paul Lim, 109–26. Cambridge: Cambridge University Press, 2008.

Mitchell, Alex F., and John Struthers, eds. *Minutes of the Sessions of the Westminster Assembly of Divines While Engaged in Preparing Their Directory for Church Government, Confession of Faith, and Catechism (November 1644 to March 1649) from Transcripts of the Originals Procured by A Committee of the General Assembly of the Church of Scotland.* Edinburgh: William Blackwood and Sons, 1874.

Morgan, John. *Godly Learning: Puritan Attitudes towards Reason, Learning, and Education, 1560–1640.* Cambridge: Cambridge University Press, 1986.

Muller, Richard A. *After Calvin: Studies in the Development of a Theological Tradition.* Oxford: Oxford University Press, 2003.

———. "Biblical Interpretation in the Era of the Reformation: The View from the Middle Ages." In *Biblical Interpretation in the Era of the Reformation,* edited by R. A. Muller and J. L. Thompson, 8–13. Grand Rapids: Eerdmans, 1996.

———. "Perkins and the Protestant Exegetical Tradition: Interpretation, Style, and Method." In *A Commentary on Hebrews 11 (1609 Edition),* by William Perkins. Edited by J. H. Augustine, 71–94. New York: Pilgrim, 1991.

Muller, Richard A., and John L. Thompson. "The Significance of Precritical Exegesis." In *Biblical Interpretation in the Era of the Reformation,* edited by Richard A. Muller and John L. Thompson, 335–45. Grand Rapids: Eerdmans, 1996.

Muller, Richard A., and John L. Thompson, eds. *Biblical Interpretation in the Era of the Reformation.* Grand Rapids: Eerdmans, 1996.

Muller, Richard A., and Rowland S. Ward. *Scripture and Worship: Biblical Interpretation and the Directory for Worship.* Phillipsburg, NJ: P&R, 2007.

Murray, Ian. *The Puritan Hope*. London: Banner of Truth, 1971.

Nassif, Bradley L. "The 'Spiritual Exegesis' of Scripture: The School of Antioch Revisited." *Anglican Theological Review* 75, no. 4 (1993): 437-70.

O'Banion, Patrick J. "Jerome Zanchi, the Application of Theology, and the Rise of the English Practical Divinity Tradition." *Renaissance and Reformation/Renaissance et Reforme* 29, nos. 2-3 (2005): 97-120.

Oden, Thomas, ed. *Ancient Christian Commentary on Scripture*. 25 vols. Downers Grove: InterVarsity, 2001.

Old, Hughes Oliphant. "Matthew Henry and the Puritan Discipline of Family Prayer." In *Calvin Studies VII: Papers Presented at a Colloquium on Calvin Studies at Davidson College and Davidson College Presbyterian Church*, edited by John H. Leith, 69-91. (Davidson, NC: Davidson College 1994), 69-91.

Packer, James I. "The Puritan Approach to Worship." In *Diversity in Unity: Papers Read at the Puritan and Reformed Studies Conference, December, 1963*, 3-14. London: Evangelical Magazine, 1964.

———. *A Quest for Godliness: The Puritan Vision for the Christian Life*. Wheaton: Crossway, 1990.

Parker, Kenneth L. "Richard Greenham's 'Spiritual Physicke': The Comfort of Afflicted Consciences in Elizabethan Pastoral Care." In *Penitence in the Age of Reformations*, edited by Katharine Jackson Lualdi and Anne T. Thayer, 71-83. Burlington, VT: Ashgate, 2000.

Parker, Kenneth L., and Eric J. Carlson. *"Practical Divinity": The Works and Life of Revd Richard Greenham*. Aldershot: Ashgate, 1998.

Parnham, David. "Redeeming Free Grace: Thomas Hooker and the Contested Language of Salvation." *Church History* 77, no. 4 (December 2008): 915-54.

Pelikan, Jaroslav. *Luther's Works: Luther the Expositor*. Companion Volume. Saint Louis: Concordia, 1959.

Plomer, Henry R. *A Dictionary of the Booksellers and Printers Who Were at Work in England, Scotland, and Ireland from 1641 to 1667*. London: Blades, East and Blades, 1907.

Puckett, David L. "Calvin, John." In *Dictionary of Major Biblical Interpreters*, edited by Donald J. McKim, 287-94. Downers Grove: InterVarsity, 2007.

Reid, James. *Memoirs of the Westminster Divines*. Vol. 1. Edinburgh: Banner of Truth, 1811.

Schoneveld, Cornelius W. *Intertraffic of the Mind: Studies in Seventeenth-Century Anglo-Dutch Translation with a Checklist of Books Translated from English into Dutch, 1600-1700*. Leiden: Brill, 1983.

Seaver, Paul S. *The Puritan Lectureships: The Politics of Religious Dissent, 1560-1662*. Stanford: Stanford University Press, 1970.

Sheppard, Gerald T. "Between Reformation and Modern Commentary: The Perception of the Scope of Biblical Books." In *A Commentary on Galatians: With Introductory Essays*, by William Perkins. Edited by Gerald T. Sheppard, xlii-lxxi. New York. Pilgrim, 1989.

Sinnema, Donald. "Beza's View of Predestination in Historical Perspective." In *Théodore de Bèze (1519–1605): Actes du colloque de Genève (septembre 2005)*, edited by Irena Backus, 219–40. Geneva: Librairie Droz, 2007.

Soanes, Catherine, and Angus Stevenson. *Concise Oxford English Dictionary*. 11th ed. Oxford: Oxford University Press, 2004.

Spurgeon, Charles H. *Commenting on Commentaries: Lectures Addressed to the Students of the Pastor's College, Metropolitan Tabernacle, with a List of the Best Biblical Commentaries and Expositions, Also a Lecture on Eccentric Preachers, with a Complete List of All of Spurgeon's Sermons with the Scripture Texts Used*. New York: Sheldon, 1876.

Stannard, David E. "Death and Dying in Puritan New England." *The American Historical Review* 78, no. 5 (December 1973): 1305–30.

Steinmetz, David C. *Calvin in Context*. New York: Oxford University Press, 1995.

———. *Luther in Context*. 2nd ed. Grand Rapids: Baker, 2002.

———. "The Superiority of Pre-Critical Exegesis." *Theology Today* 37, no. 1 (April 1980): 27–38.

Stephen, Leslie, and Sidney Lee, eds. *Dictionary of National Biography*. Vol. 22. New York: Macmillan, 1890.

Strom, Jonathan. "Problems and Promises of Pietism Research." *Church History* 71, No. 3 (September 2002): 536–55.

Tentler, Thomas. "Postscript." In *Penitence in the Age of Reformations*, edited by Katharine Jackson Lualdi and Ann T. Thayer (Burlington, VT: Ashgate, 2000), 240–59.

Todd, Margo. "Providence, Chance and the New Science in Early Stuart Cambridge." *Historical Journal* 29, No. 3 (September 1986): 697–711.

Torrance, Thomas F. *The Hermeneutics of John Calvin*. Edinburgh: Scottish Academic Press, 1988.

Treier, Daniel J. "The Superiority of Pre-Critical Exegesis? Sic Et Non." *Trinity Journal* 24 (Spring 2003): 77–103.

Troxel, A. Craig. "Cleansed Once for All: John Owen on the Glory of Gospel Worship in Hebrews." *Calvin Theological Journal* 32, No. 2 (1997): 468–79.

Walsham, Alexandra. "'The Fatall Vesper': Providentialism and Anti-Popery in Late Jacobean London." *Past and Present* 144 (August 1994): 36–87.

Wilson, John F. *Pulpit in Parliament: Puritanism During the English Civil Wars, 1640–1648*. Princeton: Princeton University Press, 1969.

Winship, Michael P. "Weak Christians, Backsliders, and Carnal Gospelers: Assurance of Salvation and the Pastoral Origins of Puritan Practical Divinity in the 1580s." *Church History* 70, No. 3 (September 2001): 462–81.

Wood, A. Skevington. *Captive to the Word: Martin Luther, Doctor of Sacred Scripture*. Exeter: Paternoster, 1969.

Zachman, Randall. *The Assurance of Faith*. Minneapolis: Fortress, 1993.

Scripture Index

OLD TESTAMENT

Genesis
3:1 80
3:15 115

Exodus
18:21 19

Numbers
16:44–50 121

2 Samuel
23:21 66

2 Chronicles
8:9 . . . . 42n15

Ezra
8 . . . . 160n43
8:21 159

Job
18:14 . . . . 65n86

Psalms
6 106
8:4–6 56
31 106
113:5–6 118
116 124
127 . . . . 46n28

Isaiah
24:23 131
32:2 . . . . 22n70
41:26–27 131
61 107

Ezekiel
10:1 117

36:1 119
36:11 113–114

Daniel
11:44 131

NEW TESTAMENT

Matthew
10:29–31 113
10:29 69
18:22–35 110
26:41 . . . . 101n75

Luke
15 73

Romans
8:28 118
8:30 . . . . 11n30
11:5 130
11:20 . . . . 101n75

1 Corinthians
1:28 64
6:13 64
10:12 . . . . 101n75
15:55 65-66

Galatians
3:13 62

Ephesians
5:30 168
6:10–20 . . . . 74, 76
6:12 65
6:15 . . . . 52, 100
6:16 89-90

1 Timothy
4:5 68

2 Timothy
1:3 163

Hebrews
2:2 59
2:6–8 56
2:6–18 . . . . 55, 63
2:9 . . . . 56, 61, 62
2:10 . . . . 61, 63
2:14–15 . . . . 63, 183
3 49
3:11 49

3:12 . . . . 85, 85n30, 101n75, 102–3
3:18 49
4:1–11 . . . . 49, 101n75
4:12 47–51
9:13–14 . . . . .56n56
10:1–18 . . . . .55n53
10:38 . . . . 101n75
12:15 . . . . 101n75

1 Peter
3:21 116

Revelation
21:10–21 118

Subject Index

Anglican, 125, 129n62
Anselm, 53n50, 58–59, 58n63
apostate, apostasy, 25, 73, 76, 85, 105–6, 106n88, 121, 185
armor of God, 24, 47n33, 65, 74–78, 83–86, 88–89, 91, 102, 107, 186
assurance, 3–15, 32–36, 68, 69n96, 84–89, 94, 97–107, 134–35, 151–58, 167–69, 174–78, 180–91
full assurance, 14–15, 96–97, 101–2
of faith, 10, 55, 62, 83, 95–96, 98, 134, 158, 163, 167–68, 177, 181, 184
of salvation, 4–7, 12, 15, 18, 32–36, 78, 95–96, 99, 107, 141, 150, 152–53, 156, 174–78, 180–86
atonement, 5, 8, 53–56, 53–54n50, 55n53, 59, 61–63, 67–70, 182–83
Augustine, Saint 28–29, 147

baptism, 116, 140–41, 151–52, 174, 186, 190
Bayly, Lewis, 9, 19n59
Bebbington Thesis, 33–35, 35n118
Beeke, Joel, 2n6, 9–11, 13n37, 14, 35, 35n118, 92,
Beza, Theodore, 8–11, 8n20, 9n24, 11n30, 35, 91n44, 103
Blackfriars, 1, 5n14, 20–22, 25, 29, 38–40, 74, 100n73, 110, 113–14, 117, 136–37, 137n84, 137n85, 141, 166, 169n70, 185, 188, 191
Bozeman, Theodore, 3, 32–33, 150, 156
Bremer, Francis, 6–7
Burgess, Cornelius, 11, 92

Calvin, John, 7–10, 8n20, 9n24, 12–15, 13n37, 34–35, 50–51, 53–54n50, 91n44, 97n63, 103, 176, 176n84, 181

Calvinism (Calvinist), 2n6, 8–9, 15, 34, 35n120, 169
Cambridge, 16–18, 20, 126, 131, 72,
Cartwright, Thomas, 28, 165
casuist, 16n48, 29, 34
catechism, 24–25, 41, 51, 69, 117, 143, 163–65, 164n55, 169–77, 169n69, 176n84, 182, 186
Catholic Church, 1, 5, 28, 30–33, 50, 73, 81, 81n18, 86, 87n34, 88, 110–11, 124n43, 126, 141, 147–48, 150–52, 154, 188–90
Chaderton, Laurence, 20, 43n18, 134–35, 135n78, 154–55
Charles I, King, 2n6, 22n70, 120, 126, 145, 159, 188
Christ, 4, 6–10, 11n30, 12, 14, 33, 39, 42, 42n13, 50–53, 55–57, 56n56, 59, 61–70, 72, 75, 79, 86–88, 91–94, 98–107, 109, 113–14, 116–19, 124, 126, 128, 130–132, 137–37, 141, 148, 151–54, 156–57, 161, 170, 172–74, 176, 176n84, 180–82
Church of England, 1, 3, 6, 21, 81n18, 128n58
civil war, 126, 126n49, 158–59, 188
Clairvaux, Bernard, 28–29
Clarke, Samuel, 23, 179
Collinson, Patrick, 2n3, 128n58, 167n62
Commentary on Hebrews, 23n77, 24, 47n32
confession, 1, 7, 31–32, 121, 127, 144, 172, 173, 189–90
conscience, 11, 13, 15, 16n48, 17–18, 32, 38, 42n13, 54, 73–74, 76, 78n12, 80, 81n18, 98, 105, 133–34, 136, 149, 152, 156–57, 164, 180, 182
conversion, 32–34, 85, 118, 130–31, 139, 143, 153
covenant, 6, 8–9, 42, 121, 153, 156, 163

Davenport, John, 22, 129n62

Devil, 54, 54n51, 63–68, 72, 74, 76, 78–83, 85–88, 93n50, 98, 105–6, 115, 123, 141, 154, 156, 158, 161, 183, 186

Dignitie of Chivalry, 42n15

Domestical Duties, Of, 47n32, 77, 163, 165, 170, 189

Downame, John, 32–33

Dry Dayton, 16–17, 16n48, 18n56, 37

Ducke, Margaret, 136–39, 142, 185

Edward VI, King, 1, 127–28

Egerton, Stephen, 20, 21n68, 170

election, 4, 7–8, 10–11, 11n30, 14, 103–4, 154

Elizabeth I, Queen. 1, 112, 126, 128, 128n58, 159

Essex, 37

evangelicalism, 33–35, 35 n118

faith, 3–15, 9n24, 11n30, 13n 37, 34–35, 38, 49n36, 53, 55, 60, 62, 69n96, 70, 72–76, 82, 84–85, 87–107, 91n44, 93n50, 97n63, 120–22, 130, 133–34, 138–39, 141–43, 148, 150–51, 153–58, 163, 167–68, 173–77, 176nn84–85, 179–86, 189 (*see also* assurance of faith)

faithful, 13, 41–42, 44, 50, 68, 73–74n3, 76, 88, 94, 95, 100n71, 102, 120, 121, 127–28, 173n78, 186,

fasting, 76, 121, 158–63, 160n43, 177, 188, 190

Flavel, John, 92

forgiveness, 80, 106, 151–52, 154–56, 173, 175

God's Three Arrovvs, 160

Goodwin, Thomas, 2n6, 92, 132n72

Gouge, Elizabeth, 20, 19–20n60, 132–33, 135, 140n94, 145

Gouge, Thomas, 20n60, 164n55, 175

grace, 4, 6, 8, 10–12, 18n54, 20, 41, 56–57, 59–63, 67–69, 77, 80, 85–89, 94–96, 98, 101, 107, 107n91, 122, 124n43, 125, 144, 149, 153, 157, 171–72, 177–78, 186

Greenham, Richard, 16–19, 16n48, 17–18n53, 18nn56–57, 30, 37–38, 180

Guide to Goe to God, A, 144–45, 187, 189

Gurnall, William, 47n32, 77–78, 91, 91n44, 93n50

Hall, Basil, 4, 7–8, 8n20

Hambrick-Stowe, Charles, 7, 30–31, 70, 188

Helm, Paul, 9, 12–14

Hooker, Richard, 165

Henry Finch, 22, 26, 26n85, 118, 129–32

Henry VIII, King, 1, 126–128

Israel, Israelite, 49, 114–17, 122, 131, 160n43

James I, King, 118, 126, 129, 131–32, 132 n71

Jenkyn, William, 19n60, 21, 22n70, 23, 23n75, 26

justice, 53–54, 54n51, 58–69, 94–95, 121, 141, 155, 173n78,

justification (justified), 4, 12, 15, 34, 52, 78, 83, 89, 94, 125, 127, 152, 155–57, 176–77, 181–83, 186

justifying faith, 4, 7, 8, 9n24, 10, 13, 35, 68, 89–97, 93n50, 99, 107, 149, 176n84, 180–82

Kendall, R. T., 4, 7–9

Knox, John, 144–45, 144n2

Laud, William, 22, 26, 26n86, 73, 137n85,

Lord's Supper, 20, 21n69, 143–44, 173–74, 184, 186

Luther, Martin, 9n24, 34, 50, 53–54n50

Mede, Joseph, 131–32

medieval spirituality, 28, 30–33, 48n33, 188

Mercies Memorial, 112, 128n59

millennial, 24n79, 118

ministry, 3, 17, 21, 27, 38–41, 50, 121, 134, 138n86, 145, 173

Muller, Richard, 9, 44–45, 45 n24, 46 n30, 47–51, 48n33

non-conformist, 2n6, 21–22, 81n18

Owen, John, 2n6, 47n82, 55-58, 61, 62n78, 63, 69

Parliament, 21, 25, 114n16, 126-27, 144, 159, 188
pastoral call, 37-38, 41
Perkins, William, 8, 8n20, 10-11, 16-19, 16n48, 17-18n53, 18n57, 30, 35, 43n18, 49n36, 90-91, 93, 154-55, 180
persecution, 73, 109, 127, 129, 185
perseverance, 2n6, 87, 89, 100, 107
piety, 16-17, 19, 23, 70, 109, 125, 131, 138, 142, 162
Pocahontas, 140, 140n93, 185
pope, 41, 81, 121, 126, 189
popish, 50, 87n34, 95, 127
practical divinity, 3-7, 15-17, 17-18n53, 19, 30-33, 35-37, 40-41, 47n32, 52, 54, 67, 70, 104, 109, 133-34, 138, 144, 150, 156, 167, 172, 180, 182, 185, 187-88, 190
practical syllogism, 8-12, 9-10n24, 95-96, 99, 107
prayer, 24-25, 30-31, 35, 43, 68, 76, 81, 110, 121, 124-25, 124n43, 130, 141, 144-75, 160n43, 172 nn76-77, 177, 183-86, 190
preaching, 20, 23, 29, 39, 41, 42n15, 43-44, 50, 73, 121
presbyterian, 21, 128n58
protestant, 1-3, 2n3, 7, 16-17, 31-34, 31n106, 55, 56n56, 73, 77, 81, 110-11, 117, 150, 159, 188
providence, 5, 24n79, 40-41, 69-70, 109-20, 122, 125-26, 128, 133, 135, 138-39, 141-43, 163, 171, 182-85, 188, 191
providentialism, 24-25, 111, 114n15
Puritanism (Puritan), 1-4, 2n3, 2n6, 6-8, 8n20, 11-12, 14-17, 18n57, 19-24, 27-36, 35n118, 37-38, 43n18, 47, 51, 56, 68-70, 77, 80, 92, 102n77, 107, 114n15, 125, 128, 129, 129n62, 132n72, 135-36, 137n85, 144-45, 150, 154, 163-65, 167n62, 170, 175, 180-81, 188, 190

Ramism, 43
restoration of the Jews, 22, 129-30
Rogers, Richard, 16, 16n48, 18-19, 18nn56-57, 30, 37-38, 154-55, 180

sabbath, 24-25, 37, 121, 163n53, 188
Saints Sacrifice, The, 112, 124
salvation, 3-15, 18, 31-33, 31n106, 35-36, 59, 63, 68-69, 78, 84, 86-89, 92-96, 98-100, 102-3, 106-7, 141, 143, 150, 152-54, 156, 170-71, 174-78, 181-84, 186 (See also assurance of salvation)
sanctification, 4, 9-12, 11n30, 93, 96, 156-57, 176
Satan, see devil
Shakespeare, William, 137, 137n84
Sibbes, Richard, 22, 55n55, 129n62, 136
Spurgeon, Charles, 26-27

temptation, 73, 79-82, 84, 88, 98, 105-107, 133, 138n86, 150, 157
Thompson, John L., 44-45, 46n30, 47-48, 49-51

union with Christ, 102, 167-68
Ussher, James, 14, 23, 23-24n78, 145

Walsham, Alexandra, 111, 142
Westminster Assembly, 9, 21, 23, 114n16
Westminster Confession, 7, 10, 14, 35, 49
Whole Armour of God, The, 52, 74, 77, 84, 91, 104, 161n48
Winship, Michael, 6-7, 18n57
worship, 1, 81, 144-45, 163-64

Zachman, Randall, 8-9, 9n24, 13